With Unbounded Confidence

A History of the University of Redlands

With Unbounded Confidence

A History of the University of Redlands

LARRY E. BURGESS

Published by The University
of Redlands
P. O. Box 3080
1200 East Colton Avenue
Redlands, CA 92373–0999
Phone: (909) 335–5211
www. Redlands.edu

First edition

Printed in Verona, Italy

Library of Congress Cataloging-
in-Publication Data

Burgess, Larry E., 1945–
  With unbounded confidence:
  a history of the University
  of Redlands / Larry E.
  Burgess. — 1st ed.
    p. cm.
  Includes bibliographical
  references and index.
  ISBN 0-9787019-0-9
  ISBN 978-0-9787019-0-1
  1. University of Redlands —
History. I. Title.
  LD4701.R6642B87 2006
  378.794'95 — dc22
                    2006019531

Produced by Kim Coventry '82,
the Coventry Group, Chicago,
Illinois

Designed by Klugman Braude
Design, Durham, North Carolina

Color separations by Prographics,
Rockford, Illinois

Printed by Graphicom,
Verona, Italy

Front jacket illustration: Class
of 1915 on their way to a picnic.

Page VIII: Commencement 2003.

Pages X–XI: View across the
quad from the Administration
Building, 2006.

Back jacket illustration:
The Redlands football team
arrives in Honolulu to play in
the Pineapple Bowl, 1948.

Table of Contents

Preface

In concluding his detailed history, *Redlands: Biography of a College*, published on the occasion of the University's Golden Jubilee in 1958, Professor of English Lawrence E. Nelson contemplated the account that might be written fifty years hence. "Possibly a historian will . . . seek to sift anew the essential grain of truth. . . . Your identity, veiled historian of the hundredth anniversary, and even the certainty of your existence in that dim and shadowy year . . . are to me unknown."

This "veiled historian," Larry Burgess, came to know Larry Nelson in 1963. During our association in a service club and in the Fortnightly Club—a literary society—Nelson vouchsafed to me many nuggets of University history, including a meaningful clue as to the identity of one of Redlands's most generous patrons, known only as the "anonymous friend," whose munificence and name are revealed here in Chapter 4.

In his afterword, Nelson marveled at the abilities of University presidents Jasper Newton Field and Victor L. Duke, as well as longtime Business Manager George P. Cortner, to overcome their virtual inexperience in "promotional" work and found a college that they then proceeded to "so quickly build . . . to material and educational greatness." He also praised the founding trustees who, in an era "replete with intolerance, economic, social, and theological, often went unduly far in their efforts to placate those who could not be placated . . . a fault, if fault it be, closely akin to virtue. They earnestly tried to be fair, and to protect integrity of thought." Finally, he expressed hope that the Redlands of 1907, which became the Redlands of 1957 and then the Redlands of 2007, would remain at once steady and vibrant in pursuing its mission and maintaining its essential nature. He cited President Field's charge: "Let us not say we will rest on our laurels; let us look up and toil on until we have achieved greater things than we have yet known."

When Field became the University's first president, he declared that he viewed its potential "with unbounded confidence." This phrase struck John Master, the special-project historian for the present book, as a good title. I agreed. It captures the spirit and deeds that have, over the one hundred years of Redlands's existence, defined its complex, often troubled, and ultimately triumphant history.

During my career, I have read many college histories, reviewed some for scholarly journals, and supplied information to individuals who research the topic and write these narratives. One element is present in all: the impossibility of being encyclopedic, of discussing or mentioning every administrator, instructor, student, staff member, alumnus, trustee, donor, and friend or foe. Thus, a *mea culpa*: I could not include everything or everyone in this endeavor. There is good news, however. In 2000 the University funded its first-ever institutional archival program and hired a professional archivist. Those readers desiring to know more may now turn to the University Archives.

With Unbounded Confidence is designed to capture the essence, spirit, and broad issues that we call the University of Redlands. After considering a number of possible approaches—a multivolume account, a monograph with few illustrations, a picture book with little text—the Centennial Steering Committee and I elected for this book to employ a blend of formats: a single volume filled with illustrations and captions and also featuring a text full enough to tell the story of the University. To find the right person to edit the book and manage its production, we consulted with colleagues at Lake Forest (Illinois) College, which had produced a history not unlike what we aimed to do. They gently laughed and expressed surprise that we did not know about Kimbeth L. Coventry '82—a University of Redlands alumna who specializes in institutional histories and had shepherded theirs from its inception! I am deeply grateful to Kim for her professionalism, energy, and commitment to this project. I am also grateful to Julie Klugman Braude for taking the text and images and crafting a design that so perfectly fits the tone and spirit of this book.

I wish to acknowledge my appreciation of a number of individuals at the University of Redlands. Senior Vice President Phillip L. Doolittle '76 made it possible to create the team without which this book would literally have not been realized. James D. Hofer '78, the first and present University Archivist, provided encouragement and valuable material; he was ably assisted by Vanessa J. Wilkie '00 and Kathleen D. McGuire '02. A "wizard of photographs," Brennan J. Gosney '04, helped organize the visual images. Susan McCue, guardian of alumni records, provided accurate and important information on alums in timely fashion. John Master worked with my text and my ideas, helping form them, sometimes questioning their point, and contributing mightily to their organization and to the flow of language. He also contributed sidebars and captions. I hold in esteem his sense of history.

As the narrative approached its final form, Thomas J. Frusciano, archivist of Rutgers University and author of a history of New York University, generously agreed to read the text. James A. Sandos, a historian at the University of Redlands, also read it, posed helpful questions, and made valuable comments.

I owe enormous thanks to a number of colleagues at the A. K. Smiley Public Library, Redlands, which I have directed since 1986. The trustees graciously encouraged my efforts, and I am grateful. The library's associate archivist, Nathan D. Gonzales, made corrections and added new perspectives to my text. Don McCue and Richard Hanks, both first-rate historians, are to be thanked for making available material from the holdings of Smiley Library. The library's administrative analyst, Janice Jones, remained calm and supportive in the face of many revisions occasioned by the discovery of new information as the archives were perused. She deserves an honorary membership in the Alumni Association.

To Charlotte G. Burgess '69, '70, I owe double thanks: as a patient spouse who endured my moods and exhilarations over what must have seemed astoundingly minor historical occurrences, and as chair of the Centennial Steering Committee. To her staff, especially Juliann Fisher and David E. Kuhlmann '05, I am beholden. Diane Moye provided important materials from the president's office.

At this point, it is customary to say that all the errors and omissions are mine alone. However, I would like to add a note of context. The University Archives houses valuable material about the institution's past and its unfolding present. This book is designed to capture the essence, the spirit, and the broad issues that we call the University of Redlands. There are many stories yet to see the light of day. Archival processing of the past sometimes could not keep apace of my deadlines. Thus, some newly cataloged materials may alter or nuance my text. Alumni donations of materials also necessitated additions and changes. It is my hope that future issues of the *Och Tamale*, fundraising appeals, sports announcements, students, the alumni office, academic departments, and other constituents will use the archives to bring life and light to the diverse human components that are the vital spark of a university community.

Enjoy the read and marvel at what a century has wrought.

Larry E. Burgess '67
Redlands, California

This book is dedicated to all alumni, past, present, and future.

> "... an important influence was the remarkable scenic setting of the University of Redlands ... on the early life of the institution."—ROGER J. WILLIAMS '14

IN THE VALLEY OF SAN BERNARDINO

In 1907 the University was but a vision. The founders had already made one vital decision: as home for the incipient campus they had selected a tract of land on the outskirts of the tiny San Bernardino County town of Redlands. Then a varietal grape vineyard, the site promised imposing views from the nearly empty plain that lay before the distant, majestic San Bernardino Mountains. The architect envisaged a garden campus, verdant and bucolic. On November 25, the incorporation papers arrived, affirming that Southern California's newest private university was in business. Vision now became an imperative insisting on realization.

The site for the future University of Redlands had long been celebrated for its natural beauty. The broad valley of San Bernardino "lies smiling before me . . . a mass of verdure with its groves of forest trees scattered over the immense grassy lawns, up to the very foot of the mountain ridges," lawyer Benjamin Hayes confided to his diary in 1862. Musing about the Spanish Franciscans and their unerring eye for the best locations for their missions, he marveled at the scene before him and concluded, "But go to Jumua [the San Bernardino Valley], and you will say they must have been *poets*." Hayes penned his remarks near the old San Gabriel Mission ranch, on what is now Barton Road at Nevada Street in Redlands.

Nearly forty years after Hayes's rhapsodic comments, pioneer California Impressionist Theodore Steele, originally a member of the "Hoosier Group" of Indiana artists, became, along with William Wendt, possibly the first Impressionist committed to painting the Southern California landscape, when he was living in Redlands in 1902 and 1903. Steele executed a series

of colorful mountain, forest, and town views, many of them from near the site of the old Stillman vineyard on Colton Avenue. He found "the local color strong and vivid . . . the wonderful color effects of the landscape . . . due far more to the atmosphere than anything else. The air seems to vibrate with flashes of colored light, rose and violet and red and blue and orange, and this with a vividness and intensity I have never seen before. So brilliant does this become . . . at sunset and twilight, that it often made me think of aniline dyes. . . ."

Today a sense of place permeates the buildings and grounds of the University of Redlands. Its location celebrates the natural beauty much lauded by pioneers. Founded in 1881 by two Connecticut friends, Edward G. Judson and Frank E. Brown, the Redlands Colony was named for the area's adobe-red clay soil. The burgeoning navel orange groves and the salubrious climate had brought people to Redlands who had read and wanted to experience the world Charles Nordhoff described in his 1873 book *California for Health, Pleasure and Residence.* His Chapter 12 enticingly describes the San Bernardino Valley as having "a climate more charming and healthful in winter than Los Angeles . . . and appears as one of the most fruitful parts of the Southern country."

The town's destiny changed when the twins Alfred H. and Albert K. Smiley, nationally known educators and resort owners, established their winter homes in Redlands. Civil engineer Frank Brown, whose Bear Valley dam provided water to Redlands, knew his colony would be "the coming spot." In a few short years, the town boasted one of the nation's highest concentrations of millionaires. Both president William McKinley and Theodore Roosevelt visited friends living in Redlands. An established population of eastern and midwestern residents demonstrated a keen value for

Redlands had ten thousand residents, many with college degrees, including eleven from Harvard; eight from Yale; five from Michigan, four each from California, Columbia, Cornell, Pennsylvania; three each from Princeton and Wisconsin, and two each from Bowdoin, Chicago, Dartmouth, and Heidelberg. Twenty-four institutions, including three foreign universities, had one graduate each, only one of which was from south of the Mason and Dixon line. In short, the people who orchestrated Redlands's cultural, educational, and business life represented a particular collegiate vision and experience. It should also be noted that Redlands, for its population size at that time, sent the highest percentage in California of its high school pupils to college.

Chief architect for the gown side of the equation and representing the sectarian energy was the dynamic and intellectual Jasper Newton Field, the fifty-one-year-old new minister of the local First Baptist Church. Armed with an impressive list of credentials and publications and an undergraduate degree from Denison, a Baptist college, Field made the fateful and propitious decision to leave a series of successful midwestern pastorates for the Redlands church.

higher education. With money in their pockets, time on their hands, and goodwill in their hearts, Redlanders were ready for a college.

In 1906 the synergy between the residents of Redlands and the Southern California Baptist Educational Commission radiated reciprocal cooperation. An unlikely set of circumstances emboldened twenty-five-year-old community to seek a college, wooing Baptists in Southern California who longed to join the list of denominations that had created private institutions of higher learning. From its very beginning, the University of Redlands was a joint effort between the Baptists and the town's leading citizens, the majority of which were non-Baptists. This union marks the first time in Southern California that a municipality had joined with a religious denomination to match each other's demands for money, land, and mutual support.

FURTHERING THE BAPTIST MISSION

In his fiftieth-anniversary history of the University, *Redlands: Biography of a College* (1958), Professor Lawrence E. Nelson noted three forces that resulted in the selection of Southern California, and ultimately Redlands, for the college site: First, the arrival of Field in Redlands in early 1906. Second, the San Francisco earthquake and fire, which slightly damaged the Baptist California College in Oakland but severely damaged the finances of the

Citrus: Not Only a Fruit but a Romance

"It is not only a fruit, but also a romance," writer Charles Lummis astutely observed one hundred years ago about the citrus industry in Southern California. The navel eating orange enjoyed a reputation separate from the Valencia juice orange produced in Florida. Less than one-tenth of a percent of the world's land is suitable for the cultivation of this seedless fruit. Redlands was thus blessed by its geography. By the peak of production in 1940, the City of Redlands had ten thousand acres and twenty-five packing houses producing and marketing some of the most famous, delectable, and beautiful Washington navel oranges in the world.

Indeed, Redlands's cofounders Edward G. Judson and Frank E. Brown, Connecticut men, staked the colony's future on the navel orange. "The orange tree is the living symbol of richness, luxury, and elegance," gushed Cary McWilliams in *Southern California Country: An Island on the Land* (1946). A five-, ten-, or twenty-acre plot of citrus could support a family. Thus California's second gold rush came not from nuggets in the earth but rather upon golden orbs on trees. Some of the land that the University acquired for its campus was planted with citrus and over the years more was planted. A hard lesson about nature's vagaries was learned in 1913, when a freeze severely cut the University's citrus-based income.

Following World War II, housing tracts began to replace citrus groves throughout Southern California. In 1955 San Bernardino County had fifty thousand acres of citrus. Today, it has less than 2,500. In 1984 a town and gown project replanted three acres of University groves at Colton Avenue and Grove Street. Named "Centennial Grove," it honored the forthcoming 1988 centennial of the city's incorporation. Since then additional pocket-grove plantings dot the campus. Once again fruit is harvested and the March air is filled with the smell of orange blossoms.

constituency. Lastly, Pomona College's proposal to the Baptists and Disciples of Christ to join with Congregationalist Pomona in forming a truly strong inter-denominational school "able to compete successfully in college work with the great universities near San Francisco."

The Baptist denomination originated in the Protestant movement in seventeenth-century England. The first Baptists came to America in 1639. When the nineteenth-century debate over slavery resulted in civil war, hard feelings and tensions led the denomination to split into the Southern Baptist Convention (pro-slavery) and the Northern Baptists (anti-slavery). By the twentieth century, the Northern Baptists had evolved into the American Baptist Convention. Jasper Field and his Baptist site selection committee colleagues were heirs to the Northern Baptist tradition.

"Encouraged by the pastor of the denominationally powerful First (Baptist) Church of Los Angeles, on Sunday, July 15 (five days after the interdenominational committee agreed upon conditions of a possible union with Pomona), Field consulted his Trustees and Deacons after the morning service, found them unanimously favoring a Baptist College at Redlands," wrote Nelson. What was to be "the town" part of the equation had set the ball rolling.

A chance meeting between Field and Redlands's Board of Trade member Homer P. D. Kingsbury occurred in Smiley Park, behind the A. K. Smiley Library. There, sitting on a bench under a shade tree, the two men shared ideas about a possible college for Redlands.

On Monday morning, the town's forces gathered at the Board of Trade (today known as the Chamber of Commerce) in the Phinney Block building and listened intently to Kingsbury, a businessman known as "the Marmalade King." He talked to them about the Pomona proposal, indicating that a number of prominent Baptists preferred a college of their own.

Kingsbury, a Harvard alumnus and a Congregationalist, enthusiastically introduced Field to present the particulars.

In twenty-four hours, two constituencies were challenged in ways guaranteed to produce results. To the Baptists, Field pointed out the existence of the Methodist University of Southern California, Presbyterian Occidental College, Quaker Whittier, Church of the Brethren LaVerne, Roman Catholic Loyola, Disciples of Christ Chapman; he reminded them of Congregationalist Pomona's plan to seize the day. He challenged his parishioners to respond affirmatively in terms he would later use to implore the Southern California Baptist Convention: "But you say . . . 'It will cost a tremendous struggle.' That is certainly true. But what are we here for?" Given the American Baptist propensity for establishing institutions of higher education—Brown, Kalamazoo, Dennison, Ottawa,

and others across America—Field drove home the need and appropriateness for a college at Redlands.

Kingsbury then expertly appealed to the civic pride and vanity of the important businessmen before him. Did not Redlands boast thriving tourism? World-famous Washington navel oranges? Beautiful mansions? The celebrated Smiley Heights botanical park? Had not President Theodore Roosevelt made Redlands his first stop in California, where he greeted his influential friend Albert K. Smiley, the town's "patron saint"? Kingsbury exclaimed, "What is the town missing?" A college.

"The air was tremulous with skepticism and doubt," recalled Field about his December 7, 1906, speech to the Southern California Convention. "Timidity was in evidence on every hand, but in less than sixty minutes . . . the air was super charged with the spirit of enthusiasm, resolution and hope." With sizzling oratory, Field reminded the convention delegates that "the way is open for one of two things: either to content ourselves . . . with doing nothing; or to build up a school of our

own." He concluded, "From the tips of my toes to the crown of my head, I am in favor of having a college that will be credit to ourselves and to the state, or none at all. . . ."

His oratory carried the hour. A new commission was appointed to select the location for a college with Field as its chairman. Offers and rumors of offers came from Azusa, Gardena, Long Beach, Newport, Ontario, Pasadena, Redlands, Riverside, and Santa Ana. The commission looked at four of the sites—Azusa, Pasadena, Redlands, and Riverside.

When fifteen committee members visited Redlands on June 2, 1907, they toured the town, met the local committee, and heard the offers and the requirements that Redlanders expected. Twelve of them stayed on for dinner at the Casa Loma Hotel. It had been an overcast, chilly day, which surprised committee members, who had been told by competing towns nearer Los Angeles to expect enervating, hot weather. Mayor J. J. Suess, a native of Switzerland, confronted the issue directly, telling the delegates that the heat "was not as tiring as some would have the commission believe." He declared that the weather never prevented him from doing what he needed to do in his Star Grocery business and that it would not stop students from studying. The weather concern quickly evaporated.

The best offer was that of the citizens of Redlands: forty acres of land and $25,000, both of which came from Karl C. Wells, a young banker from Vermont. Today that cash amount is equal to about $460,000. The Redlands committee had offered to raise $100,000 from the town, equivalent now to about $1,825,000. Redlands asked that the Baptists raise $240,000, with $200,000 as a minimum (in today's world $3 million). Moreover, they requested that $300,000 (about $5.5 million today) be raised by the Baptists in eastern church and financial circles. A town of ten thousand and a few Baptists had committed to raise a staggering amount of money. Perhaps the locals counted on that great Baptist millionaire John D. Rockefeller to aid the project, since he had founded the University of Chicago in 1892. One thing is for certain: no one

wanted to repeat the financial struggles that had almost ended the Congregationalist effort at Pomona College, and both Redlanders and Baptists alike wanted the new college to be economically stable from the start. Their concern was exacerbated by the severe bank and financial panic of 1907, ultimately ended by the audacious effort of financier J. P. Morgan.

Of the seven signatories on the Redlands offer, only one was a Baptist, Arthur C. Gregory, a real-estate and citrus man. Others were former city councilman and clothing-store owner Frank P. Meserve; banker and citrus grower H. H. Ford; businessman M. M. Phinney, in whose building on Orange Street the Board of Trade was headquartered and where the committee worked; J. J. Suess, grocer and mayor; and A. E. Brock, former member of the City Council and businessman. These men were used to getting their way, as was Field.

Chapter 2: 1907–1909

From Vineyard to Quad

> "I shrink rather from the consequences of refusal than of the acceptance of responsibility."

—JASPER NEWTON FIELD ON ACCEPTING THE UNIVERSITY PRESIDENCY

IMPLEMENTING THE VISION

When the Commission on Christian Education voted on a site, the Redlands offer, "coupled with the fact that there was no college in that part of the state, assuring a large local patronage, made the decision not only easy, but practically the only one possible," concluded historian Lawrence E. Nelson.

Redlands had won. *The Redlands Review* observed that, while the college was to be "fathered" by the Baptists, it was not to be strictly denominational, and as a result citizens from other local churches joined the bandwagon. One prominent Presbyterian pledged $1,000 at the local banquet to entertain the Baptist Commissioners. Speakers included Reverend Dr. J. H. Williams of the Congregational Church and Reverend L. W. Warren of the Presbyterian Church.

After the decision was reached to locate the new college in Redlands, the next step was to appoint a board of trustees. Its charter members included Mattison B. Jones of Los Angeles, chairman (in the founding decades the title was "president," but the current term of "chairman" has been employed for consistency's sake); A. H. Smith of Pasadena, vice president; Frank G. Cressey of Los Angeles, secretary; and Homer P. D. Kingsbury of Redlands, treasurer. Other members were Jasper Newton Field, operating as financial agent or chief fundraiser; A. T. Currier, businessman, state assemblyman, and sheriff from Walnut; Jesse W. Curtis, jurist from San Bernardino; W. H. Fowler, businessman and citrus grower, Los Angeles; Arthur C. Gregory, Redlands; G. F. Holt, Riverside; C. C. Pierce and F. C. Roseberry, Los Angeles; Carey R. Smith, Santa Ana; J. H. Strait, Redlands; and W. W. Wilcox, Colton.

As chairman of the Board of Trustees, Mattison Jones guided the course of the University from 1907 to 1942. The University's early development owes as much to Jones as to the four presidents whose tenure overlapped his reign. A maxima cum laude graduate of the University of Kentucky, he had delivered his graduation address in Latin, taught college, and became the first civilian to be named commandant in the university's history. A lawyer and a leading Democrat in Los Angeles, Jones provided leadership that combined a strong intellect and firm resolve. He also was a man of definite opinions and could be a formidable presence.

The board and their fundraising colleague Field confronted a gloomy picture in September 1907. The financial panic among the nation's banks had spread to Southern California. Banks,

compelled to conserve their balances, limited depositors' daily withdrawals. They substituted script issued from the Los Angeles Clearing House Corporation for United States currency. Gold went into hiding and panic began to spread across America.

Recalling those days in a 1911 address, Field praised the board as a "braver, more self-sacrificing, more painstaking and determined body of men" than he had ever known. "We have put our hands to the plow and must not turn back. Believing that we were divinely led, we tore up the bridges, we overthrew the ships, we cut off all possible means of retreat, and with nerves of whipcord and sinews of steel we stuck to our job. . . . You know the rest."

Meeting for the first time formally, the board convened at the First Baptist Church of Redlands on December 19, 1907. In calling the meeting to order, Chairman Jones observed that the

gavel he used to inaugurate America's newest Baptist college had a symbolic tie to the nation's oldest, Brown University. It was made from a piece of oak from Brown's University Hall (1770).

By consensus the board charged Field with the goal to raise $200,000; as an incentive, he was guaranteed three percent of the total raised. Instruction was to begin in September 1909. The trustees also voted to ask E. Benjamin Andrews, former president of Brown and recent head of the University of Nebraska, to assume this post at Redlands. The innovative and energetic Andrews had been president at Denison College when Field was an undergraduate there. From him Field had learned much, especially traits that would prove invaluable in raising money.

The next day, December 20, the board adopted the by-laws, confirmed the new trustees, achieved a quorum, and took business up in earnest. At the board's January 14 meeting, Field

reported that $25,000 had been raised from eighteen Baptist churches in Southern California. A bright note was the decision by the trustees of the now-defunct Baptist-founded Los Angeles University to transfer its assets to Redlands, which, it was hoped, could net an additional $60,000.

Much discussion about the proper structure of the institution ensued. Field and his supporters prevailed with plans for a university. He envisioned additions to the "regular college course . . . a college of fine arts . . . a college of medicine and other professional courses to be introduced as the institution grows and its facilities will permit, thus making it eventually a university in the full sense of the word." Nevertheless, for twenty years, the defining designation—college or university— simmered beneath the surface of trustee meetings. The function and demands of a "university" contrasted with the nature of the liberal arts undergraduate bedrock known as the "College of Arts [Letters] and Sciences." By the January 14, 1908, trustee meeting, the amount Field had secured had grown to $40,000. He proposed to visit Andrew Carnegie on his way to the Baptist General Education Board in New York City. Alas, Carnegie volunteered encouragement but made no financial commitment. The trustees' hope to raise large sums in the East ultimately proved illusory.

Andrews decided not to become president, and throughout 1908 the search for the right individual continued at a slow pace. In the absence of a president, Field headed the study of buildings needed for the University site, consulting closely with Norman Foote Marsh, a South Pasadena architect whom the board had selected. Marsh's work included many schools and churches in Southern California—notably, Founders Hall at the University of Southern California, and the First Baptist Church of San Pedro. He and his partner, C. H. Russell, designed many landmark buildings in South Pasadena. They created the site plan for Venice, California, and its now-famous buildings on Windward Avenue. Emphasizing the importance of landscape as an integral part of the campus plan, he called

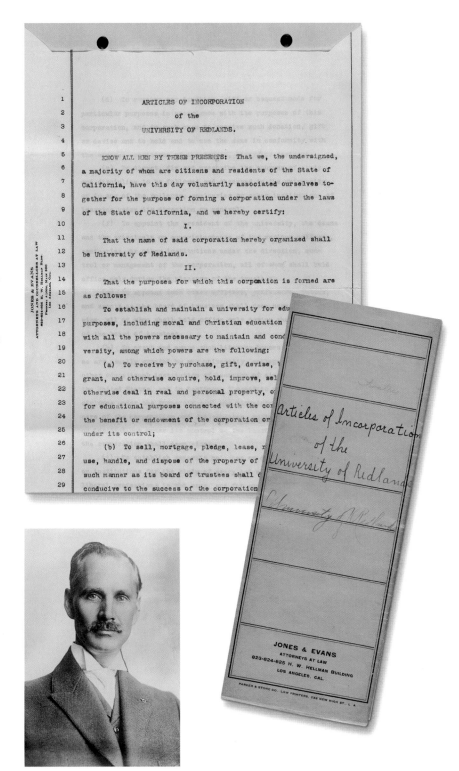

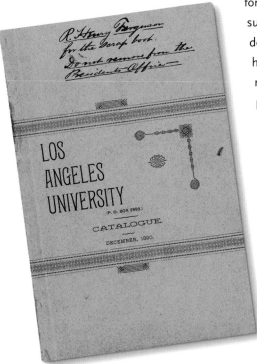

for a quadrangle that was largely a sunken garden. Signature academic buildings and residential halls were to surround it. A museum was sited where the present Founders Hall is located. Marsh's basic design evolved between 1907 and 1908.

Field urged the board and Marsh to plan for an administration building, a president's home, and a heating station. Field's leadership is demonstrated in the master plan for construction that accompanies notations in the board meeting minutes.

At the December 31, 1908, meeting, the trustees took stock of their progress and requested that Field excuse himself from the room. When he was asked to return, the board informed him that unanimously they wanted him to become the first president of the University of Redlands. Field, somewhat surprised, told them candidly that "he did not seek the place and was not certain as to his duty in the matter." Chairman Jones had publicly called for Field's appointment in an address to the Los Angeles Baptist Association earlier in 1908. After hearing this stirring address, the association voted to ask the trustees to appoint him president.

Replying to the February 5 formal letter of appointment from Jones, Field responded with an eloquence and sincerity that impressed the chairman:

> Most thoroughly do I appreciate this great honor conferred upon me by my brethren. But, when I think of the responsibilities involved, especially in connection with the launching and guidance of such an Institution as we have in mind, I am overwhelmed and say as did one of old, "Who is sufficient for these things?"
>
> Were I to think only of my unworthiness of such distinguished honor, and of my keen sense of weakness to cope with such a great task, I should certainly decline. . . . I shrink rather from the consequences of refusal than of the acceptance of the responsibility.
>
> Realizing to some degree at least what it means, with unfaltering faith in God, with unbounded confidence in my brethren, and with a resolute purpose of heart to give to this Institution the best of my life, I accept the office and shall be ready to enter upon its duties March 1, 1909.

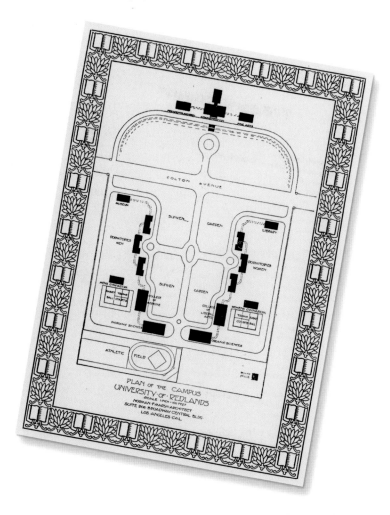

A noted speaker, Field utilized well-honed oratory with scintillating analogies and vivid verbal pictures. "What kind of an institution shall the University of Redlands be?" he asked the audience of the Southern California Baptist Convention in November 1909. "Not one of us knew which way to steer," he told them. Acknowledging the Lord's "unseen hand," Field declared, "He placed His Beacon Light to lead us safely on to our anchorage in the harbor of fulfilled desire."

A 1913 pledge form expresses Field's definition of the mission of the University, as well as his "pitch" in approaching donors for money. Its economic use of language, straightforward presentation, and forthright

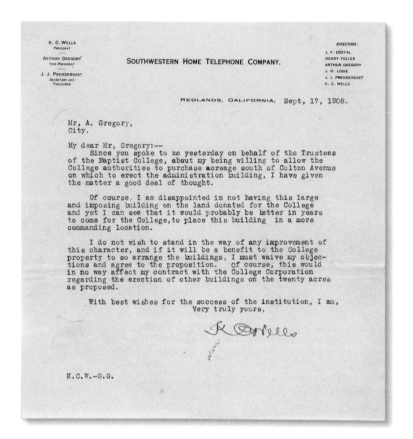

structure let a prospective donor or a long-time supporter understand with no ambiguity what the University was all about. "The University of Redlands aims to mould the mind and the heart so that in the conflict of life, keenness and conscience shall go forth together. It seeks to impress its pupils with the idea that making men is more important than making money; that it is better to live a life than to make a living."*

FUNDING THE VISION

When it came to fundraising in 1908–09, Field's energy touched many people and institutions. He was particularly fond of reminding potential donors of the following: "On a tombstone of a great and generous man was this epigram: 'What I used I had, what I saved I left behind, what I gave away I took with me.'" Apparently the tactic worked. Mr. and Mrs. Martin Bekins of Los Angeles stepped up to the plate and offered to

donate a dormitory. In March 1909, President Field reported that $80,000 (more than $1.5 million in present terms) had been raised from the Redlands community, apart from the original forty-acre donation from local resident Karl Wells.

With such good news, the trustees confidently entered into a contract with the J. F. Atkinson Company of Los Angeles for $61,000 to construct the Administration Building and committed an additional $18,000 to Califia Ornamental Brick Company for the exterior of the building. In order to understand the magnitude of this achievement, that equals $1.75 million in today's value. The University declined some offers. An anonymous donor proffered $250, a present-day equivalent of $5,000, "on the condition that no colored students be permitted." After a brief discussion, the president pursued the donor and asked him to drop the requirement. Instead, the donor was dropped.

As the board and president considered how to lay out a campus on the land donated by Wells, they became enamored of a hill across Colton Avenue just south of the gifted land. The former site of a winery and home belonging to the J. D. B. Stillman family, struck them as an imposing location for their planned administration building. A gracious and open-minded supporter of the University, Wells expressed disappointment that the stately edifice would not be on his land, but yielded to architect Marsh's vision. The University moved quickly to acquire the eight-acre parcel and soon added others.

At high noon on Monday, April 9, 1909, President Field addressed a crowd three times as large as expected from atop what would shortly become Ad Hill. After taking up the shovel

---

* For today's reader, this statement may come as a shock when compared with the University's present multi-paragraphed omnibus mission statement. The majority of undergraduates when polled in my course on the University's history expressed admiration for the sentiment but quickly noted the impossibility of such achievement in "modern times." Most daunting for the students to accept was the notion that making a life is more important than self-preservation and economic success. Yet, a sizable number allowed that the "mind and the heart" sentence remains at the center of the University's mission.

The Laying of the Cornerstone

When town and gown gathered to dedicate the Beaux Arts-style Administration Building on June 21, 1909, Mattison Jones, chairman of the Board of Trustees, presided; distinguished clergy offered prayers and scripture readings; President Field delivered an address; a quartet sang songs; and the contents of the cornerstone were sealed.

For many years following, the cornerstone was referred to pejoratively as the "northwest cornerstone creed," since it was believed to contain the Baptist articles of faith to which faculty had to swear allegiance. Imagine the surprise when the contents were later discovered not to include a creed but rather a copy of the incorporation articles for the University; a red-covered booklet on the University; a picture of Field; a history of the First Baptist Church of Redlands;

the names of the trustee building committee; Field's address to the Southern California Baptist Convention on December 7, 1907, advocating for a college in Redlands; copies of the *Redlands Daily Facts* for May 31 and June 20, 1909; and a list of the members of the Board of Trade (Chamber of Commerce) and the City Council when the movement to found a college began in Redlands in 1906–07.

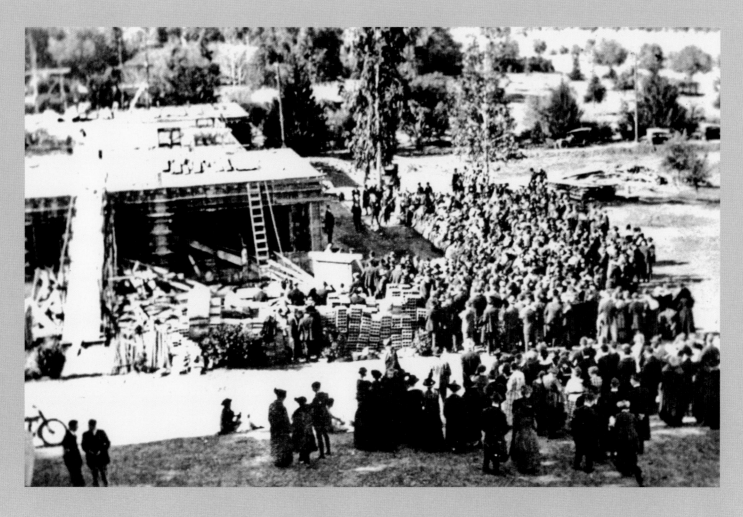

Pasadena's Tournament of Roses on New Year's Day.

by the Baptist denomination. Still, the ministerial presence was felt on the board for years, and it was not always one of harmony as the institution matured. Indeed, President Emeritus George Henry Armacost, during the seventy-fifth anniversary of the University, in 1982, remarked that one of his earliest challenges was to ease out some of the long-time Baptist trustees who resisted modern ideas because they feared a dilution of the original religious purpose inherent in the institution's mission.

When Thomas C. Roseberry, lawyer and founder of the Franklin Life Insurance Company, as well as a real-estate investor, joined the founding board, he agreed to become the Business Manager for the new University. This helped to solidify its image among potential donors and also provided expert handling of the funds.

At the location of the Frenzell Brick Yard, two successive Redlands mayors, George Cortner and Homer Kingsbury,

and turning the symbolic spade of earth, he presented brief but piquant remarks. Field told his listeners, "A short time ago we were not here; a few more years we shall have gone hence. May it be our supreme purpose while here to turn to the best account for good the power that God has given us. . . . May [the University's] policy be neither too narrow nor too broad, but such as will redound to the glory of God and the good of mankind. . . ."

A June 21 date was set for laying the cornerstone of the Administration Building. President Field and the Board of Trustees, having established solid ground in early 1909 for curriculum, faculty hiring, student recruitment, creation of the physical plant, and fundraising, felt confident to open the University on September 29.

From the University's founding, the issue of the Baptist involvement was explicit, as stated by Field: "While it is a Baptist institution . . . let it be a school where children of other denominations can come . . . without having their denominational preferences interfered with in the least." The University's incorporation papers do not mention any ownership or control

sought and in 1908 secured a bond issue for a park on the University Street parcel lying west of the campus. This led to the creation of Sylvan Park in 1912. It has provided an open space of beauty and recreation ever since.

Harley F. MacNair '12 described Field as "a good persuader," with "intense enthusiasm." He concluded that Field "had one characteristic, at least, in common with Napoleon—namely the power and imagination to dream great things and then set to work undaunted by obstacles, physical and not physical, to draw them out of the dream-world and put them into the world of reality." To many students, Field was removed as a figure with which to identify. Nellie Hill Lolmaugh '14 observed that he put into the presidency "sufficient dignity to grace even an old and well-established university. A bit pompous and naturally self-important, he led the course of the University of Redlands in its first five years—years of success and adversity."

A Campus Takes Shape

In 1909 upon being picked up at the train station, new faculty member S. Guy Jones was asked by the carriage driver his occupation. After he replied that he was to be a professor at the new college, the driver exclaimed, "Hell, mister, there ain't no college there, but just piles of sand and dirt."—ANECDOTE OF S. GUY JONES

OPENING THE DOORS

President Jasper Newton Field spent considerable time on securing a first faculty of "excellent men." George Melton had taught history at the University of Chicago and also served as superintendent of library purchasing. Edwin DuPoncet taught at the University of Missouri, in Argentina, and in Utah. He spoke eight languages, read more, and was selected to head the Department of Modern Languages. The genial A. Harvey Collins came with a background in school administration in Southern California. Formerly a professor of Greek at William Jewell College in Liberty, Missouri, James "Jimmy" Kyle so loved ancient languages that students came to believe he thought in them. Victor L. Duke, a handsome, austere man whose half-smile confused students who never knew whether he laughed at them or with them, had taught in Illinois and was appointed professor of mathematics. George Knights, a gentle spirit touched with humor, had worked at private academies in Pennsylvania and Illinois and came to teach English literature. George Robertson, a Congregational pastor and instructor who was the essence of kindness and consideration, became professor of geology. Don José Rodriguez, who was born in Spain and educated in Italy, France, and America, agreed to head up the School of Music. The first professor of physics, S. Guy Jones, from the Pillsbury Academy in Minnesota, was

the youngest member of the faculty. A splendid athlete, the red-headed Jones also directed the required outdoor activities. Duke, Jones, Kyle, and Robertson each stayed at Redlands for over two decades.

Three of the faculty had Ph.D. degrees, a high percentage in those days. In the United States, an undergraduate degree had remained standard for college faculty into the nineteenth century. Americans who desired to pursue advanced study usually did so in Germany. While the first American doctorate

was conferred in 1861, the degree did not become standard until after 1876, when Johns Hopkins instituted a graduate program, which other schools then copied.

The University of Redlands's tuition, due in advance, was $50.00 per semester. Students had to pay fees of $5.00 for biology, chemistry, and physics, and lab fees of $8.00. A double room in a dormitory did not come with bedcovers, linens, and towels; students had to supply their own. Those electing to use the bathroom down the hall paid $27.00 monthly or $30.00 for a private room with a bath. Meals cost an additional $20.00 per month.

The graduation requirements of one hundred twenty units included English twenty hours, mathematics six, history ten, sociology three, ethics three, Christian evidences three, psychology four, science eight, modern languages six, and ancient languages eighteen. Students could elect to receive a bachelor of philosophy or a bachelor of science degree. An M.A. and M.S. required an additional year in residence, a written examination, and a thesis.

The faculty held its first meeting on September 23, 1909, at the First Baptist Church of Redlands, where classes began shortly thereafter. The opening ceremony featured a floral sign of the college name in orange letters on a dark-green background, decorated with a large bow. Orange and white were listed as the school's colors. A few days later, faculty and the thirty-nine-member student body un-selected these colors, opting instead for maroon and gray.

The institution continued to evolve, posting enrollment gains each of the first three years: from fifty-nine in 1909 to one hundred fourteen in 1910 to one hundred fifty-four in 1911. Given scant resources to

serve the growing numbers, the administration sought to reuse as much of the inherited physical plant as possible. Thus, the stones from the winery foundation became the foundation for the President's Mansion, constructed alongside the Administration Building atop Ad Hill. The retaining wall facing University Street also traces its lineage to the old winery. The wood from the winery building found new life as a gymnasium, which the University constructed adjacent to Grove Street north of Colton Avenue and east of Ad Hill. Students and faculty cleared the remnants of the vineyard next to Colton Avenue and transformed the grounds into fields suitable for athletic exploits and glory.

An even more prominent recycling became the fledgling campus's first dormitory. The Stillman family, proprietors of the former winery, occupied a large home located in the spot the University desired for the Administration Building. Because the residence was still serviceable, the University elected to relocate it to the intersection of Colton Avenue and Cook Street at the foot of Ad Hill. Renamed Reavis Hall—after the donor who financed the relocation—the mansion first served as a residence for women, and later provided classroom space and housed the first on-campus infirmary.

Even as the first year drew to a close, the campus was still taking form. Nellie Hill Lolmaugh '14 visited as a prospective student in May 1910, and later remembered being "not much impressed with what I saw." The campus comprised only four buildings: the gymnasium, Reavis Hall, and the two new buildings, Administration and Bekins, both as yet incomplete. Although she admitted having wanted to attend Pomona College, the warm, familial ambiance fostered by the charter students won her over. "The welcome accorded us at lunch, the happy atmosphere and the quality of students gave me hope, and before long I could see [myself] as a music student . . . registering in the fall term of [the school's] second year."

Lolmaugh's memories, provide us with a most vivid account of those pioneering days. The Ad Building, as it came to be called, housed most classes and served as the site of laboratories, library, chapel, and administrative offices. To the north stood the transverse San Bernardino mountain range running west to east, trending south. "Often enough we were reminded of the inspiration we could — or would — get from God's handiwork," said Lolmaugh. "Yes, that view became a real part of our education." The stunning 360-degree vista afforded from the hill made up for the lack of additional buildings and landscaped amenities of a mature campus.

Despite the relative incompleteness, neither Lolmaugh nor her peers regretted their choice to attend a "start-up school." She emphasized that they recognized their pioneering status, and she never heard anyone say, "I'm sorry I went to Redlands instead of another college." Indeed, attending a new institution had certain built-in advantages: "We were glad to have the personal interest of the faculty, the smaller classes, and the beautiful long-lasting friendships."

Reavis Hall housed "the girls," while "boys were

bedded down in the administration building." The former decamped for Bekins upon its completion, and the School of Music of Don José Rodriguez also found a home in the new structure. While other buildings would eventually crowd around the Quad, Lolmaugh recalled that this first edifice "stood out like a sore thumb." The absence of landscaping exacerbated that impression. "Nothing grew around [Bekins] until a few plants were put up against the wall; not grass, no trees or shade, but plenty of dust. . . . We had to imagine ivy-covered walls, old oak trees and well-worn paths beneath . . . but we were pioneering, those things would come later."

Spurred by the energy and contributions of Jasper Field, the founding trustees, and important supporters in town, the fledgling University enjoyed a running start. Yet one other group of founders merits our attention as well, as Lolmaugh's words remind us. "Too much credit cannot be given to the young people who were willing to come to a 'one-horse' institution of higher learning with no history, no background, no traditions and no accreditation." Her point well-taken, we now render credit where credit is due and turn our attention to Lolmaugh's peers, those self-same "young people" who braved a "'one-horse' institution" and pioneered the folkways, mores, and traditions of student life.

STUDENTS CHART THEIR COURSE

Developing a student life and traditions might seem daunting in retrospect, but for the charter students these constituted a challenge and a responsibility. From the beginning and for the next two decades, the faculty was vested with the day-to-day responsibility for student life. Faculty minutes illustrate the diversity of concerns and areas of oversight. Student marriages caused Field to call a special meeting in 1912. How to control their charges' romances? The faculty passed a motion in which

BELOW LEFT: Bekins Hall "stood out like a sore thumb," recalled Lolmaugh. "Nothing grew around it until a few plants were put up against the wall; not grass, no trees or shade, but plenty of dust. . . . We had to imagine ivy-covered walls. . . ."

BELOW RIGHT: The Bekins lobby featured a brick hearth and Craftsman furniture. Note the "Redlands" pillow on the bench.

BOTTOM: Pictured here (left to right) are Delta Kappa Psi's Anita M. Gordon '14, Virginia Claire Gaines '12, Grace Ellington x'14, Helen M. Field '13, Isabel Carpenter x'13, Ruth M. Bekins '13, Beatrice Fessendin, and Lois E. Field '10, at Arrowhead Hot Springs in about 1912. The occasion was the sorority's first annual luncheon.

they expressed a "keen sense of responsibility" for the moral, spiritual, and social welfare of the students, and therefore considered marriage while in school to be "very detrimental" to the students' best interest. In fact, they opposed such action and declared that "cases of this kind will be disciplined."

Despite the small student body of twenty in 1910, augmented by seventeen in the Preparatory Department and twenty-two non-degree candidates, issues of irregular attendance at chapel (religious service) and assembly (the secular "business" meeting of the University's constituents) confronted the faculty. They debated letters from parents asking that their son or daughter be excused for health reasons from attendance at regular assemblies. They decided to fasten chairs together in sets of five with the classes seated separately. To control noise in the dormitory hallways, the faculty asked students to participate in their own enforcement of "quiet." Faculty oversight even extended to the corridors of Smiley Library, directing that students speaking loudly be held accountable. But when the campus library opened, the noisy students continued their frolic.

The first commencement, with three graduates, took place on Thursday morning, June 16, 1910. President Field proudly awarded the first diploma to his daughter Lois E. Field '10. She later recalled her resentment at being pulled out of Stanford

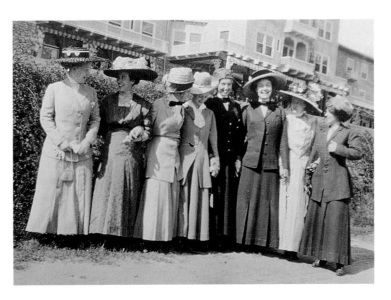

The Zanja Fiesta

The first Zanja Fiesta was held in June 1910 as a highlight of the University's first commencement week. The idea came from Adelaide Field, the president's wife, and helped to honor the first three graduates, John W. Jones '10, Ralph R. Rice '10, and Lois E. Field '10, the Fields' daughter. The campus community gathered for the fiesta on the banks of the Zanja ("ditch" in Spanish). Lights and boats for the occasion embellished the grounds, and the decorations included "colored serpentines and pounds of confetti," all of which created a jovial holiday atmosphere. The event included circus elements such as sideshows, a band, popcorn, and roasted peanuts.

From the very beginning, a theatrical production highlighted the fiesta. The inaugural spectacle was Gilbert and Sullivan's *Mikado*, directed by Don José Rodriguez, chair of the School of Music. At the behest of Professor Victor L. Duke, the faculty even voted that the spring semester conclude the previous Friday so that students in the cast and crew would have more time to rehearse prior to the Monday performance.

The first fiestas featured lighthearted musicals. Then operettas became the favored offering. Faculty sometimes wrote and scored the productions, and in 1914 an audience of two thousand university and townspeople attended. A military

theme was presented in 1917, signaling the enveloping presence of World War I.

The June 1927 presentation marked the first time the new Alumni Greek Theatre served as the performance venue. The Zanja, which at that time flowed in front of the theater, often was damned up to create a shallow lake. This permitted canoes or gondolas festooned with lights to be rowed gently across the water.

By the 1930s, the Zanja Fiesta had Redlands community members writing scripts and participating in productions. Created for the University's Silver Jubilee, *Feathered Serpent* by local resident Bruce McDaniel related the story of the fall of the Aztec empire and thus served an educational purpose. Future Broadway and film star John E. Raitt '39 played the lead in the 1937

production of *Die Fledermaus* (The Bat) while still a student. Reviews dubbed it "brilliant." By 1941 many alumni, including Raitt, were participating in productions.

Following World War II, the enthusiasm for the fiesta waned. After several years of intermittent staging, the final production commemorated the University's Golden Jubilee in 1959. For the Diamond Jubilee in 1982, alumna Katherine Talbert Weller '71 mounted a well-received gala evocative of by-gone extravaganzas.

at her father's request to beef up the number of graduating seniors. The other two graduates were John W. Jones '10 and Ralph R. Rice '10.

Following the customary oratory and ceremony, one hundred thirty-five people adjourned to the Casa Loma Hotel for dinner. Rice presented an eloquent toast referring to the University as "the fountain of life and wisdom." He concluded with a poem now sadly lost. Board Chairman Mattison B. Jones reminded everyone to speak succinctly because so many, like himself, had to catch the 3:00 p.m. train back to Los Angeles.

The earliest students took the Santa Fe or Southern Pacific train, the Pacific Electric Red Car, or the bus to Redlands; they walked to classes and to town. Few owned cars. By 1914 more administrators and faculty had them, and so did students. By 1916 the automobile era at Redlands had arrived.

Bonding took place in various forms as the student body grew from its original fifty-nine to one hundred seventy-five by 1915. Opportunities for close collaboration were numerous. No doubt inspired by similar adventures of contemporaries at other colleges, some Redlands students began discussing the prospect of creating a symbol upon the western slope of the San Bernardino mountain range.

The students' plan gelled in March 1913 when they petitioned the faculty to excuse those who wished to work on the college letter. After a debate, the faculty bestowed their blessing on the project if participants would make up missed time and receive proper authority from the Forest Service. They even contributed to a commissary department for the boys going up the mountain to cut the "R." On a cold December day in 1913, a dozen-plus students trekked up the mountain and began to clear the brush and form the letter "R" in gray stone visible from miles away.

The Alma Mater was written by a group of college men who were attending a musical at the Wyatt Theatre at Colton Avenue and Orange Street in Redlands. "The words were hatched up to go along somewhat with the tune of 'The Little Old Red Shawl My Mother Wore,'" recalled Elizabeth J. Hidden '12. Added to the melody, which was first put

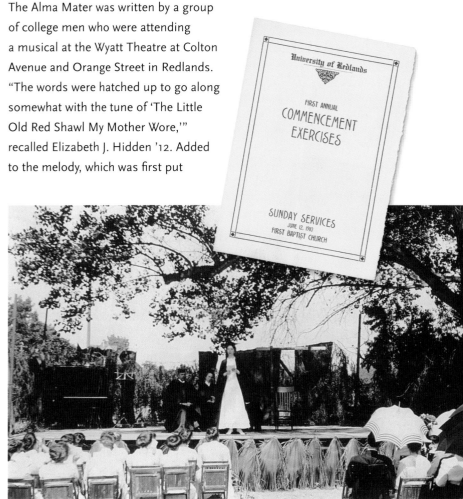

Kappa Psi, was organized, followed by Alpha Theta Phi in 1911. Even in those early days, some students believed that popularity and money overly influenced the selections for membership. That same year, a YWCA college branch was established.

A forensics program inaugurated in 1910 brought debate to the University. Ralph Rice '10 became the first University student to compete in an intercollegiate contest. The initial debate, held in 1910, pitted Redlands against the University of Southern California Law School. Alas, Redlands lost. At about the same time, the faculty determined a method of recognition for the excellent record of the 1909–10 debate team.

With the appointment of E. R. Nicholas in 1913, debate was assured a long and winning tradition at Redlands. "Prof" Nicholas pioneered speech tournaments in the West, bringing all teams together in one location instead of following the tradition of traveling from place to place. In 1916 he organized one of California's earliest high school tournaments, in Redlands. A later colleague, Joseph H. Baccus, pioneered a

to paper in 1914, was the inclusion of bars from the popular musical-theater tune "He Never Wanders Far from His Own Fire," and other verses.

The long tradition of student-founded activities and organizations began with a women's literary society called Pi Kappa Chi, founded in 1910. "With Might and Main" became the club's motto. The Hi Larkers undertook hikes and picnics. There were German and Spanish clubs sponsored by the faculty. Various local churches supported organizations as well. *The Spectrum* magazine began with the first meeting of the student body in the fall of 1910. The monthly literary magazine was renamed *The U of R Campus* in 1914. It would take until then for a critical mass of students to produce the first yearbook, which they called *La Letra* after the "R" on the mountain. In 1909 the first local fraternity, Pi Chi, was founded, and in 1910 a sorority, Delta

The Origin of the "R"

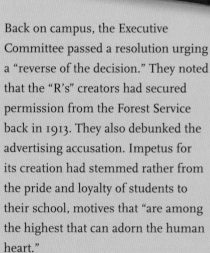

On the side of the San Bernardino Mountains, 5,000 feet above sea level, stands a 415-feet-tall, 275-feet-wide monument to the University of Redlands. With lines forty feet across, the "R" has towered over the San Bernardino Valley since 1913. Encouraged by President Field, the trustees, and the faculty, a group of mostly freshmen made the trek up to the San Bernardino range in 1913 and again in 1914 to create a college letter on the granite mountainside. Tradition quickly elevated the annual trip to trim vegetation and clean away debris into a freshman rite of passage. A little poem became the maintenance guideline:

Little Freshies, grab your mattocks,
Also seize the ancient hoe,
Take a bunch of grub and scurry
Up the mountains in a hurry
To the "R" where weeds now grow.

In early years, the trip was arduous. Mules carted food and equipment—in some places, props were needed to keep the laden burros from falling off the trail. The initial two-man surveying team, Russell D. Powell '14 and William H. "Henry" Cram x'14 experienced both rain and a snow storm so heavy it split their tent. The 1914 expedition departed campus at 4:00 a.m. but did not reach its destination until afternoon. A second and third trip ensued, scuttling all hopes of creating the letter secretly and unveiling it to the valley and campus below.

Lighting the "R" with railway flares soon became a cherished annual tradition. "To silent watchers on Administration hill," recalled historian of the University Lawrence E. Nelson, "the giant letter glowing high in the sky, first rosy red, then white, has ever been a deeply moving sight." In 1926 the United States Forest Service concluded that the lighting posed a fire hazard and that the letter itself represented "a means of advertising which is prohibited in National Forest Reserves." Officials decreed it would have to go. The "R" seemed doomed.

Local outrage quickly reached Washington, D.C. The *Redlands Daily Facts* published an unsolicited editorial by State Senator Lyman King entitled "Officialdom Gone Mad." Protests and petitions were sent to every major organization and person of influence in the San Bernardino Valley. Congressman Phil Swing, indignant, pledged his support. Even Senator Hiram W. Johnson, ex-reform governor and father of California's initiative, recall, and referendum, weighed in against the Forest Service's decision.

Back on campus, the Executive Committee passed a resolution urging a "reverse of the decision." They noted that the "R's" creators had secured permission from the Forest Service back in 1913. They also debunked the advertising accusation. Impetus for its creation had stemmed rather from the pride and loyalty of students to their school, motives that "are among the highest that can adorn the human heart."

An impressive delegation of elected local, state, and national officials, along with representatives from the colleges Pomona, La Verne, and Cal Tech, met with Colonel Greeley of the Forest Service. He listened and diplomatically deferred a decision until he returned to Washington, D.C. He subsequently ruled that existing school letters on National Forest Reserve could remain.

The battle of the "R" was won.

junior college debate tournament, the first ever held in the West even though Southern California contained the greatest aggregation of junior colleges in the world. Redlands would celebrate regional and national championships in ensuing years, taming and defeating the oratorical skills of America's best-known colleges. In the spring of 1913, women competed in debate for the first time.

Life on campus proved to be a challenge socially. Mrs. Doane, housemother at Bekins, lamented that girls could have a good time without boys. Accordingly, rules were strict and enforced. "All girls must be in, and lights out, by 11 o'clock." "What girl could go along with that?," asked Lolmaugh. Much protestation brought relaxation of the rules, even though the 11:00 p.m. curfew for women continued through the mid-1960s. Sign-outs were required before leaving the campus. Regardless, "the roof of Bekins provided space and sunshine to dry clothes and hair. It also provided a cool place to sleep, providing a student was willing to drag a mattress up the stairs and not get caught."

A balancing act between students, faculty, and trustees over student rules placed faculty in the middle, where they did not want to be. The issue of dancing provides a striking example of

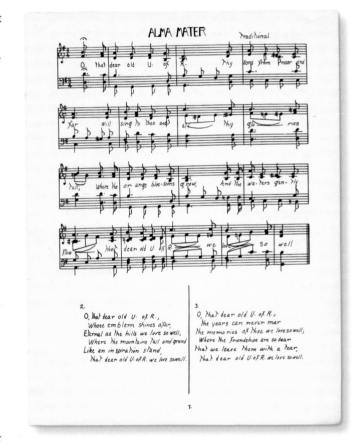

the problems they faced. Students wanted to have dances and card parties, but in the early years the faculty refused. When upholding this regulation in the face of student resistance proved too onerous, the faculty bucked the dispute to the Board of Trustees. If such events occurred off campus, the trustees decided they would require only the parents' permission. For thirty-four years, the trustees maintained the rule that dancing on campus was contrary to the wishes of the constituency.

In those early years, athletic conference issues, times of games, and permission for prepatory students and freshmen to play on the teams dominated many discussions. In 1910 the faculty organized the Athletic Association, independent of the student body. President Field called a special meeting to allow the basketball team to play against Pomona, prompting the faculty to insist that it must approve any mid-week games.

When the Athletic Association formed, it confirmed the University's intent to offer competitive sports. Baseball and track were staples in the earliest days, but rugby was the most important sport. Football had become the rage among college campuses across the country. In the early years, Redlands team members literally contributed to uniforms and sometimes even equipment. A school holiday was declared in 1914 for male faculty and students to build a fence to enclose the athletic field. Coaches were challenged to put together a complete team in many sports, especially football, in which Professors Jones, Kyle, and Duke sometimes played as "students."

The first director of physical education, Robert L. Glover, a kind and effective leader, wrote the Board of Trustees in April 1911, "Recognizing the prominent place football holds in college athletics and wishing to see the University of Redlands take an equal stand among the institutions of its kind in the state . . . I hereby express my willingness to pay one hundred dollars from my next year's salary toward securing a football coach." President Field and the board's respect for Glover translated to action at their April 5 meeting. Glover's contract was extended as physical director and head of all athletic sports, "except football at a salary of $1,000 per alum," and it was further approved "that the Board secure a good coach for the football team." As a result, Redlands scored its first touchdown ever in a 1913 game with Pomona.

THE FREEZE—HARD TIMES AND HARD FEELINGS

The very survival of the University became questionable in early 1913, in the face of a weather calamity. On January 5, temperatures plunged to eighteen degrees Fahrenheit, and they dropped below twenty each of the two successive nights. The freeze ravaged the local orange crop, and the University's future almost spoiled along with the icy fruit. The cold snap's aftermath wrought havoc with finances, a setback that ultimately

created fissures in the relationship between President Field and the Board of Trustees.

Attracted to the area by the temperate climate, many early settlers to the City of Redlands had invested in citrus growing. Profits from a five-acre navel orange grove could support a family of three. The University bolstered its income by maintaining commercial groves on campus land not used for academic

purposes. Many of its staunchest donors also derived their wealth from this lucrative crop. Thus, the University's financial well-being fluctuated with the year's orange harvest. Because the pioneers believed that the city lay in a frostless belt, no provision existed for orchard heating. The three-day freeze killed hundreds of trees outright and damaged thousands more. The bad weather in turn wiped out the year's entire crop. In the days before federal or state disaster relief, the crisis bankrupted many growers.

The calamity struck town and gown alike, and economic recovery required years. In addition to the income lost from its own groves, the University also faced a decline in gifts. Many donors in 1913 and the years that followed either postponed their pledges or reneged altogether. Tuition revenues sank, as many students, dependent upon family income that had been lost, could no longer afford tuition. Growth of the city's formerly burgeoning population stagnated. Local banks were hard-pressed. The University struggled to meet payroll, further straining the resources of local merchants whose businesses benefited from faculty spending. Fortunately, both the University and the city recognized that cooperation ensured survival. Lawrence Nelson recalled the spirit of harmony in *Redlands: Biography of a College*: "Gradually, town and gown, working together, conquered the Big Freeze." Local merchants rallied and agreed to carry over bills on goods and services to faculty. Donors from Los Angeles, including some trustees, offered short-term assistance to severely affected students. Nelson wrote that those "dauntless, desperate years matured the Redlands spirit."

As damage assessment continued, the Board of Trustees convened an emergency meeting on January 21 to discuss plans with the faculty. Three strategies emerged for dealing with the impending financial disaster. First, increasing student enrollment acquired a fresh urgency. Second, Chairman Jones appointed a short-lived committee to evaluate whether the teaching force could be reduced. Lastly, the board placed a new premium on Field's prowess as a fundraiser. Jones urged the president to depart immediately for the East to solicit money. Sadly, the lengthy trip proved to be largely futile; the president raised only $2,250, an amount too small to dent the shortfall.

The board also employed creative methods for tapping funds. In response to the widespread financial difficulty experienced by students, it voted to accept joint notes between parents, students, and the University for tuition rather than see anyone abandon their education on account of monetary distress. The trustees also affirmed that the University would use its property "to guarantee all scholarships thus far paid-in." Additionally, the faculty received a letter soliciting them to "assist the University financially during the next school year." This ploy led Victor Duke, now dean, to increase his annual personal contribution from $500 to $1,500. Professor Herbert E. Wise volunteered an additional $100, a gift intended to benefit one specific student, Herbert H. Bronk x'15. Professor Kyle offered to make good on a pledge from his late father.

At its June meeting, the board held a lengthy discussion on student recruitment and asked the faculty to draw up lists of class needs and supplies that might be contributed by University donors. Earlier, in his annual report of February 1912,

Field commented upon the "delightful spirit of harmony prevailing in the faculty and throughout the college." Similar sentiments are expressed throughout the faculty minutes of the time.

In spite of the freeze and the ego-deflating eastern trip, Field still had secured nearly $37,000. Nonetheless, signs of discontent among board members over his leadership emerged at an informal meeting in September 1913 in the office of Mattison Jones. Early in the year, the trustees had pressed the president to concentrate his energy on fundraising. While returning from the eastern trip in the spring of 1913, Field had attended the Northern Baptist Convention in Detroit and had, along with other Baptist college presidents, met with its Board of Education. He returned home enthusiastic about continued support from the Convention. The Convention urged Field

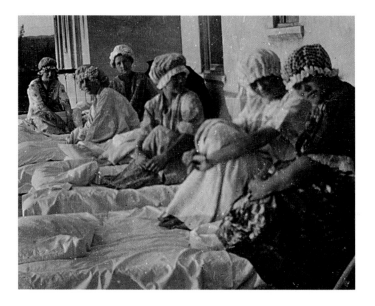

to increase the number of Baptist students. Fewer than half of the one hundred fifty-five students at Redlands in 1913–14 were Baptist, while eighty percent of Baptist young people in California attended non-Baptist institutions. Nelson noted that at the time other Protestant denominations—Methodist, Episcopalian, Presbyterian, and Congregationalist—were educating from two to five times as many of their young people, in proportion to their membership, as were Baptists.

The Convention annual report later noted that the University had many difficulties to confront but urged that its friends be ample in their appreciation and "slow and kindly in criticism." Yet Field saw little "slow and kindly" criticism. Not only did the Board of Education refuse aid to Redlands, it sent a letter expressing serious concern. Charging that the school spent altogether too much on administrative overhead, it claimed not to be saying that salaries were too high. Yet, until Redlands adjusted its practices, the Board of Education could not recommend the University to prospective donors. It also criticized expenses for the President's Mansion.

At the September board meeting, Chairman Jones revealed to the trustees correspondence between himself and the Board of Education. Noting that they had received an inquiry from a

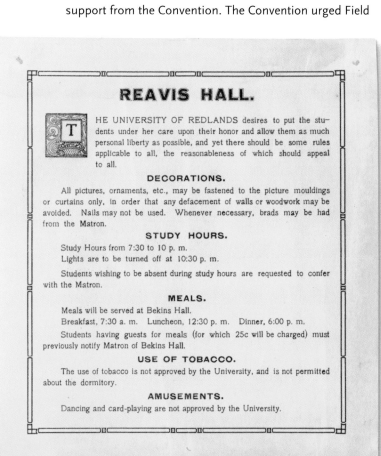

REAVIS HALL.

THE UNIVERSITY OF REDLANDS desires to put the students under her care upon their honor and allow them as much personal liberty as possible, and yet there should be some rules applicable to all, the reasonableness of which should appeal to all.

DECORATIONS.

All pictures, ornaments, etc., may be fastened to the picture mouldings or curtains only, in order that any defacement of walls or woodwork may be avoided. Nails may not be used. Whenever necessary, brads may be had from the Matron.

STUDY HOURS.

Study Hours from 7:30 to 10 p. m.
Lights are to be turned off at 10:30 p. m.
Students wishing to be absent during study hours are requested to confer with the Matron.

MEALS.

Meals will be served at Bekins Hall.
Breakfast, 7:30 a. m. Luncheon, 12:30 p. m. Dinner, 6:00 p. m.
Students having guests for meals (for which 25c will be charged) must previously notify Matron of Bekins Hall.

USE OF TOBACCO.

The use of tobacco is not approved by the University, and is not permitted about the dormitory.

AMUSEMENTS.

Dancing and card-playing are not approved by the University.

party interested in supporting Redlands financially, the trustees stated that before they could reply, they needed to address the charge that Redlands was "spending too large a proportion of its income for the management of the institution."

Field, doubtless with much indignation, read to the trustees a copy of a letter he had written to the Board of Education in which he stated his views. He then withdrew from the meeting, and the trustees entered into a candid discussion. The prospect of losing the active support of the Northern Baptist Convention in the fundraising efforts of the University weighed heavily upon their deliberations.

More telling and ominous, they talked about "the future relations and duties of President Field to the University." A resolution charged Field to commit himself first and foremost to the raising of $250,000, plus additional money for an endowment fund. When Field was called back into the meeting and told of the resolution, he committed himself to the challenge. One wonders if the trustees were advertently or inadvertently setting him up for failure. They pledged to "earnestly pray for the success of the movement before us." The goal was daunting, about $4.725 million in today's money.

The most important of Field's financial announcements centered on a gift by Effie M. (Mrs. Will) Crawford of her fifty-acre orange ranch in Villa Park, Orange County, to the University in exchange for a lifetime annuity. The board accepted the offer "with deep gratitude" and agreed to take the corpus from the ranch's sale to create the Will C. and Effie M. Crawford Chair of Ethical, Biblical, and Missionary Instruction. This became

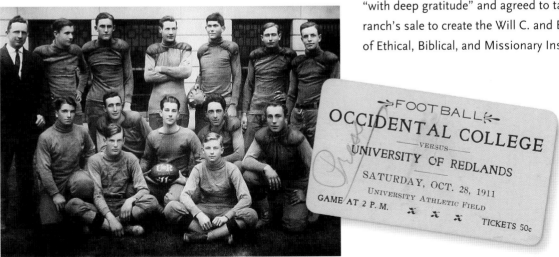

the University's first endowed chair, and in 1915 Professor Wise became the first to fill it. Nonetheless, even this good news could not reverse the disintegration of the relationship between the board and president.

The trustees also passed a resolution honoring board chairman Jones. It declared that he had given "unstintedly of his time, energy, and thought to the affairs of the University; *and that very much of the growth and welfare of the University is due to the untiring labors of Mr. Jones as president of the Board*" (italics are the author's). Further, the University's by-laws were amended so that no employee could be a member of the Board of Trustees and no paid employee could serve on the Executive Committee. Thus Field, who was an employee, was removed from both bodies. At this point, the board consisted of twenty-four members, including Field's position. The Executive Committee, chaired by Jones, had six members.

Later on the Reverend Dr. James W. Brougher reported on the news from the Northern Baptist education committee, of which he was a member. Sensing the divergent opinions of members on how Redlands was being run fiscally, he stated that the committee had agreed to contribute $50,000 to the University on the condition that it raise $200,000 by December 31, 1916, or

that the committee would donate to the endowment $100,000 if the University raised $400,000 by December 31, 1917. While the education committee would take all University requests under consideration, no decision would be made until May. It is evident that more was to be said by the trustees about the education committee, but not with Field present.

Yet another issue contributed to ending Field's tenure, albeit in an oblique but telling way: his unconditional stance at the 1907 Second Baptist Commission regarding the title of the proposed school as a "university." Board Secretary Dr. Frank G. Cressey, a powerful leader of Southern California Baptists and a founding Redlands trustee who resigned in 1909 under acrimonious circumstances, strongly advocated that institution be a college, not a university. It may be surmised that Cressey's resignation was due to Field's presidential power and the subsequent lack of support from his fellow trustees. When the Northern Baptist trustees on the board asked for an accounting as to why the president's home was "lavishly maintained" in the face of the

University's massive debts, Cressey pressed the matter on behalf of the large Southern California Baptist community.

Despite the mood, mundane issues of governance still occupied the trustees' attention. The board resumed its meeting at 7:00 p.m. with faculty in attendance. A committee of trustees and faculty was appointed to recommend changes to improve the academic program. Then the faculty left and three students came into the meeting. William Henry Geistweit '15 requested that $63.00 be appropriated to pay for medical attention for a student injured while playing on the football team and $90.00 for another so injured. Owen Walker x'15 asked that the board employ more faculty, noting the "limited teaching force." Arthur D. Smalley '14, playing "wingman" support, urged the petitions of both his colleagues be granted. All three would eventually become trustees.

On January 21, 1914, the board entered into executive session, without the president, and began a general discussion regarding the criticism made by the education committee of the Northern Baptist Church "relative to the amount of money expended by the board in the erection of the President's Mansion." All agreed that the situation mandated that the University *temporarily* use the president's home "for the music department of the College of Fine Arts."

President Field was recalled to the meeting and informed of the decision, which was described "as a crisis in the affairs of the University" that gave the trustees no other choice. Field, doubtless filled with anger and frustration, wisely refused to engage in conversation or debate and said he would "reflect upon the matter before giving a definite answer," and then left.

The poignant circumstances of Field's private life are assessed in the University's fiftieth-anniversary history by Lawrence Nelson. At fifty-nine years of age, Field was physically weary. As he had informed the trustees, he had been ill off and on for weeks and was exhausted by the negotiations "over the Crawford deal." With considerable success in fundraising

during national financial panics and the disastrous freeze of 1913, Field, in Nelson's view, felt his enthusiasm ebb as he approached donors for still more commitment, only to see gifts becoming harder to secure. He wondered if he had lost his promotional skill.

Field's personal finances also drained his energy. He lost much in the aftermath of the 1907 financial panic in a land syndicate in Buffalo, New York, which, by 1910, had soured. An arrangement involving the trade of some of the property in New York for more lucrative prospects in Riverside usurped non-University hours. The unexpected death of Elizabeth, his teenage daughter and the youngest of his five children, took its toll on him. "The emotional effect was devastating," observed Nelson.

In passing a formal resolution about the President's Mansion, the board added a sentence that would ultimately prove to be the last straw: "And that beginning with September 1914, the president's salary be reduced by the extent of the house rent."

As if anticipating imminent change, the board asked the Executive Committee to assume some presidential prerogatives

and to work out the details of appointing a chair of economics and sociology, and authorized Chairman Jones and Secretary Curtis to prepare a suitable protocol for granting scholarships. Finally, a new member was elected to succeed Field on the board. The message could not have been clearer.

March 1914 was a difficult and stressful time for the board and administration of the University of Redlands. After an opening prayer in Mattison Jones's office the morning of March 19, a special meeting of the Executive Committee began with three administrative issues. The first related to the presidency of the institution in case a vacancy occurred. The second was to identify who would be responsible for selecting new faculty members. Oddly, the third item was a more prosaic discussion about whether to change music instruction from "the presently used Italian or English method."

General discussion followed, a bit of business conducted. Then President Field spoke, handing in his resignation. There was prolonged discussion; a committee of three was appointed to further confer with Field. The meeting was adjourned to the following week, on March 25. Committee members Brougher, Merriam, and Curtis reported no progress in the discussion. It was decided to take an informal ballot to see about Field retaining the use of the mansion and continuing to act as president of the University. The results revealed a sharply divided board. Six voted in favor, nine were opposed, and one abstained. William F. Harper and J. Whitcomb Brougher, Sr. proposed a motion stating that now was "an inopportune time for a change of presidency. That, therefore we return to Dr. Field his resignation and request him to continue in his present position until the work of raising an endowment of $250,000 has been completed. . . ." The motion lost. A new motion to accept Field's resignation to take effect September 1, 1914, passed. Appropriate resolutions recognized Field as the man who had carried the day among the Baptists to found Redlands, praised his fundraising efforts, and lauded his faculty appointments. But the deed was done. The Field era passed into history.

At a last meeting with the faculty on April 7, 1914, Field was presented by Dean Duke with a resolution expressing appreciation for his work, character, and good relations with faculty. Field received poignant letter from the faculty early in May 1914. The signatories, led by Duke and joined by Professors Kyle and Wise, expressed their "deep regret" and their desire to convey "their sincere and high appreciation of the fitting services rendered our beloved institution." They complimented the "largeness" of Field's vision, his buoyant optimism, and unflagging zeal. They thanked him for helping to create an "intimate fellowship" at the faculty meetings during which Field often referred to everyone as a family. That attitude, advanced by Field with sagacity, tact, and grace, had fostered at the meetings "unanimity of spirit and purpose."

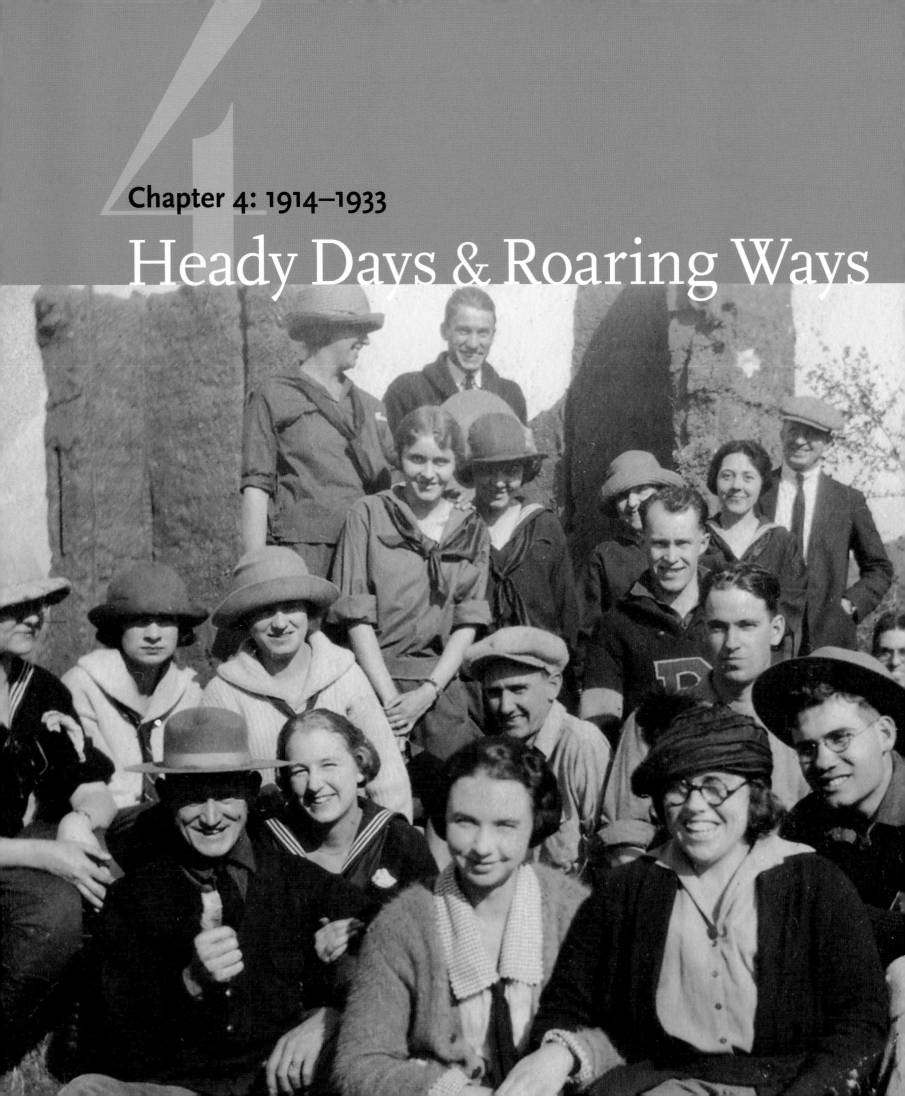

"I have made inquiry of nearly all the members of the Faculty, who seem to be of one mind concerning Prof. V. L. Duke. They tell me that he had filled the place of the Dean admirably."—JASPER NEWTON FIELD, JUNE 1913

RECHARTING THE COURSE

The sudden departure of Jasper Newton Field left the University without its rudder, and the Board of Trustees seemed uncertain what course to chart. A year would pass before the board would select Field's successor, and its members used the time to reevaluate several fundamental issues regarding University governance. In the short run, they split the duties normally shouldered by a president among three men. Chief among these was Victor L. Duke, promoted from dean of the faculty to the position of acting president.

During the same meeting that saw Duke invested with authority and control over the University's administrative departments, "and such other matters as would belong to the office of the president of the University," the board made two decisive moves to shore up the institution's beleaguered finances: they hired a fundraiser and a business manager. For the former post, they selected A. M. Petty and instructed him to open an office in Los Angeles. For the latter, they selected George P. Cortner, who would assume both roles upon Petty's death a few years later. A former mayor of Redlands, Cortner had demonstrated ample mettle and business acumen as proprietor of a successful funeral parlor. By putting University finances in order, the trustees hoped the undertaker would end criticism of institutional spending. The hiring proved to be one of the most propitious choices ever made by the Board of Trustees: Cortner's thirty-six-year stewardship of finances kept the University afloat through turbulent storms under four different presidents.

Brandishing facts and figures, Cortner quickly offered a plan to conquer the debt, expand service, and attract first-rate students. He proudly pointed to the largest student body yet: 170 enrollees, a result of tireless promotion. He noted the religious status of undergraduates, with thirteen preparing for the ministry, fifteen missionary bound, and only ten declining to express any religious preference. Petty, the field representative, also delivered a strong endorsement of the University's financial prospects. "It was an enthusiastic and hopeful conference," concluded the minutes.

Meanwhile, the trustees, under Mattison B. Jones's leadership, pressed ahead in financial matters. They called a meeting of leading Baptist clergy and lay people to confer jointly with the board in Los Angeles. Dr. Selden W. Cummings of Pasadena was elected chairman. After a positive give-and-take between attendees about the University and its future, the conference unanimously agreed to "heartily and enthusiastically endorse" the University of Redlands as *the* Baptist school of the Southwest; decided to back the trustees in a $50,000 fund drive in 1915–16; urged the Baptist pastors of the Southwest to help in raising money and securing students; called upon the Southern California Baptist Convention to devote an entire session to the University; and appointed a committee of five to get the job done. At last, there was a bright spot to offset criticism.

At the January 15, 1915, board meeting, the trustees, upon the recommendation of President Field, had authorized the beginning of a formal admission program. This enabled Dean Duke to take a one-week leave to recruit students by visiting high schools and other institutions.

The perennial issue of whether Redlands should change its name from university to college reemerged. Ultimately, the University's structure would be discussed intermittently for decades. Duke firmly advocated making Redlands a college, a position that never prevailed but remained a viable option, although less so with the post-World War II population boom. As late as 1967, when announcing a reorganization, the institution felt obligated to emphasize that it was indeed a university.

The nexus of the debate centered on how Redlands's educational mission and its effectiveness would best be served. As dean, Duke advocated a school "second to none in the whole United States." To him that meant creating an institution in the mold of a classic liberal arts college. "Personally I do not believe that there is any place or need for a Baptist *University* [italics are the author's] on the Pacific slope. . . . I am convinced that we would more easily accomplish our purpose, if our institution were called a college instead of a university." In emphasizing the four-year liberal arts curriculum and realizing Redlands would have less appeal to those who wanted "a technical education," Duke urged such students to take their "first two years of college work with us."

From the beginning of his employment, Business Manager Cortner advanced the view that Redlands faced strong competition from six existing colleges and universities in California, four of them in the south. There would be five when Los Angeles State Normal became a branch of the University of California (later UCLA). Like Duke, he believed that the best

strategy was "to strengthen the University of Redlands in every way possible." After World War I, he received news that the New World Movement of the Northern Baptist Convention was seeking to unite all its constituent organizations under one fundraising umbrella. "This means that the strong carry the weak and that the whole matter of our future growth will probably rest in the hands of a committee composed chiefly of Eastern men who know practically nothing of the Western spirit, standards or objectives," Cortner warned the trustees. In his history, Lawrence Nelson wrote, "This cautious, hardheaded business man proved himself to be as magnificent a dreamer as ever Jasper Newton Field had been. . . ." For Cortner the issue carried greater import than either "university" or "college" designation. Rather, he cited climate as a factor that might draw students from all over the country. Moreover, he stated:

> [The school's] location is strategic because it is situated in one of the most promising sections of our country. It is strategic because of its isolation — no other Baptist college within 1,500 miles. It is strategic because we face the teeming millions of the Orient and our Pacific Coast harbors are the first points of contact. Can we think of our strategic position and be satisfied with a small college? Can we think in small figures when we have at our very door six strong competitors that threaten to overshadow us? Can we think of being satisfied with what has been accomplished when the Nation and the Church are clamoring for educated leaders — men and women of strong hearts and clear minds?

Ultimately, the issue of quality as an imperative for Redlands's success cemented Duke's and Cortner's vision in *deed* and outweighed their individual concepts of *kind* as to what the school might be called.

With day-to-day administration of the University in capable hands, the trustees could devote themselves to a more esoteric question: what duties did the presidency of a university entail? Tellingly, the discussion at the May 1914 meeting reveals a board split along philosophical and practical lines. At least two different positions may be discerned, divisions that bedevil presidential search committees at liberal arts institutions to this day. Each side envisioned a president whose mandate would be narrower in scope than that of Field. One faction favored reducing the next president's portfolio by hiring a financial representative whose job it would be to raise funds and secure students. Thus divested of financial chores, the next president would merely head the University's educational mission. A second faction sought to reduce the president's workload by creating a development and admissions position that would report to the president, who would retain full control over both the educational and administrative aspects of the University. The two factions broke down internally on the question of when to hire the next president. With Petty already fulfilling the pecuniary function, some advocated deferring selection. Others sought to hire the new man sooner rather than later. Still unresolved was the use of the President's Mansion — now serving as home to the School of Music in the wake of the earlier controversy. The debates lasted the entire

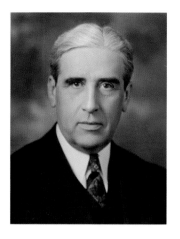

1914–15 school year, and no consensus emerged.

Nine months had elapsed since Field had left office. During a two-day board session in June 1915, Dr. J. Whitcomb Brougher reported on the presidential search. Several names were mentioned. The Rev. Frank Mathews, pastor of the Redlands First Baptist Church, asked to speak. The board listened with much interest to his endorsement of Dean Duke. The trustees discussed options and agreed to invite Duke to come before them and provide his views on a number of subjects "relative to the presidency of the University." After listening to the man who ran the University's affairs when Field was away on fundraising trips and who had for many months been acting with presidential authority, the board accepted Brougher's motion and invited Victor Leroy Duke to assume the presidency. A member of the founding faculty and still dean of that body, he certainly qualified for the position; yet he asked that he be permitted to deliberate. After consulting family, friends, and faculty colleagues, he reappeared before the board to accept the post. The trustees received his announcement "with the greatest enthusiasm." They might also have recorded "with relief." By unanimous consent, Duke became president as of that moment.

TWO PEAS IN A POD

Over the next nearly twenty years, the dynamic team of Duke and Cortner would make many changes in style and direction at the University. Their first act, however, clearly reflected an old issue, Baptist criticism of administrative salaries. With trustee approval, both men voluntarily reduced their compensation.

Though saddled with the title "University," Duke and Cortner surveyed the landscape and opted to commit all their energy and time to building a small, strong liberal arts college. Some of the concepts they devised brightened the future in clever and far-sighted ways. Rather than irrigate an orange grove on University property with expensive domestic water, Cortner had a line constructed to take advantage of irrigation water. He urged the accumulation of shares in non-profit mutual water companies that served the University, thus guaranteeing in future years a ready source of cheap, non-potable water for the green swards and groves that became the formal landscaped campus. He consolidated positions on the maintenance staff. He even pushed his agenda of cost-cutting and fundraising by eloquently reporting to the trustees in June 1916, "Our present situation should not discourage us, but merely bring us to a realization of the fact that things intensely worthwhile challenge the heroic within us . . . let us unitedly set our faces like flint toward the future and fight on till the dawn of day."

Another early challenge facing the Duke and Cortner team was thawing the University's chilly relationship with the Baptists. A golden opportunity arose in September 1915, when the Northern Baptist Convention met in Los Angeles. People from across the nation attended, and the University's trustees chartered a seven-car train to bring the delegates to Redlands for a visit. A fleet of one hundred automobiles was amassed to tour the dignitaries through town, including a stop at nationally famed Smiley Heights Park. The campus tour included refreshments served at the Administration Building, before all adjourned to Sylvan Park for a picnic lunch.

During this outing, the trustees responded to many of the objections previously raised by the Baptists. Back in May, the Board of Education had urged the institution to change its name to "Redlands College," intimating that support heretofore withheld might be forthcoming. The trustees indicated a willingness to "contemplate" such a shift in name and scope and offered their selection of Victor Duke for the presidency as testament that a "high grade" liberal arts college was their fondest aspiration. They likewise addressed the Board of Education's financial doubts by agreeing to provide a requested audit and promised to work with the board in matters of detail "with great care." Finally, they avowed their doctrinal faith by

reiterating an intention "to maintain a high grade college on a conservative basis in harmony with the action of the Southern California Baptist Convention under whose authority and at whose direction our institution came into being."

The effort at rapprochement paid off. In February 1916, the

Board of Education of the Northern Baptist Convention, reversing its decision of two years earlier, enthusiastically endorsed Redlands and publicly commended it to prospective donors in California and elsewhere. After but two years in office, Duke received glowing reports from the heretofore critical Baptist quarters. Their January 1917 report extolled, "President Duke is showing rare fitness for the task for which he has been selected." High praise, indeed.

But Duke had his plate full. The expenses of running the University continued to outstrip the income. At the rate it was headed, Redlands's reserve funds would be completely depleted sometime in the early 1920s. Duke and Cortner worked determinedly to devise means of cutting expenses. Once again, reducing administrative overhead proved a viable option. Rather than hire someone to replace Field Agent Petty, who had resigned due to illness and died soon after, Cortner took on the additional responsibility himself and then *cut* his own pay. His salary had been $2,500 per year, plus a commission on any sum he raised above $100,000. In a true display of placing the institution's financial well-being ahead of his own, Cortner reduced the compensation package to $2,400, plus traveling expenses and an annual $100 stipend for his Ford, *and* he eliminated the commission.

Even with these drastic measures, the debt was worrisome. At one point, faculty went five consecutive months without seeing

a paycheck. Led by Trustee Katherine (Mrs. Martin) Bekins, board members ponied up funds to help clear the deficit. Still short, they called a "mass meeting" of Californians concerned with Christian education, hoping to inspire others to follow their example. Shortly before, a founding trustee, Carey R. Smith, advised the University that a revision to his will stipulated a bequest of $100,000, provided that the endowment stood at least at $200,000. With incentives to eliminate the shortfall and to raise an endowment, the University embarked in January 1917 upon an ambitious crusade to accrue $500,000.

However, World War I nearly scuttled the campaign. With the country immersed in the needs of war, the selling of liberty bonds, and the formation of soldier assistance groups, little time and attention remained for a college fund drive. The Bekins-inspired campaign was therefore postponed until autumn. All levels of the University quickly redirected their energy toward the war effort. The Class of 1918 pledged "unreserved and hearty loyalty and allegiance to the Government of the United States, its flag, its principles, its institutions, and the cause to which it is committed in the World War." Each senior signed the pledge. The University and city joined forces to urge enlistment of high school graduates and college-age men.

Three weeks after Congress declared war, the faculty recommended military training on campus. Unable to provide officers or equipment to institutions that did not have such programs prior to the war, the army rebuffed such offers. President Duke vowed to press ahead anyway. One student proposed an Army Training Corps, and Duke proudly announced a unit of 131 men. The unit ultimately reached 275. The army's desire for a three-term school year for trainees—rather than two—even led the University to alter its calendar. The corps remained active even beyond the end of overt hostilities, not demobilizing until Armistice Day, November 11, 1919. The increased enrollment of men produced other effects on campus, including the need for a larger Assembly Hall. The simple wood-frame building was designed to convert into a large barn or garage in later years, but it did not survive long enough to witness this adaptive reuse. In January 1920, the building, located near the Zanja Fiesta grounds near the later site of the Alumni Greek Theatre, burned to the ground.

Although World War I overshadowed the $500,000 capital campaign, the indomitable George Cortner pressed on. By 1918 he had secured a challenge from the Pasadena First Baptist Church, which pledged a princely $150,000 with the caveat that the University procure a $150,000 match. Cortner raised all but $6,240 of the $150,000 on his own, and the trustees themselves made up the difference. The $300,000 became a lifeline, securing the University's future.

A BUILDING BOOM

During Duke's presidency, the campus attained the basic form it would retain until after World War II. A veritable building boom character- ized the 1920s. When Duke became acting president in 1914, the campus consisted of five buildings. A dozen years later, it had expanded to one hundred thirty acres, included eleven buildings, a faculty of thirty-nine, a student body of five hundred fifty-four, and a graduating class of eighty-seven. Optimism for the future ran so high that desire to expand the campus extended even to the nearby San Bernardino Mountains, where the University bought a tract of seven hundred acres

in Mill Creek Canyon for $5,000. Cortner named it Oak Knoll. The intention was to dedicate the site to a summer school. Unfortunately, the plan became a casualty of the Depression, and the land was sold after Cortner left.

The building boom owed its existence largely to the generos- ity of a single donor, a donor whose identity was kept from the public, the faculty, and even the Board of Trustees.

The best account of this signal moment in the life of the University is provided in Nelson's *Redlands: Biography of a College*. According to the author, just as Cortner was capping off the $150,000 to match the gift of the Pasadena Baptists in January 1918, he presented the trustees with a most mysterious offer: "A loyal and generous friend of the University proposed to give an unannounced sum on condition that there should be absolute secrecy as to the donor, the property and the gift." Placing full confidence in Cortner, the board departed from its usual prudent approach and accepted a large donation of "some unknown property for certain purposes and under certain conditions and agreements to be contained in a writ- ing to be signed by this friend and the University of Redlands Treasurer Cortner under the seal of the corporation and then sealed in an envelope and left in the exclusive possession of Treasurer Cortner and his successor."

That gift, attached to the $500,000 campaign, proved the first of many. Ultimately several buildings resulted from the inter- est of "this shy and shadowy friend," but the patron always insisted on anonymity. Nelson observed that even the strict secrecy of the board meeting could not pierce the veil of obscurity, the donor "being referred to only as 'our friend.'" More than any other single benefactor, "our friend" made possible the rapid early growth of the University during the Duke years.

The boom began on April 1, 1919, when Cortner reported to the trustees that he had secured a $50,000 pledge for a men's dormitory. With the University men housed in Reavis Hall and the Administration Building, a permanent solution had long focused Cortner's efforts. The pledge, however, came with strings attached: the University had to raise an additional $100,000 and construct two other buildings as well—and they had to do so within two months. Cortner decided to raise half of that amount without leaving

town, challenging the citizens of Redlands to raise $50,000. Nelson captured the energy of the moment: "When the proposal to raise $50,000 locally within 60 days came before the Chamber of Commerce, pessimism ruled until department store magnate Phillip Harris stood up and said, 'I, for one, am ready to get to work.' Led by two Jewish merchants and a Congregationalist banker, Redlands thereupon raised $53,000 for its Baptist College."

Town and gown rose to the challenge. Cortner reported on June 23, 1919, that the entire $150,000 for three new buildings had been secured. The Building Committee quickly recommended construction of only two: the dormitory for $175,000 and the Hall of Science for $180,000. University funds supplied the difference. For the first time in ages, the future looked rosy. No doubt flummoxed by this unaccustomed success, the trustees "immediately increased all salaries in the Liberal Arts College . . . and those of the Resident and Business manager . . . , presented Cortner with a new automobile . . . and begged Duke and Cortner to take a month's vacation . . . on full salary."

Currier Gymnasium

For almost eight decades, Currier Gymnasium has figured prominently in the lives of Bulldogs—a nice return on a building that cost a mere $200,000 to construct back in 1928. One of the earliest campus buildings designed by Herbert J. Powell '20, it was located near the football and baseball fields. The 1961 construction of new tennis courts in an adjacent lot guaranteed its spot as the epicenter of athletic achievement.

The building quickly became a hub of campus activity, a place where students, faculty, and administrators might mingle at athletic events, physical-education classes, and—eventually—dances. Bulldog cagers quickly discovered the building's tight confines afforded an intense advantage to the home side. This has only intensified in recent years, as many schools build larger facilities that put spectators at a greater distance from the players.

Currier comfortably housed all Bulldog athletic teams for many years; however, as the number of sports proliferated, so did the need for additional campus venues for athletes. Football, soccer, track and field, aquatics, and baseball all decamped for newer facilities in the past few decades. Casual fitness also found a new home following construction of the Field House. While these buildings shifted the locus of Bulldog athletics to the north end of campus, Currier continues to house men's and women's basketball and tennis, and women's volleyball and softball.

The building had only minor alterations to its physical appearance until recently. The emergence of women's sports in the 1970s and after necessitated the enlargement of locker rooms. The original bleachers were replaced in 1996. The pool closed when the Thompson Aquatic Center opened in 1996. In 2005 the University filled the pool area to create a new basketball court, only the second indoor court on campus. These renovations will extend Currier's lifespan another twelve to fifteen years. — JDM

Residential life and academics alike benefited from the building boom. For the first time since Bekins Hall's completion a decade earlier, the University of Redlands built a dormitory: California Hall debuted in 1921. Its location on the Quad's west side began the configuration of women's dormitories to the west and men's to the east. "Our friend" then stepped up in the 1920s to provide funding for three more dorms to join Bekins and California Halls. Fairmont Hall (1921) and Grossmont Hall (1925) housed women, while Melrose Hall (1924) provided more space for men. The friend's gifts were contingent on the University raising funds for other academic buildings, which meant that growth of the residential side fueled growth of the academic side.

The construction boom of academic buildings began with the Hall of Science. In March 1920, the University laid the cornerstone for a new science building west of the Administration Building. After Science was completed, work began on Fine Arts West in 1921 and Fine Arts East in 1923. A large swath of open space separated these structures, both of which became home to the School of Music.

The mysterious benefactor made three other significant gifts in the mid-1920s. In 1924 he engineered the acquisition of an additional twenty-seven acres of land adjacent to the campus on its eastern boundary. The narrow parcel, which stretched

from Sylvan to Brockton between Cook and Grove, essentially completed the campus footprint. Of even greater importance was the gift of a facility. Opening during the middle of the fall 1925 semester, the new facility finally gave the University a proper library. Finally, the most important building constructed during the Duke years was the Chapel. "Our friend" provided $180,000 for its construction and another $36,000 for its Casavant organ. To better anchor the north end of the Quad, the Chapel was placed in the open space between the two halves of the Fine Arts Building. Shortly after the Chapel's completion, the University moved Fine Arts West and joined it with Fine Arts East to create the single building that still stands. Watchorn Hall now occupies the original location of Fine Arts West. The Chapel opened in 1928; ironically, the first memorial service celebrated there was that for Jasper Field, who had read the Scripture lesson at the dedication ceremony shortly before.

Street placement in the mid-1920s emerged as an ongoing bone of contention between Redlands and the University, each evolving in ways unique yet intertwined. Years earlier the city had agreed to abandon portions of Cook Street, a north-south corridor that bisected campus. First, a portion of Cook extending north from Colton Avenue through the present-day site of Armacost Library was abandoned; later the city also closed the portion between Colton and Sylvan Boulevard to the south. To replace that corridor, the University relinquished a strip of land on its western boundary so that University Street, which had dead-ended at Colton, could be extended northward. These alterations endowed the campus with a sense of continuity and territorial integrity and not incidentally reduced safety concerns for student pedestrians.

One nagging issue remained: the fate of Colton itself, the only city street still vivisecting campus. The town's population had swelled to ten thousand, which meant a corresponding increase in local traffic. Desiring to reduce the flow of that traffic through campus, which now hosted six hundred students, the University proposed to close Colton Avenue entirely. Administrators envisioned the University as a single, continuous park free of outside traffic, an island surrounded by a sea of city streets. The proposal elicited only a lukewarm reception at City Hall, where officials proved understandably reluctant to close a major artery without a suitable alternative. Colton remained a throughway, and the disagreement simmered for decades.

While the automobile created challenges for University growth, its necessity as transportation for students failed to garner trustee sympathy. In response to student needs for parking and driving their automobiles, the trustees in 1924 adopted a policy of "discouraging the custom of bringing automobiles on campus." Such discouragement continued in various forms over the next decades, including prohibiting scholarship students from owning cars, but by the 1970s the trustees and administration had to throw in the towel. By the 1980s, students thought nothing of arising from their dorm rooms, say in Cortner or North, getting their cars from the lot, driving them across Colton, and parking as close as possible to their classrooms on Ad Hill. Adequate parking challenged the University with no acceptable solution in sight.

Aside from its obvious centrality to intercollegiate competition, the campus gymnasium also fulfilled a daily function as home to physical-education classes required of all students to graduate. Trustees and administrators alike recognized the need for a first-class facility. When the existing gym burned on May 23, 1916, the need became acute. A temporary facility made due for a decade.

A new gym became possible thanks to the bequest of A. T. Currier of Walnut, California, a founding trustee (see page 4). Currier Gymnasium opened shortly before the 1928–29 school year. It included a field house to host basketball, locker rooms for all the teams, and a modern indoor swimming pool. The pool closed in 1996; in 2005 it was floored over for sports such as basketball and volleyball. Architect Herbert J. Powell '20 recalled that the "interior was pretty much of a structural job. We just left the steel trusses exposed . . . over the basketball

court and swimming pool." He added a Romanesque touch in the design of the main entrance. It features an elaborate bas-relief over the door with the Latin motto *Mens Sana in Corpore Sano* (a sound mind in a sound body). Powell recalled that "the contractor for the building had given this job to a model shop in Los Angeles. They had some guy they picked up to do the original. The figures looked as if they had been hung by their necks. When I went down and looked at it I said, 'We're going to get Merrill Gage to do this.' So Gage came in and redid the design." Gage, the noted head of sculpture at the University of Southern California, created a striking piece of art to grace the entrance.

The Alumni Association

The Alumni Association organized on June 17, 1912, when the total alumni population was still quite small. Rachael Coolidge Price '11 was elected president. Seven members were present at this initial gathering, which, as with other first meetings—of the trustees, of the faculty, and of classes—took place in the First Baptist Church of Redlands. By 1915 the fifty or so alumni determined that a gesture—a gift to the University—was necessary from them. After some discussion, they embarked upon an ambitious fundraising effort

to construct an open-air theater. By June 1921 they had secured only $1,248. It would take another six years to achieve a completed building, but the Alumni Greek Theatre finally opened in June 1927.

Almost from the beginning, the Alumni Association lobbied for a voice in governing the University. Its efforts paid off in 1917, when the trustees allocated a place on the board to a representative of the association. Mary P. Montgomery '12 was seated as the first alumni trustee.

The first alumni publication, the *Alumni Edition*, appeared in the regular bulletin series of the University in April 1923 under the editorship of Alumni President Hubert E. Barnes '15. In July 1924, the association itself undertook the publication of a quarterly, *The U of R Alumnus*, edited by Arthur D. Jacobsen '17.

Also in 1924 alumni clubs were organized in Los Angeles, Berkeley, and Redlands, as well as in Santa Barbara and Ventura counties, the San Joaquin Valley and San Diego in 1925, and New York City in 1926.

Joining with the students, the Alumni Association received blessings from the Board of Trustees to inaugurate the first observance of Founders' Day on December 7, 1925, marked by Redlands clubs and alumni throughout the world.

The desire to assign a plum location to the state-of-the art field house marked the end of the line for one of the University's original buildings, Reavis Hall. Multiple campus functions had found a home in the relocated structure over the previous fifteen years, but the completion of the Hall of Science west of the Administration site more than offset the space. The former Stillman home was now expendable. With its useful days ended, Reavis Hall soon followed Cook Street into oblivion. Aside from the first gymnasium, which burned down, Reavis is the only significant university building to have been demolished.

Another indication of the University's evolution had occurred in 1912 when a tiny coterie of graduates formed the Alumni Association. The twenty founding members elected Rachael Coolidge Price '11 as the association's first president. They held their first meeting in the parlor of the town's First Baptist Church, as had the trustees, faculty, and student body previously. In those days, the association was dues-based. After lobbying for several years, in 1917 the organization persuaded the trustees to seat a representative on the board, which signaled the trustees' recognition of the importance of alumni participation in institutional governance.

At a 1915 meeting, Gordon Palmer '16 asked the association to donate a structure to the University. The alumni debated several alternatives before choosing the most grandiose option: it would fund a Greek amphitheater, a truly audacious choice considering the group's meager constituency. The alumni worked and pledged, then worked and pledged some

more, but not until 1926 did they finally have the $20,000 necessary to start construction. Two alumni—Miriam Frances Scott '16 and Herbert J. Powell '20—volunteered their architectural expertise.

The association presented its achievement—dubbed the Alumni Greek Theatre—to the University community on June 1, 1927. Boasting a seating capacity of four thousand, the venue has hosted countless performances, and generations of Redlands students have celebrated their commencement in the bowl.

Participation in the Greek Theatre project soon led one its designers to assume a prominent place in the history of the University's architecture. Born in Chicago in 1898, Powell graduated from the University in 1915. During World War I, he served in the United States Army, in Heavy Artillery. As a member of the Alumni Association, he had offered to design the Greek Theatre before leaving California to obtain an A.M. in architecture from Harvard University. He completed the degree in 1924, and then accepted a Sheldon Traveling Fellowship to spend 1925 in Europe studying architecture. Upon his return in 1926, he served as a draftsman at the prestigious New York firm of McKim, Mead and White. Longing for Southern California, Powell found employment as an instructor in the School of Architecture at the University of Southern California. As the alumni had finally completed fundraising for the Greek Theatre, Powell no doubt reacquainted himself with Redlands upon his return.

started. After much discussion and a good deal of behind-the-scene planning, Powell offered to do the design as part of Marsh's office. Not long after, the firm became known as Marsh, Smith, and Powell.

The Chapel proved to be the first of many buildings to grace the University of Redlands campus that began life on the drawing board of Herbert Powell. He designed nearly every building constructed on campus until his retirement, starting with Currier Gymnasium in 1928 and culminating with the Peppers Art Center in 1963. His firm continued to provide architectural services until the early 1980s.

The timing of the theater design proved fortuitous for Powell and for Redlands. With construction underway on the alumni project, the University was ready to award the design contract for the new Chapel. Unfortunately, Norman Marsh, the lead architect, was in ill-health. An impatient Cortner asked the alumnus if he could provide a design that would get the project

Of all the Powell buildings, the Chapel is the gem. It is the visual anchor of the Quad, and for much of its history served as the campus crossroads: gathering space, place of worship, and public face combined into one facility. Its construction merits further discussion. Eschewing the services of a general contractor, George Cortner assumed the role himself. He hired a foreman whom Powell remembered "being a whiz." The architect also recalled the chief painter as able to do the "tricky" things.

The Casavant Organ

Business Manager George Cortner made the initial contact with the Casavant Frères organ company in Montreal in September 1926. He indicated that the "organ will be used strictly for chapel purposes and occasional high-class recitals." Such sentiments were music to the ears of the tonal director of Casavant, Stephen Stoot, who preferred a classical approach to organ design.

Casavant sent specifications to Professor Charles H. Marsh, who was on sabbatical studying with the great French organist and composer Marcel Dupré. Marsh was thrilled by the design, as was Dupré. Following its installation in 1928, Cortner wrote expressing his appreciation "for the quality" of the organ. "In every sense of the word . . . [it is] first class." Arthur Poister, University organist, added his delight "with the greatness and finesse of this lovely instrument."

Opus 1230 was the third and largest Casavant organ installed in California when it was finished in 1927. That same year, Casavant installed organs in Japan and South Africa. The organ in Tokyo was destroyed in the bombing of World War II, while the one in Zimbabwe remains in use today.

Defective electrical lighting delayed by an hour the dedication of the Casavant on Tuesday evening, February 28, 1928. Professor W. B. Olds led the A Cappella Choir to the delight of the listeners.

Finally, the noted composer Pietro A. Yon, organist of St. Patrick's Cathedral in New York City and honorary organist to the Vatican, took his seat before the instrument and the evening of memories began. Yon played the "Chimes of St. Marks," a rhythmic arrangement of Spanish Christmas carols, a march, a piece by J. S. Bach, and a medley of American patriotic pieces "to encore after encore." "Rarely is an artist willing to give so delightfully of his talent . . . [he] completely won over the audience to an appreciation of the concert," proclaimed the *Redlands Daily Facts*.

In 2001 the Casavant Opus 1230 was sent back to Canada, where over seventy years of accumulated grime, soot, smog, and dirt were removed from inside the organ, and damaged pipes repaired; those missing and beyond fixing were replaced, remaining pneumatic actions were updated with electric systems, and windchests were rebuilt.

On January 6, 2003, the Casavant returned to the Chapel with the assistance of three installers from Casavant Frères. The 4,266 pipes were uncrated, sorted, and laid onto the Chapel floor, which was cleared of half its seating. In March two voicers arrived to complete the voicing and tuning of each pipe. The final tuning of the entire organ was finished on April 3, 2003. The original organ was purchased for $36,000;

seventy-five years later, $500,000 was required to refurbish it.

At the May 17, 2003, re-dedication service, President James R. Appleton welcomed the guests, who filled the Chapel seats. Phillip L. Doolittle '76, vice president for finance and administration, presented the project overview. Professor Jeffrey H. Rickard '69, '70 demonstrated the organ and talked about its capabilities. Jacqueline Rochette, artistic director at Casavant Frères and an organist, played *Toccata and Fugue in D Minor* by J. S. Bach, along with another composition.

During the course of the organ refurbishment, someone at the Casavant Frères company wrote: "The recent involvement with an organ built by our founders some seventy-six years ago has reinforced our already strong appreciation for these extraordinary individuals and their life's work. That the organ came back . . . and was 're-assembled' in the same workshop it left in 1927 on its initial journey to California is all the more remarkable in an age when far too many objects are considered disposable."

Powell confirmed that the anonymous donor never made any demands. The architect was free to design at will. He personally designed the grills screening the organ pipes and believed that the "nicest feature" was the Palladian stained-glass window illustrating the Sermon on the Mount, which was executed by the Judson Studios in Los Angeles.

Completed in 1927 and dedicated on February 20, 1928, the Memorial Chapel served the religious needs of the University, and became a venue that drew town and gown together to hear renowned speakers. In his memoirs, Powell cautioned against multipurpose use of the Chapel: "When the Chapel was designed the building was intended to be a chapel. It was not thought of as a performing arts center. Frankly, it is not very well adapted for that. By force of circumstance the University was not able to build another building of that size for performing arts. The closest they came to it was the Wallichs Theatre.

The Chapel should not be looked upon as a building that was unsuccessfully designed for functions it must take care of now." Many of Powell's concerns were addressed in a renovation completed in 2002.

In anticipating the construction of the Chapel, Cortner in 1926 planned to realize part of architect Norman Marsh's 1907 vision of landscaping the campus, which featured a sunken garden, planted with trees and shrubs. Foregoing the sunken aspect, the University undertook a two-month project, leveling an alfalfa field and creating a green-lawn "quad" at the center of campus. Oak trees were planted around the perimeter and sidewalks poured. The campus now had both physical definition and a focus that made it a social space.

The 1929 stock market crash and ensuing Great Depression of the 1930s terminated the University's building boom.

BELOW LEFT: This rare color slide depicts the 1918 baseball team.

BELOW RIGHT: Pictured in their later years are, Cecil Alonzo Cushman (left), (football coach, 1923–56) and Ashel Cunningham (standing), (athletic director, 1913–53). Cunnigham coached football, track, and baseball.

BOTTOM: The 1914 football team at practice poses for a photo against the mountains.

Nevertheless, the Duke years endowed the campus with many of its most enduring landmarks. Each of the dormitories still stands. Students conducted experiments in the Duke Hall of Science until 2005; following a refurbishment, the Business Department occupied the stately building. The Alumni Greek Theatre continues to be the site of commencement each year. The athletic program has outgrown Currier Gymnasium, and a number of other facilities now supplement the athletic mission; yet, many teams still locker in the gracefully aging facility, and the small-scale field house continues to bedevil Bulldog opponents in basketball and volleyball. The infirmary, now a "Health Center," still succors sick students. The campus had outgrown the library by the end of the 1960s; but as home to a number of academic departments and classrooms, the building (now Larsen Hall) remains central to the intellectual growth of the University's students.

No one is certain who suggested the term "Memorial" Chapel, but this formal appellation likely commemorates the man who had staunchly supported the University's mission. His generosity no doubt persuaded other donors that the University

of Redlands had a future worth contributing to. Sadly, the Chapel became his final gift. "Our friend" died before he could witness the building's dedication in 1928. As he wished, he remained anonymous to his death.

"OUR FRIEND" REVEALED

"Our friend" was Milo C. Treat, of Pittsburgh. His daughter and future son-in-law graduated from Redlands. A modest donor before 1918, he knew about the challenges brought on by Field's resignation and, as a committed Baptist and savvy businessman, understood the University's desperate need for a major donor. Treat came from the "old school," where one's name only appeared in print three times: at birth, marriage, and death. Philanthropy, based on the Christian principle that we are born with nothing and should die with nothing, infused his character and his deeds. Anonymity became his mantra and his demand. During Treat's life, his family fiercely protected his secret gifts, as did the University, where only the board chairman, president, and Cortner knew his identity. Only upon his death was the code of silence broken; the Board of Trustees sent an expression of grief and a floral tribute to his widow and family.

The Sermon on the Mount *or* Christ Window

One of the most striking features of the Memorial Chapel is the stained-glass window on the north wall. Designed by, Walter Horace Judson, founder of the famous Judson Studios of Los Angeles, the window illustrates Christ delivering the Sermon on the Mount to listeners amid the hills of Galilee. The window comprises three panels containing 3,500 pieces of stained glass imported from England. Overarching trees draw the panels together. Only the leaves, scrolls, faces, and robes were painted on.

The window depicts a variety of social types—rich and poor, young and old, male and female, prosperous merchants, peasants, shepherds, Jewish ecclesiastical leaders, and Roman soldiers. The artwork also intimates Christ's ministry to the suffering: a tired mother with her baby, a sick boy leaning against an elderly man, and parents accompanying a lame son are represented alongside the scornful and indifferent. A series of smaller scenes runs along the bottom, such as: giving water to the thirsty, entertaining the stranger, clothing the destitute, visiting the sick, and cheering the prisoner. The combination of human tableaux and ornamental borders is found in illuminated manuscripts prior to the Renaissance.

The Judson Studios designed windows for a number of landmark buildings in Southern California, including several homes by Frank Lloyd Wright in the Hollywood Hills, the rotunda of the Los Angeles Natural History Museum, Forest Lawn Memorial Park, and churches and public buildings. Of all the windows designed by Judson and his sons, however, the *Sermon on the Mount* at the University of Redlands was the artist's favorite.

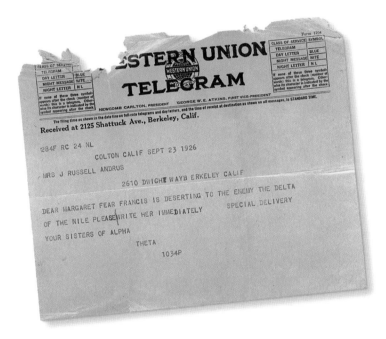

In all, Treat gave the University Fairmont, Melrose, Grossmont, the library (Larsen Hall), Memorial Chapel, and the land from Sylvan Boulevard to Brockton, east of Armacost Library. Those bear testimony to his faith in the young institution and in its future. After his death, his daughter Mila Treat Palmer '16 and her husband, Gordon Palmer '16, continued Treat's benefactions by establishing an endowment for Memorial Chapel.

Now that the "special friend" had passed from the scene, the full board, in open session on January 16, 1926, read a letter from Mrs. Treat and her family, expressing their "thanks and appreciation" for the sympathy of the University.

A special committee of H. Merriam, J. H. Strait, Mattison B. Jones, and J. W. Curtis presented resolutions to the board for adoption. They expressed the "profound sorrow and sense of loss which is felt by every member of the Executive Committee . . . and by the Board, by reason of the Death of Brother Treat. . . ." They attested to having "endeavored faithfully to observe the earnest wish and purpose of Mr. Treat that no public recognition whatever should be given, and that there be no publicity concerning the many things he has done to

build up and establish upon a firm financial basis, our Baptist Educational Institution at Redlands, and even in the confidential counsels of our committee and our Board, he has been mentioned only as a 'good friend of the University.'" They went on, "But we feel that now, at least, it is appropriate to express to you our conviction that to Brother Treat, more perhaps than any other one individual, is due the credit for so establishing this Christian College, not only because of his magnificent gifts just at the time of the greatest need for them, but also for the wise counsel which he was always so ready to contribute. . . . "

"SHOWING SPLENDID SPIRIT"

While the construction frenzy during the 1920s is remarkable, the fabric of the University academic and student life kept pace. The University's best assets to advance its profile and enhance its reputation were its students. For example, the 1920 Glee Club traveled to Chicago, performing at various towns en route. Even more conspicuous ambassadors were the debate squad. From 1909, when the irrepressible professor James "Jimmy" Kyle proposed an award for excellence in speech, the University

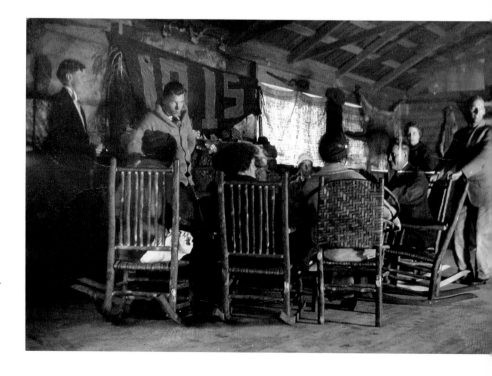

had made oratorical proficiency a high priority. "How is it that the U. of R. stands the victor over the forensics champion of the Mississippi Valley and over Stanford?," inquired the editor of the 1920 *Campus*. The community considered forensic prowess to be on a par with athletic success. Every student was required to perform a public recitation. Egbert Ray Nichols, who began his speech professorship in 1913, led Redlands to countless regional speech championships and to two national debate championships before his retirement in 1952. Shortly after Duke became president, a "broad policy for advertising" was implemented by sending the forensic team on an interstate debate trip every two years. Pi Kappa Delta, the national speech fraternity, began a national competition in 1916 held in Topeka, Kansas. In order to obtain travel funds, the University debate council sponsored a play but came up $100 short of the goal. A local Redlands jeweler took up the cause and community members raised the funds. The team had scheduled a number of exhibition debates along the way, a tradition continuing to the present day. During the 1917 competition at Ottawa University in Kansas, a departure in format by a Redlands student, Ray E. Untereiner '20, redefined debate in a revolutionary manner. Heretofore, debates consisted of prepared speeches with no verbal interaction between teams. Untereiner changed that by directly arguing against the points of the Ottawa team. Taken aback, Ottawa lost, 2 to 1. It was a lasting legacy of Nichols's coaching.

Sports also showcased student prowess. "A miracle year in 1918–19 for athletics saw Redlands win its first undisputed championship in football and basketball, tie in baseball, finish second in track, and third in tennis," University historian Nelson reported. In 1918 the coaches and others led Redlands to a new American record at the Pennsylvania Relays in Philadelphia, twenty yards ahead of the field, clipping four seconds from the old time. With an enrollment of three hundred, the 1919–20 teams took three conference championships. William J. Yount '21 rated fourth-best all-around athlete in America when he competed at the Antwerp Olympic Games.

At the next Penn Relays, competing against Harvard, Yale, Chicago, the University of Pennsylvania, and the University of Paris, Redlands took third. Redlands became a full-fledged member of the Southern California Intercollegiate Athletic Conference in 1924.

An enduring Redlands student and alumni tradition began after World War I. Dwight O. Smith '22 recalled that classmates Jacob "Jack" Slutsk x'22 and C. Merle Waterman '20 collaborated on a "Psalm of Collegiate Thanksgiving." This chant was for athletic events. Polished by Waterman into final form, it endured as the "Och Tamale," delivered in rapid fire with a cadence and word gibberish so seductive that once it took hold, it fastened itself upon the campus sports scene.

Dramatic arts at Redlands gained a broader perspective when Theta Alpha Phi, the national drama fraternity, granted the University a chapter. In 1924 Sigma Alpha Lota, the national music fraternity admitted the University to membership.

In many ways, President Duke defined the kind of student life that still characterizes the Redlands experience. For example, in a 1917 report to the trustees, he expressed his desire to keep the student body small but not to limit future enrollment increases. He advocated mandatory residential living on campus in student quarters. He expected undergraduate social life to center entirely upon the campus. This view is entirely consistent with Duke's vision of building community in a liberal arts environment.

In its early years, Redlands's president and the faculty presided over the students' day-to-day life. Policies were discussed and promulgated through these two governing bodies, as problems arose or as students' concerns were called to the attention of the University. As Nelson stated, the issues of discipline, activities outside the classroom, and dormitory life had an uneven chart as the president and the faculty chose to interpret things their way, and, often, the students quite another.

The Och Tamale

C. Merle Waterman '20 served four years as a cheerleader, and his travels to competing schools exposed him to traditions of fan support elsewhere. In particular, he became "envious of a tongue twister yell which Oxy [Occidental College] had at the time." The yell was more nonsense than anything else, but Oxy students raucously shouted it in support of their side:

> Io triumphe, Io triumphe!
> Habaen swaben Rebecca le animor,
> Whoop-te, whoop-te sheller-de
> ver-ede;
> Boom-da, ral-de, I-de, pa,
> Honeka, heneka, wack-a-wack-a.
> Hob, dob, bold-e bar-a, bold-e bar-a,
> Con slomad-e hob dob, rah! O.C. Rah!

Waterman wondered why the University of Redlands did not have a swell yell as

well. In 1921 he suggested to classmate Walter J. Richards '21 that they devise one. They also knew a freshman from San Diego, Jacob "Jack" Slutsk x'22, whose high school had a yell. Together, the trio concocted one. They were not "so sure their chant would go over but hoped that the gimmick 'each frosh class must learn it' might sell the idea." The "Och Tamale" was born:

> Och Tamale gazolly gazump
> Dayump dayadee yahoo
> Ink damink dayadee gazink
> Dayump, deray, yahoo
> Wing wang trickey trackey poo foo
> Joozy woozy skizzle wazzle
> Wang tang orkey porkey dominorky
> Redlands! — Rah, Rah, Redlands!

Later, Waterman recalled that they "mimeographed the yell and I rehearsed Walt in the motions for several days, hoping he would introduce it or at least we'd take the blame together." At that point, Waterman's buddy abandoned him. "He got 'cold feet' at the last minute and I had to introduce it myself so [I] got to be known as the 'Father of the Och Tamale.'"

The chant soon became ubiquitous among the Bulldog faithful. In his *Biography of a College*, Nelson related a particularly charming anecdote attesting to its universality among Redlands alumni. One night the patrons in a Paris café "craned when certain previously

sedate diners suddenly rose and rapturously chanted" what must have seemed gibberish to the befuddled diners. Of course, it was the "Psalm of Collegiate Thanksgiving," known as the "Och Tamale."

This strange behavior on the part of "previously sedate" diners was explained when an alumni couple, who had been on their way out, heard the familiar chant, whirled around in the doorway, and rushed across the room in ecstatic amazement toward a table of fellow alums.

During the early years of the twenty-first century, Redlands received national radio and newspaper coverage when the owner of a personalized California license plate with "yahoo" emblazoned on it spurned the entreaties of the dot.com giant Yahoo, Inc. to buy rights to the plate. Instead, the owner voluntarily transferred rights to the slogan to the dean of students, for use on her car. Thus, the "yahoo" plate joined a population of cars in university parking lots that already included President James R. Appleton's "Och Tamale" and those of other administrators, whose license plates proclaimed "gazolly," "gazump," "dayump," and "dayadee."

After much discussion by the trustees, fraternities and sororities were permitted on campus as local rather than national chapters. Founded in 1909, Pi Chi fraternity came first, followed by Delta Kappa Psi sorority in 1910, Alpha Theta Pi sorority in 1911, and Kappa Sigma Sigma fraternity and Alpha Sigma Pi sorority in 1914. By 1918 the sentiments of the University's administrators on the place of Greek organizations had changed. President Duke reported a lack of "sympathetic cooperation between the faculty and the students" conducive to the "best work in the institution." With America at war in 1918 and "democracy" the watchword of the day, the faculty did not necessarily approve of the exclusive nature of Greek life. They notified the students that the "existence of fraternities and sororities in this democratic institution was not in the best interest of the University of Redlands and invited cooperation with the object of their ultimate elimination."

The students replied that they wished to cooperate. Would the faculty kindly suggest what might better replace the Greek organization? Stymied, the faculty voted to let the matter rest for a year, requesting that meanwhile the associations cease pledging during the first semester. Further discussion about this also failed. Instead, the faculty endorsed a resolution asking students to work with them to formulate regulations governing conduct of the Greeks. Outmaneuvered by the students, the faculty retreated. Approximately every five years since, like the ebb and flow of the tide, the faculty has renewed its call for the demise of fraternities and sororities, but they have always staved off that fate.

The question of nationally affiliated versus independent local fraternities reemerged after World War I. During the 1920s, fraternity members agitated for national ties, in part because they desired to build fraternity houses just like brethren at other colleges. Since most such houses enjoyed off-campus locations—thus making University oversight a dubious issue—the trustees proved reluctant to acquiesce. The board spent many months investigating practices at other Southern California Christian colleges—to wit, Pomona, Whittier, and Occidental—and then firmly ruled out nationalization. They followed that restriction with new policies intended to curb objectionable behavior. Notwithstanding, student enthusiasm for fraternities and sororities and the board's recalcitrance clearly indicates that members harbored deep suspicions regarding the ability of the associations to foster proper Christian values.

The issue of fraternity houses persisted. From the fraternities' perspective, the construction of a house was eminently sensible: the campus lacked sufficient meeting space for student clubs and a house would resolve that shortcoming. The only concession wrangled by the fraternities from the trustees was permission to rent off-campus meeting rooms—at approved locations only. In 1925 one fraternity experienced the limit of trustee patience when it sought permission to build a mountain cabin in Mill Creek Canyon. The Executive Committee of the Board of Trustees rejected the request. The inquiry, however, revealed the existence of another such off-campus cabin, used by Alpha Gamma Nu. Further investigation turned up the cabin's owner, an alumnus who held it in trust for the convenience of his erstwhile fraternity. Quite unmindful of his property rights or any lack of jurisdiction over a *former* student, the board ordered the hapless man to "dispose of it" and "cease immediately its use."

Subsequently, three students—one of whom, Dwayne Orton '26, would become a trustee (he later proved instrumental in the founding of Johnston College, and his name graces a building on the north campus) — appeared before the board to plead further the issue of fraternity houses. "Showing splendid spirit," the trio made a favorable impression but lost the argument. Their supplication, however, won the battle, as the board relented on the issue of constructing on-campus houses for the purpose of holding meetings. But it was not until the 1950s that "fraternity row" along the Zanja materialized. Adding to the conundrum but rarely addressed in faculty minutes was the fact that many alumni trustees over the years had been frat boys, including five who would chair the board. How did such captious, ephemeral social groups seem to continually contribute so many future University leaders?

The aftermath of World War I brought new phrases to the national vocabulary: bobbed hair, necking, speakeasy, hijacking, flaming youth, the lost generation, "twenty-three skidoo." The Associated Students of the University of Redlands (ASUR) also had its problems. Undergraduates complained in 1919 that seniors should be made to suppress the activities of "loud day" and "crab day." Much arguing took place among the students, and the meeting adjourned without any action taken. These and many later student traditions have disappeared without a tangible trace.

In January 1922 the board authorized its chairman, Mattison B. Jones, to address the student body at an early date on the "matter of their being exceedingly careful regarding their conduct, which would in any way be detrimental to the reputation of the University and of the ideals that it represents." He delivered that address in April at a chapel convocation. Much of what he urged appears to have fallen on deaf ears. Two students who did listen drew up a list of complaints about noise in the dormitories, disrespectful behavior at compulsory chapel, and a "serious laxity in the observance of the University traditions. . . . "

Most of the problems and resulting student complaints were dealt with by the University, with no public airing in the press. The time-honored hazing of underclassmen by upperclassmen seems a curiosity of an earlier time in today's world of litigious

practice. Trustee concerns were not invalid. An example of this is illustrated in a 1922 hazing incident. Because of rampant truancy, the entire freshman class was deprived of the annual "R" trip to the mountain symbol and all social functions for the remainder of that year. A few weeks later, according to the trustee minutes, the "sophomores were very rough with the freshman. The next night the freshmen came back, and taking the sophomores out of their rooms one at a time, they beat most of them into unconsciousness." Trustee outrage visited itself upon students over this raid, which took place at California Hall. The trustees were prepared to expel any and all Redlands students whose involvement could be proven. A lengthy resolution passed by the board at its June 20, 1922, meeting condemned physical injuries sustained by two students, one of whose father threatened legal action. Despite intense efforts by faculty and the Redlands police, the culprits were never identified.

University oversight of student lives experienced a profound shift with the hiring of the first dean of women. Formerly, the faculty had handled discipline, a chore that took time away from teaching responsibilities. President Duke's 1922 appointment of Mary Newton Keith relieved the faculty of that role. The new dean came armed with a degree from Wellesley College, service as a teacher both in public and private schools, and

Senior Ditch Day

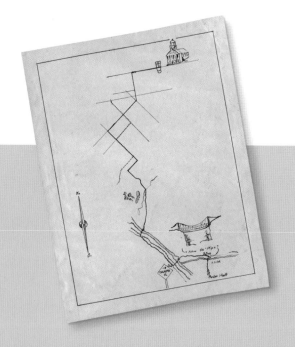

Within a few years of the University's inception, crafty students managed to find an off-campus location that could provide a discreet, out-of-the way venue for group revelry and bonhomie. Once each year, the entire senior class decamped en masse for this "secret" hideaway, and the Ditch Day tradition began. Dubbed "Senior Hall," the location was a ruined adobe building on the outskirts of Redlands, possibly a leftover outbuilding of early Spanish settlers. Seniors reached Senior Hall, which was located two miles from campus, with the help of a secret map that was handed down from class to class.

The seniors soon developed the custom of hiding a "treasure" for the next year's class to locate—complete with cryptic clues and maps. The Class of 1920 obtained a scrapbook, in which they "tried to preserve all records (without alterations) from the old book" and "lovingly dedicated this book to all succeeding Classes of the U. of R." That scrapbook depicts several generations of Bulldog students posing at the ramshackle structures. "We were 30 in number!" the Class of 1920 wrote on their picture. By decade's end, the Class of 1929 reported a membership of ninety-two. The earliest photos depict the Class of 1913, while the last entry was made by the Class of 1936. Senior Hall deteriorated over the years, as less of the ruin is still standing in the later pictures. In fact, by 1935 the activity seemed to have migrated to the shore, for the Classes of 1935 and 1936 were photographed sitting on a beach. By this time, January 15 seems to have become the fixed date on which seniors would ditch.

The following poem, authored by the Class of 1922, encapsulates the light-hearted spirit, group solidarity, and love of alma mater that infused Ditch Day revels:

The Seniors Have a Hall of their own,
Far from the city, Lying alone,
Far out to the South and to the West,
Where the good and the bad and the
  worst and the best
Come for a day of much needed rest.

And the good and the bad and the worst
  and the best
When they mingle together are just like
  the rest.
At least with our class it seemed so to be;
And it's probably true of NINETEEN
  TWENTY-THREE.

So we give you our greetings and wish
  you Godspeed
And we've buried a treasure in case you
  have need
Of something to help you on Life's
  weary way
And make you happier just for today.

If successful in finding the first treasure,
  we hope
You'll look for the second—it's far
  richer dope.
It will help you in life other treasures to find;
Not least among these, the riches of mind.

Then to you and the classes which follow
  each year
We leave the trust of the HALL we hold dear.
May it mean as much to each one of you
As it means to the Class of NINETEEN
  TWENTY-TWO! — JDM

experience as the general secretary of the Young Women's Christian Association of Salt Lake City. Fifty years of age and the widow of a Baptist pastor, Dean Keith also taught freshman mathematics, her major at college. Professor Herbert E. Marsh brought patience and firmness to the position of dean of men during the 1920s and 1930s.

The trustees in January 1923 presented an analysis of whether Redlands students were better or worse in their actions than coeds at other colleges and concluded that, while some criticism was merited, the "student body is composed of young people in the process of development . . . and [the University] ranks remarkably high in wholesomeness of its ideals and its near approach to the realization of the truest ethical and religious standards." The trustees also pointed to a new professor of Bible study, and described "a faculty with loyalty to the teachings of the new testament and to its ethical standards," involved as counselors and friends of the students and encouraging them to lead a spiritual life with faith in Jesus Christ. Finally, they praised Dean Keith as "a woman of large experience in the service of young women," and called for support and cooperation by the board in the use of methods deemed "wise" and expedient to foster and attain these ideals. These actions over student behavior marked the continuing struggle between sectarian and secular forces.

Clearly, faculty supervision over student life had its limits and inconsistencies. The faculty permitted President Calvin Coolidge's inaugural address to be broadcast over a radio from the porch of the Administration Building, but radios were removed from dormitory rooms, and allowed only in parlors or dining rooms. A "Whizbang Club," named for a racy national magazine of the time, organized with students meeting in a rented space in town. The faculty ordered it to disband. The editor of the La Letra was forbidden to run pictures of the club or to mention it.

Following a stinging criticism of faculty disciplinary procedures by the editor of Campus magazine, who described some

punishments as too lenient and others as too harsh, the faculty demanded his resignation. A flurry of meetings between faculty and students called for the president to talk with each succeeding editor of Campus, instructing him or her to write about matters concerning the faculty or administration only after prior approval.

The town was not seen as totally helpful by the gown during these social crises. "Some of the young men of Redlands have caused considerable annoyance at our dormitories for women this year in the taking of our girls out and keeping them out beyond hours," bemoaned President Duke, "and in other ways causing in them to violate the standards of the College and the regulations at the dormitories." Some of the offenses were "grave," and he requested that the Executive Committee pass a resolution supporting him in asking one of these youths to remain off campus, after consultation with the housemothers and the Discipline Committee. One of the miscreants was Dan A. C. Smith, scion of a pioneer Redlands family, who later became a distinguished attorney. As a nonagenarian in the 1980s, Smith recalled a summons to President Duke's office that occurred during a visit home from Yale Law School. The president accused the young townie of compromising the morals of Ruth E. Grinnell '25 by taking her out for dinner, drinking, dancing, and smoking. Smith compounded these sins by returning her to her dorm after curfew. The soon-to-be attorney tartly confessed his guilt, but refuted the president's claim of authority off-campus. For good measure, he branded Duke "a Christian high collar." Ignoring this challenge to the legal extent of his suzerainty, Duke informed Smith that he "accepted the compliment." This from a man who drove a sporty red Maxwell coup.

Recognizing the need for administrative support and guidance for ASUR, the trustees, at President Duke's urging, dealt with the financial problems confronting the student body's funds. While congratulating the men's and women's debate team for securing the Southern California championship for 1925 under the direction of Professor Nichols, President Duke also noted that the Athletic Department, in maintaining both varsity and freshmen teams, if not all athletic contests, expended greater resources than ever before. The result: a $2,000 deficit in the funds of ASUR. The trustees agreed to make up half the amount, provided the students covered the difference. Athletics, as opposed to physical education, were still seen primarily as a student-driven activity.

To assure proper oversight of ASUR's finances, Duke recommended the hiring of a manager of all student enterprises jointly selected by the trustees and ASUR. He urged ASUR to take over the management of the student store, heretofore privately run by students. He asked that a registration fee be added to tuition costs, thus providing an assured treasury for ASUR. Among the items covered by the fee would be admission to all conference athletic contests, a copy of every student publication, and access to "other student enterprises." The duties of the manager were to be worked out by the Executive Committee and representatives from ASUR and from the faculty. In June 1925, Cecil Alonzo Cushman, a genial, gum-chewing Texan, became the first general manager of student activities as well as a part-time coach. Ultimately Cushman made his contribution as one of the most colorful figures in West Coast football, gaining national prominence in 1935 with his famous Kicking Toe, which, when attached to a football shoe, increased accuracy. Upon his death in 1959, many alumni urged (in vain) to name the football field in his memory.

A BAPTIST RELATIONSHIP STRAINED

The 1920s witnessed one of the most remarkable criminal proceedings in all of American history, the Scopes Monkey Trial. This battle over the teaching of evolution in Tennessee's public schools signaled the first salvo in a culture war that bedevils the United States into the present—namely, the clash of modern science and ways of thought with traditional religious values. Beholden to the American Baptist Convention

from its beginning, the University of Redlands proved a fertile ground for skirmishes in this larger cultural conflict.

The University's connection to the California hierarchy of the American Baptist Convention proved both a benefit and an irritant in the school's first three decades. On the beneficial side, contributions from local and regional churches filled University coffers, and the institution received the bulk of its students from those same congregations. During the 1920s, Trustee Gordon Palmer '16 undertook the supervision of an annual "Redlands Day" at each of the Baptist churches in Southern California. More significantly, the Convention in 1925 rewarded a successful University effort to raise $400,000 for the endowment with a $133,000 match from its General Education Fund.

On the other hand, such support carried a price. Within and beyond Southern California, entire congregations as well as individual donors believed their contributions accorded them the right to comment on the University's operation, curriculum, and goals. Years earlier Baptists, unhappy with Jasper Field's vision of the University budget and curriculum, had precipitated his resignation, an episode that embodies the inherent tension between the University and its most important source of extramural support. The American Baptist Convention's influence over a compliant board in the Field controversy marked a moment when its patrons moved beyond complicity in University governance into overt action. Subsequently, the Convention continued to mount pressure on the Board of Trustees to publicly affirm its allegiance to and practice of the denomination's religious tenants. A telling by-law adopted by the First Baptist Church of Redlands in 1920 illustrates well the denomination's emphasis on doctrinal soundness. The provision permitted the restoration of church membership to "persons who have been excluded" from the church only after they established "satisfactory evidence of repentance and public confession of their errors."

As the University's governing body, the Board of Trustees had to grapple with the tension between academic freedom, student desires to lead unfettered lives, and the Baptist constituency's expectation of doctrinal fidelity. In 1923 the board appointed a committee to balance these concerns. This body sought to define "the purposes and aims of the University as a Christian College and its attitude towards the Baptist Denomination and the holy scriptures." Reflecting the Convention's financial role in University affairs, Baptists, including several clergymen, dominated board membership in those years. Moreover, Mattison B. Jones, the board's sole chairman from its founding in 1907 to his death in 1942, was a prominent Baptist layman. In 1931 he even won election to head the Northern Baptist Convention of California. Not surprisingly, then, the committee's report reflected the trustees' religion. Its language reaffirmed "faith in the Historic Baptist position in regard to the Great Doctrines of the Bible, especially the inspiration and authority of the Holy Scriptures, the Deity of Jesus Christ, His supernatural Birth, and Resurrection and His Sacrificial atonement." The board promptly distributed the resolution to the *American Baptist Convention News*, the *Northern California Baptist Bulletin*, and the *Arizona Bulletin*. Clearly, the trustees sought to assure these constituencies, whose donations kept the University solvent, of the institution's continuing devotion to Baptist orthodoxy.

The sectarian Baptist influence made itself felt in myriad ways. Trustee J. H. Merriam penned an official "Purpose of the University of Redlands" that reflected the institution's mission to foster both intellectual and spiritual growth in its students. The statement pledged to "help [the University's] students to attain their best, to become men and women, whose wholesome bodies are fit temples for the indwelling of the Holy Spirit, and whose social graces make them welcome where gentlefolk congregate, whose keen minds enrich scholarship, whose reverent souls worship God in spirit and trust." Such sentiments no doubt helped to entice Baptist clergy in California to petition the University for a reduction in tuition rates for their children, a boon that would have tied the institution even more closely to the Baptist hierarchy. By not granting the request, the trustees guaranteed that the relationship between the Baptist hierarchy and the school would remain tenuous.

Just as Baptist congregations provided an invaluable source for student recruitment, so too did Baptist values influence faculty

hiring. In 1926 the Executive Committee decreed that newly appointed faculty must demonstrate not only a high standard of scholarship, but also a commitment to Baptist doctrine. The "main objective" should be the molding of "Christian character." Faculty "not in sympathy with the purpose and program of the university, shall without controversy or delay, tender [their] resignation."

Leaders from *within* the University added to the complexity of issues between the school and the Baptists. For example, in a June 1925 appearance before the board, Business Manager Cortner advocated requiring Bible study of all students. The meeting's minutes shed little light on whether this recommendation reflected his own piety or was motivated by financial concerns. He observed that patrons thinking of Redlands's future "feel the Bible should be given a little more prominence in our curriculum. They would rejoice in seeing our graduates return to their local churches not only prepared in heart and mind, but also willing to gladly take an active part in, and accept any office or position that would promote the work of God's Kingdom." Cortner urged the trustees to create an endowed chair in "practical Christianity" or "Religious Education." Donors, he cautioned, "do not care to see a duplication of the Bible Institute of Los Angeles nor do they wish to see Redlands patterned after Harvard University. They feel there is a happy medium between these two types of educational institutions in which scholarship may spring into full flower and, at the same time, faith

ripen into full fruitage." Cortner carried the day: the trustees voted to back his plan and authorized him to raise the funds.

Along with Jones and Duke, Cortner was one of the few who knew the identity of the University's anonymous friend, Milo Treat. His suggestions may well reflect his interactions with the school's greatest individual patron. From 1921 forward, "special friend" Treat had pressed the Baptist case hard. That year the trustees executed a motion to accept the "friend's" gift of property on the condition that the funds were managed by the board or others who expressly embraced Baptist principles and teaching. Any breach of this affirmation of the Holy Scriptures, the deity of Jesus, the Church as the people redeemed in order to evangelize the world would result in the funds being taken from Redlands and placed with the Pasadena YMCA. This understanding between the board and its most important donor manifests the importance of hewing to the Baptist line.

Baptist values also informed the dimensions of student life, especially, as discussed earlier, the place of dancing. The issue highlights the gulf between the Baptist-dominated board and a student body increasingly wishing to shed some of the Baptists' more confining moral strictures pertaining to "wholesome bodies . . . fit for temples." This conflict between students, administrators, and trustees would roil campus waters until its settlement during World War II.

The main agenda of the June 1927 Executive Committee meeting concerned the disciplining of students who organized a dancing party at the California Hotel in San Bernardino the previous February. Because the time before commencement was short, the trustees authorized President Duke and Dean Keith "to hold a conference with the seniors [who] were involved, before graduation, reprimanding them in such terms as they may deem wise and the committee further recommends to the Executive Committee that the same method be followed with the other members of the party, before leaving for their homes." The trustees had thrown down the gauntlet, and the students defiantly picked it up. Their ensuing petition was discussed by the full board at its June 6 session and in August referred to the Executive Committee.

Unable to render a verdict, the trustees at their January 1928 meeting voted to postpone a decision until later that day. The result was a call from the trustees to the students and student organizations to withdraw the petition. As a possible sop, they approved construction of fraternity and sorority houses on campus for meeting purposes only. The trustees affirmed their opposition to national Greek affiliations, turning aside student petitions.

The students had won one long-standing crusade in securing local Greek organizations, but were unwilling to end their push for dancing. Dismayed trustees inquired of the student-body president the following June what had happened, having heard nothing from the students. They were told that a meeting with the signers of the dancing petition for the purpose of withdrawing the action produced an attendance of but ten students. Taking a page from the trustees themselves, the ASUR president replied that "up to date nothing had been done."

The issue remained quiescent until June 1931, when a new trustee committee vowed to address it. Eight months of gestation produced a formal recommendation in January 1932. "This committee has sought in an impartial and unbiased way to ascertain what action, if any, would best serve the interests of the University," it declared. After much research, the committee determined that the constituency both within and without the University—especially the "the moral and financial support" of the "Southern Baptist Convention, composed of the Baptist Churches of Southern California—would be so divided over dancing that the trustees should take no action." The full board accepted the recommendation. The resolution, however, served only to postpone the revolution, not avert it.

In short, the relationship between the University and the Baptists resembled that of an unhappily married couple. Frustrations grew over the years, but both sides recognized that separation, let alone divorce, was out of the question. Each partner received sustenance from the other, but they had little in common.

By 1929 the University's financial picture had grown so robust that the trustees once again determined the institution could afford the luxury of a President's Mansion. The building had housed women and classes since the Baptist Board of Education had accused the University of frittering away resources in 1914. That controversy had prompted Jasper Field to resign, rather than face eviction, so firm was his belief that the official residence constituted an important part of his outreach. In lieu of the residence, Field's successor had been given a subsidy for housing. The trustees first offered Duke the residence in 1925, but the president had demurred, perhaps out of sympathy to Field who still lived in town and who had been made an honorary alumnus by the Alumni Association. "From a sense of duty" that a unifying social center might again grace the campus, Duke and his family finally agreed and occupied the mansion in late 1929. Field, who died in 1927, did not survive to witness the moment. Plans were announced for an academic building in November 1929. In 1930 the President's Mansion was cut in half, moved eastward to "Taylor's Hill," and then reassembled to make room for the Hall of Letters, which opened in September 1930 in time for classes.

Depression's Gloom

"It is my purpose to develop learners not leaners."

—CLARENCE HOWE THURBER, INAUGURAL ADDRESS, 1933

HUMAN AND FINANCIAL TRAVAILS

When the bottom fell out of the stock market in October 1929, the University's assets were affected, as were its donors and some of the existing arrangements for transfer of stocks, securities, and property under negotiation. Not since the freeze of 1913 and its disastrous economic consequences had a University of Redlands president faced such gloomy economic prospects. At the end of 1931, President Victor L. Duke, seeking to cut costs, asked and was granted permission from the board to defer his trip abroad. The faculty voted to discontinue the expense of exchanging Christmas cards with one another. In February 1932, all full-time employees of the University met to hear about Mayor N. Leo Leland's Unemployment Relief Funds. As historian Lawrence E. Nelson reported, the speaker's "smug and callous assurance that all on relief would be required to work laboriously, if only by carrying stones to one side of a field and back again, or washing windows already cleaned" prompted vigorous protests from the faculty, who insisted on protecting human dignity: one should labor productively. Nevertheless, they then pledged $284 a month for three months toward the plan unless it were to be "discontinued before that time." Soon unemployed men were hired with these funds to work on a drainage ditch from Brockton Avenue to the Zanja, the city treasury having been exhausted.

Young people could not find work, thus causing college enrollments to soar. Because tuition alone never covers the cost of attendance and scholarships were limited, the University found itself in financial distress. With two-thirds of the students on scholarship and endowment income returns down, the trustees responded by asking faculty to defer sabbatical leaves and summer study. Board costs were lowered in March, which aided students but reduced University income. In April 1932, the faculty and trustees discussed curricular and departmental savings. In May George Cortner asked that his salary be reduced by twenty percent and his entertainment fund discontinued. He stated that faculty salaries should not be cut unless absolutely necessary, owing to their emoluments being below or at par with other institutions. He also pointed to additional challenges: debt, reduction of receipts from rentals of university property, and declining investment income.

On March 3, 1933, amid the gloomy financial picture, the University community received a bombshell in the form of a letter from Chairman Jones: "My Dear Brethren, It is with the extreme sorrow that I officially announce to you the death of President Duke this morning." On campus, as the word spread quickly, tears filled the eyes of trustees, students, faculty, and employees alike. *The Spectrum*, April 12, 1933, published a poem by Cecil C. Eaker '33 expressing the collective sorrow:

> Shelter us, great mountains! You are strong;
> Lend us your courage for a little space.
> Bend over us, O sky! Your stars are kind;
> Our campus is a silent and lonely place.

Duke's death was totally unexpected. On the morning of March 3, "he rose early," according to the newspaper, "slipped a gift under the pillow of his wife, who had returned from a visit especially to be with him on her birthday, and went to take a shower. Rising to thank him, she found him unconscious from a cerebral hemorrhage."

In 1925 the Alumni Association had presented a resolution commending Duke, "our beloved President." It thanked him for leading the University into a period of unprecedented enrollment, endowment growth, and faculty expertise; praised his "broad-gauged character"; and pledged him unstinting support.

To this could be added the remarkable physical growth of the campus infrastructure and buildings, athletic achievements, the creation of the School of Education, and many curricular improvements. Now, eight years later, the trustees praised Duke's "keen mind, thorough scholarship, broad culture, sound judgment, gracious and sympathetic yet forceful personality, Christian courage, wise leadership," and credited the University's success largely to his efforts. The faculty declared its grief "over his passing. [We have] lost a friend of striking social presence, a comrade of utterly unselfish spirit and service, a leader whose Christian faith was deep, strong and unwavering." Duke's death was followed by another bombshell. The budget committee suggested that all employees of the University accept a salary decrease ranging from five to ten percent. They also suggested that six faculty positions be cut. On March 6, the day of Duke's funeral, the trustees asked religion professor W. Edward Raffety to meet with them. That afternoon a weary and grieving board unanimously selected Raffety, a man widely respected for his administrative talent, to become acting president. He accepted. The first task the board assigned him: deliver to the faculty the bad news about the layoffs. At the board's request, Trustee Walter G. Hentschke '14 presented Raffety to the faculty and student body the next day at the chapel service.

The faculty's first response was to suggest that the pay cuts be treated as "donations." A faction of the faculty moved to endorse the trustee proposal, but the motion failed. A new motion indicating agreement with the percentages passed unanimously, with the caveat that the word "decrease" be replaced with "contribution." The board, caught between necessity and principle, accepted the arrangement, and timesheets

asking faculty cooperation were sent out by the board secretary. Hopes that this action would stem the need for further curtailment were dashed when the committee on retrenchment met on March 1, 1933. Realizing that the steps taken by the Hoover administration to turn the country's finances around had largely failed, people focused on the March 4 inauguration of Franklin D. Roosevelt. But the University could not wait for national policy to change.

At their May meeting, the Executive Committee received the budget committee's report, which employed "retrenchment" as the word of the day. The faculty had sent a letter of grievance to the Board of Trustees on March 8, one day after Duke's campus memorial service. On March 23, the board reviewed student-group and Greek-organization fees. They then voted to deny scholarships to students whose spending on activity

fees exceeded the minimum. Those eligible for scholarships faced heavy competition because scholarship income had dried up. By June the board had passed a resolution denying financial aid to students who had automobiles and could not prove that they owned them out of economic necessity.

After conferring with the board and the faculty, Raffety arranged for the Executive Committee to meet with the employees of the University in the Administration Building on the evening of March 15. Cortner explained in detail the University's financial condition in order to demonstrate why position and salary cuts were imperative. The employees voted

Hawaiians at U of R

Following the successful work of two mainland students in 1931 at the University of Hawaii, dialogue among Redlands, University of Southern California, California Poly Tech College, University of the Pacific, and others centered on exchanging students between themselves and the Honolulu-based school. Only Redlands actually made exchanges, sending one student and receiving another. Kenji Fujiwara '32 impressed Redlands students, immersing himself in classwork and activities. George R. Pohlmann '32 spent a year at the University of Hawaii. Kum Pui Lai '33 arrived in 1932 and in like manner became a valued part of the campus scene.

From that time since, Redlands has enjoyed a steady contingent of students from the islands of Hawaii. In 2005–06, twenty-one made Redlands their choice.

In the 1930s, the Hawaii Club instituted an annual luau and musical performance, along with activities throughout the year. So intregal to campus life did the Hawaiians become that even President Thurber utilized the Hawaiian phrase "aloha" in his farewell to the campus.

Kum Pui Lai, who was among the first Hawaiian students to come to Redlands, recalled in his ninety-fifth year (in 2006) what the experience meant to him, "I was the son of struggling Chinese immigrant parents, leaving my island for the first time, and to see all that Redlands had to offer and experience the

friendliness of the students and the kindness of the faculty opened up my whole world and changed my life."

More than 450 alumni from Hawaii have enriched the University, not only culturally and academically, but as athletes and leaders.

TWO U. H. BOYS NAMED EXCHANGE STUDENTS

Kum Pui Lai to Go to Redlands University And Isamu Sato to College of the Pacific for Coming Year

Edited by GWENFREAD ALLEN

Kum Pui Lai, sophomore, and Isamu Sato, freshman, have been selected by the advisory committee of the University of Hawaii Y. M. C. A. to represent the local institution as exchange students to coast colleges during the next school year. These two students of the college of arts and science were selected on the basis of their scholarship, character, and interest in extracurricular activities.

Lai, who is secretary of the university weekly, Ka Leo, and of the sophomore "Y," and a member of the business staff of the Chinese Students' Alliance annual, will attend the University of Redlands at Redlands. Kenji Fujiwara, the first local exchange student, is at present studying at Redlands.

Isamu Sato, varsity debater who met Stanford university last January, and an active Y. M. C. A. worker, will represent Hawaii at the College of the Pacific.

Six mainland students who will study here next fall will be selected by the intercollegiate committee headed by Howard Hopkins of the University of Redlands.

to ask for two weeks to consider the matter and submit suggestions to the Executive Committee.

Professor Herbert E. Marsh, representing the faculty, reported on April 5 that they would accept the ten-percent cut, but asked that it be carried as a non-interest-bearing loan, made for the purpose "of meeting these conditions," that would eventually be paid back. The trustees, after much discussion, denied the request. Pleas from the faculty not to dismiss six of its members, thus literally adding them "to the bread line," were also rejected. The trustees noted that unfavorable and inaccurate publicity in the local newspaper regarding the lay-offs had exacerbated a lamentable situation. The necessity of implementation grieved the board, but the unforgiving financial situation permitted no stepping back from fiduciary responsibility, no matter how painful.

Also, the trustees, citing the rules of the University allowing faculty grievances to be presented to the board through the president, turned down a request for a permanent faculty coordinating committee, the purpose of which was to provide advice to the board during the deepening economic crisis. The board made a small concession in voting in June to grant a fifty-percent reduction in tuition for faculty children. At that same meeting, the trustees formed a committee to solicit scholarships and another to secure bequests through wills.

In addition to the pay cuts, the trustees suspended sabbaticals and summer release. They also slashed the retirement benefits of those who were to retire within ten years. This would prove especially devastating because it lowered the amount of future paychecks. Those teachers who were dismissed were given no time to correct perceived defects in their teaching or to seek academic employment for the following year. The trustees' actions both hurt and antagonized the faculty. Their approach created the impression that they had acted in an "arbitrary" manner. It was not the board's best moment of leadership or communication. They had not handled the crisis sensitively or diplomatically.

Raffety, largely above the fray, watched the drama unfold knowing the pieces would be his to pick up. The acting president's only solace was that he had specifically told the board he would not be a candidate for Duke's successor.

NEW WINE FOR OLD BOTTLES
A daunting spectrum of issues faced whoever would take the helm. The international scene featured increasing tensions and ideological divisions. The Depression wracking the country tested the mettle of individual existence and the family unit. In California the political environment was one of hostility. The City of Redlands, long accustomed to the insularity of wealth, began to feel the vagaries of less palmy times. At the University, orthodoxy challenged individualism, and the frayed edges of certitude confronted decreasing options for sustainable growth.

As word spread about the search for a new president, more than fifty applicants submitted resumés. The selection committee quickly winnowed the list by insisting that the new president be under fifty and a layperson. They focused on one man, recommending that the board unanimously approve of Clarence Howe Thurber as the third president of the University of Redlands.

Thurber arrived with enthusiastic recommendations from many of the leading lights of higher education in America. A Baptist layman, he had led Bible classes and had fundraising experience. A Phi Beta Kappa key holder and graduate of Colgate College—where he had served twice as captain of the football team, earned letters in basketball and track, and been active in intercollegiate oratory and debate—Thurber had the muscular intellect of a president's president. He met his wife, who would become a dean of women, while she was a secretary at

In Their Own Words: Two Women in a Pickle (Barrel)

The story behind the photo below involved a singular evening in the Redlands careers of two women, Henrietta E. Parker '32 (left) and Ruth E. White '34 (right). Displaying both warmth and wit, White's rendition of the episode, set down more than a half-century later, evokes the rhythms of a by-gone vernacular as it sheds insight into student life during the 1930s: how students coped with the Depression (life obviously went on!), how gender mores shaped behavior, and how mindful students were of staying within administrators' good graces. With slight editorial modifications, here is their tale:

It was the end of October 1930. The Great Depression was well underway. Ruth White and Henrietta Parker were Grossmont roommates. . . . Both came from hard-pressed families who had precious little to spare for college educations. To help out, Ruth waited tables and both girls made do or did without.

Then came the College Mix, a traditional student-body Halloween party held in Currier Gym. Excitement swept the dorms for days in advance, since admission required wearing a costume. Ruth and Henrietta longed to go, but neither had a dime to spend on Halloween duds.

Shortly before the event, the young women decided to spend a nickel and share a then-popular king-sized dill pickle, the kind that came in wooden barrels. As the butcher removed the pickle from the barrel, one of the girls said jokingly, "What about the College Mix in a pickle barrel?" "Why not!" said the other. "Maybe we could get two barrels and go as Tom Sawyer and Huckleberry Finn!" The die was cast.

They talked the butcher into loaning them two pickle barrels and rolled them home, sneaking in the back way to keep their costumes secret. Then they blew a few pennies in the Salvation Army store for a couple of old straw hats and two corn-cob pipes.

The night of the Mix, Ruth and Henrietta put on their oldest shirts and shortest undershorts. They tied rags, sprinkled with mercurochrome,

on their toes and feet. They pulled locks of hair through holes in the battered hats. They bit down hard on the corn-cob pipes. Then they wriggled into the pickle barrels and sallied forth. Needless to say, "Tom and Huck" created a sensation. They even took the prize for the most original costume.

But to their dismay, Ruth and Henrietta missed out on a lot of the fun. Although the pickle barrels ended well above the knees, their rigid circumference restricted the movements of the wearers. With their arms stuck inside holding the barrels up, the girls couldn't bob for apples. They couldn't sit down. They couldn't discard the barrels for fear of indecent exposure. And as for goodies, they were entirely at the mercy of hand-feeding friends for the bites they got.

Returning to Grossmont that night, walking barefooted and barrel-clothed slightly ahead of Dean [Mary Newton] Keith, their evening's pleasure suffered yet another blow when the administrator said, quite sharply, as only she could, "I wasn't at all proud of you girls tonight!"

In other words . . . in those days the only proper place to show a bare leg was at the beach. — **Ed., JDM**

a YMCA. He first taught at Wabash College in Crawfordsville, Indiana, and then at Purdue University in Lafayette. He received a doctorate in education at Columbia University and with his family (the Thurbers had two girls and one boy) returned to his alma mater as dean of the faculty and director of the education program.

The search committee liked Thurber's response to the board's 1926 statement of principles. Allowing that he was "not a theologian," he stated that the aim of the college "should be the development of thoroughly educated, cultured, spiritual men and women who will go forth from its halls to enrich the society in which they live, and promote the Kingdom of God on earth."

It appeared that congruity had been achieved between Thurber, trustees, and faculty. For the first time in its twenty-five years of operation, the University had chosen an outsider as its leader, one unfamiliar with its past travails and glories as well as its traditions. Thurber inherited a largely intact set of founding fathers and mothers, many of whom still labored willingly and energetically on the board and possessed deeply held opinions about what the University of Redlands was and should be. But enthusiasm for the new president proved short-lived. Writing about the moment, Lawrence Nelson stated, "No one then realized what soon became evident, that neither fully understood the other."

Following an elaborate inauguration, the *Los Angeles Times* published an article headlined "Dr. Thurber, New Redlands University Head, Lashes Education's Sacred Cow." While recognizing the University's past leadership and its "phenomenal" development in twenty-five years, as well as avowing his loyalty to its spirit and ideals, Thurber used his address to denounce education that treated students' heads as buckets into which information is poured. "Leaners not learners result from spoon feeding. . . . Shall we not then re-examine our whole set up in an endeavor to quicken the love of learning?" And he avowed that a university may only be made great through a great faculty. Specialized courses, he continued, must give way to more

general offerings. While his predecessors had said largely the same things at their inaugurals, it was clear that Thurber was determined to reorganize the University. He advocated independent study, placing the responsibility on students to self-educate. "Education cannot be poured in or plastered on but must be rooted out for oneself," Thurber reminded his audience.

The new president's desire for more rigorous course structure, greater emphasis on curriculum change, and a more cosmopolitan campus pleased many and irritated others. His style could be "imperious." Confronted with a shaky campus environment, Thurber nonetheless began to butt heads with the old guard. Not sensing the essential conservatism of the board, the president, as Nelson wrote, "a forthright man, unaccustomed to the careful weighing of delicate wisps of hints," seemed determined to impress his educational philosophy upon the small denominational University. Inherent tensions between academic freedom and orthodox religious tenants emerged.

The biography of Emmett S. "Punchy" Oliver '36 by his classmate Benjamin E. Smith '37 adds dimension to the nature of the relationship between individual faculty and the student body during the Thurber years. "Professor James Kyle," he wrote, "taught Greek and Latin and told his classes that he was married to his first cousin in a purely platonic relationship. Each spring he gave a $25 J. W. Kyle Efficiency Award to the student who contributed most to the University that year. Professor William Roberts was outstanding in philosophy, psychology and ethics, and practiced hypnotism on his classes."

Fortunately, Thurber and the University continued to enjoy the administrative expertise of George Cortner. He provided continuity amid change. As the president plunged into his campaign for individualized instruction, honors reading, and increased scholarship, he became the darling of the town's elite. He and his wife exuded a cosmopolitan, sophisticated air. The Thurbers were frequent guests at elegant dinner parties, and they entertained often at the President's Mansion.

As Nelson observed, fault-finding in the grim years of the Depression had become the epidemic of an impoverished people. The University was no different. The year 1934 proved harmful for the fortunes of Clarence Thurber, who could not have known that his controversial reign of progress would unravel because of two professors who exemplified the very academic qualities he espoused.

Robert H. Lynn, a professor of religion, became the object of a flurry of letters to the trustees from seven students complaining about his views on the deity of Christ, the inspiration of the Bible, the conversion and baptism of Saint Paul, and a number of additional issues. They asserted that biblical "truth" was not getting a fair break, and complained that Lynn "had a tendency to lead them into the dark in order to make them think, without sufficient light to guide them back to the truth."

The board appointed a three-person committee of inquiry to hear the students. Reporting to the Executive Committee in December 1934, the inquiry committee congratulated the "splendid spirit shown by the students" and also "Dr. Lynn in the whole matter. . . . " The committee declared Lynn to be a "true Christian" who was doing his professorial best. The trustees carefully sought to balance intellectual freedom, professional pedagogy, and Baptist orthodoxy. In taking such an initiative, the board misgauged the result. The ultraconservative churches from which the dissenting students had come were now not only suspicious of one professor but of the board as well. To many faculty, the incident raised the haunting specter of the violation of academic freedom.

Exacerbating the waters swirling about Thurber's administrative feet was Dr. William H. Roberts, a professor of philosophy and psychology, a ten-year faculty veteran who had taken part in a number of political campaigns. "Always on the side of angels,"

noted Nelson, Roberts had supported various prohibition candidates and crusading clergyman. His father, a pioneer missionary in Burma, had told him to "never count the risk, when an important spiritual issue was at stake," Roberts believed that, in times of particular crisis, universities should take active part in politics and that professors should validate "courageous citizenship preached in the classroom."

Roberts had suffered guilt, remorse, and a nervous breakdown over his non-combatant status in World War I as a stretcher-bearer. He sensed his opportunity for redemption in the spring of 1934, when he committed himself to campaign for the most

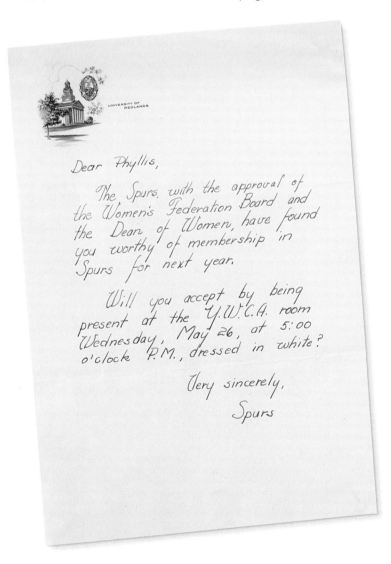

Dear Phyllis,

The Spurs, with the approval of the Women's Federation Board and the Dean of Women, have found you worthy of membership in Spurs for next year.

Will you accept by being present at the Y.W.C.A. room Wednesday, May 26, at 5:00 o'clock P.M., dressed in white?

Very sincerely,

Spurs

maligned, feared, and controversial candidate for governor in California's history, Upton Sinclair. Muckraker, novelist, and socialist, Sinclair sought the Democratic nomination and advanced a controversial plan to end poverty in the state. Roberts, imbued with a crusader's zeal, became Sinclair's campaign manager. At this juncture national, state, and local politics began a partisan and often testy intersection.

The Republican City of Redlands seethed with disgust, and the University hierarchy recoiled from one of its own. Board Chairman Mattison B. Jones, himself a former Democratic candidate for governor, took to the radio. In the name of the "League of Loyal Democrats," the party's one-time nominee urged everyone to vote for Republican Frank Merriam. Decrying Sinclair as a socialist tinged with "atheistic communism," Jones clearly had no sympathy for Roberts's support of the candidate.

Thurber, now hampered by controversy, talked to Roberts. The professor, unwilling to harm the University, agreed to drop all political activity. He was under the impression that the trustees had taken formal action requesting it. Later he found that such was not the case. Roberts was indignant at what he deemed Thurber's duplicity. "The President has muzzled me," he protested to a faculty hearing. "He has played upon my loyalty; he has demanded something the trustees did not authorize." Unbeknownst to Roberts, Thurber had actually defended him against any trustee infringement of his academic freedom. The board acceded and took the president's advice.

Using the name Allan Brand, Roberts continued to engage in politics. Three months elapsed before the president learned of the ruse. Though Roberts had made no secret of it, Thurber now felt betrayed. He charged Roberts with unethical behavior and conduct unbecoming a professor.

Sinclair, himself a victim of manipulation of false news stories and phony motion-picture news accounts resulting from collaboration between the *Los Angeles Times* and certain Hollywood studios, was widely criticized. Many alumni and leading lights

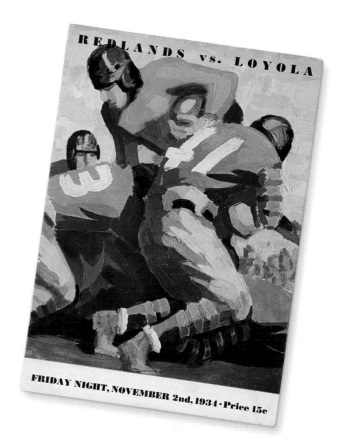

REDLANDS vs. LOYOLA

FRIDAY NIGHT, NOVEMBER 2nd, 1934 · Price 15¢

at other educational institutions urged Thurber to drop his accusations in order to save the career of an unquestionably good teacher. Roberts offered to admit errors in judgment, but Thurber was in no mood to make peace. The professor asked for and was granted a trial before a jury of his peers, the Faculty Council.

The verdict: not guilty as charged. But the council recommended firing Roberts. Calling this mixed message "curiously lacking in logic," Nelson, himself on the faculty at the time, pointed to a major split within the faculty regarding issues of dissent and involvement in politics. The affair's complexity grew when Roberts offered to recuse himself from the hearing. Thurber dismissed the call for his own withdrawal at the same time and instead took his prerogative as ex-officio chairman of the council to speak, rendering himself, in Roberts's view, "both prosecutor and juryman." Granted six-months' severance pay by the board, Roberts went to Yale University and wrote a textbook inspired by the incident, *The Problem of Choice, An Introduction to Ethics*, thinly disguising the identities of the protagonists.

THE CAMPUS AS COMMUNITY

Apart from the glare of internal dissention, communication between faculty and students remained sound. Redlands, challenged by Boston University to a debate in 1933, accepted. It was broadcast live on the radio. President Thurber, a former debater, was delighted. This followed a national Phi Kappa Delta competition that had netted Redlands the championship in 1932.

Campus life continued to evolve as the University matured. In 1933 SPURS (Service, Patriotism under Responsible

Sacrifice), an international women's honor society and service organization, received a national charter. Four years later, the sophomore men's service club chose "Yeoman" for its name. To exemplify its community-minded spirit, the group adopted as its motto a biblical passage, "He that is greatest among you shall be your servant."

Recalling Dean Mary Newton Keith, Emmett S. "Punchy" Oliver '36 remembered, "Coeds were secured in their morals by a friend and formidable censor." He recalled that "orange groves earned income for the University. Theft of fruit was prohibited but regularly occurred. No dorm room was complete without its gunnysack of large, sweet navel oranges."

Student hijinks included a spring joke by Grossmont women, who rang the telephone at all-male Melrose Hall at 2:00 a.m., asking for a specific resident. After the hapless young man

60238

The BULLDOG

UNIVERSITY OF REDLANDS

VOLUME XXIV   REDLANDS, CALIFORNIA, SEPTEMBER 24, 1937   Number 1

BULLDOGS OPEN AGAINST LOYOLA

Redlands Bulldogs will swing into action a week from tonight.

Under the blazing lights of Gilmore stadium, the largest and heftiest Maroon and Gray team in many years will match plays with the strongest and most colorful of the Coast's independents, Roaring Loyola Lions, given a decided edge over the Brazen Bulldogs.

The score in the three-year feud between the two teams now stands at two games for the Del Rey boys and one for Redlands, with this year's game conceded to the Los Angeles squad. Campus rumor, however, declares that the Bulldog gridders are out to prove the dopesters wrong, as they did two years ago when Blaisdell and "Pete" Peterson turned in the biggest upset of the season.

Truman Jolley and Prof. Cranston Will Lead Meeting

Under the leadership of Truman Jolley, the International Relations club, will begin its new series of fall meetings next Monday evening, September 27, at 7:30 at the home of Mr. Earl Cranston, 532 Cajon.

How do you like the new name for your paper? And the way it has been printed? For years and years the same "banner" has been used for your weekly publication and we felt it needed doing over.

Much thought was given to its choice. Because many schools and colleges have titled their papers "The Campus" a name was chosen that would be individual and better suited to our University.

We hope you like it.

CAMPUS WILL PREPARE FOR LOYOLA CONTEST AT BULLDOG PEP RALLY

Let's lick Loyola! Be at the Rally, gang!

The rally for the Loyola game is next Wednesday, September 29 at the Fox Redlands Theatre.

The time is 8:30, and the price is only 25 cents. We can't advertise, but a good double feature is showing, as well as Bank nite, so some lucky student is sure to win, if we fill up the theatre.

Rally Chairman Lee Launer has promised a lively program, with plenty of yells, songs, and cheers,

DR. RAFFETY BRINGS NEW WELCOME TO INCOMING STUDENTS OF REDLANDS

By W. EDWARD RAFFETY

By the time you read this, from many people, you have had already the glad word,—

WELCOME

We mean it! Administrators, faculty, old students,—the whole University family would surround you, enthuse you, with the Redland's "Hello Spirit". You have come to a friendly institution. The way you can help keep it friendly is to be a friend.

You have come to a college of high educational standards, accredited by the Association of American Universities, in November 1926. You will do your best while here with nothing less than your best. Keep first things first! You have come to a college.

You have come to a Christian institution, not narrow, or bigoted,

or sectarian, but, we trust, wholesomely, genuinely Christian. Whatever your religious faith, you are welcome! Read again and again the purpose, printed on page three of the current catalog, a purpose formulated by Trustees, Faculty and Students. Keep step with that purpose! This will mean much for the enrichment of your personalities, and those satisfactions which come only to those who invest themselves in unselfish service for others. There is gold in the Golden Rule for you. Get this treasure in full measure during the years of your life on the campus of the University of Redlands.

Friendship, scholarship, Christian living! To these privileges,—again, we say, most sincerely, Welcome!

J. BLAISDELL ELECTED PREXY OF LETTERMEN AS NEW PLANS MADE

The R Club elected Jimmy Blais-

Trustees, Faculty, Students Will Meet During Retreat Led By M. Jensen and Raitt

Leaving from the chapel steps

Because of pressing extra-curricular activities, Bill Adams, editor of the Bulldog, submitted his resignation to members of the Student Council Tuesday. The act ended a three-year career on the student paper, during which time Adams advanced from reporter to acting-editor last semester. During this year, he will add to his job as sports publicity director, the positions of sports correspondents for the San Bernardino Sun and the Los Angeles Examiner.

STAFF APPOINTMENTS BRING NEW FACULTY MEMBERS TO CAMPUS

Positions to be held by the new members of the University staff include personnel and placement secretary, George R. Momeyer. Mr. Momeyer comes fro San Bernardino where he was principal of the san Bernardino high school.

Three new head residents will be on the Campus this winter. Mrs. Florence R. Langendorfer of Long Beach will be head resident of Bekins Hall, succeeding Mrs. Katherine Corbett. Melrose Hall will be

Bulldog Growls

What's the matter with Redlands? Of all the schools in the Conference, LaVerne, with an enrollment of approximately 350 students, and Redlands are the only two not having a band! Last year this situation was faced by student leaders who at the end of long and heated argument decided that nothing could be done about either reforming the old group nor creating a new one. This year Redlands claims to have one of the best football teams in years, isn't it about time that we got a band to support it?

• • •

We also will have the largest student enrollment in five years; certainly out of a group of this size, there should be twenty or thirty students who could and would contribute enough time and talent to create a band that Redlands could hear without blushing. Until such time as the trustees realize that the University needs a regular band director, either some student or some member of the music department will have to volunteer to fill the place left vacant by the departure of Barton Bachman.

For Pete's sake, let's stop talk-

The Questions of Every Collegian's Existence

Any anthropologist would testify to the importance of assimilating local folkways, social practices, and manners when encountering a new social environment. In the 1930s, the Associated Students of the University of Redlands (ASUR) published a pocket-sized etiquette guide called *It's Being Done*. The 1937 version familiarized incoming students with social conventions in the hopes of improving the "conscious search for perfection." Topics included "Campus Customs," "Dining," "Gossip," and "Dating."

Produced by students, the guide features advice to lubricate any social setting the intrepid collegian might encounter. For instance, the authors counseled against "Howdy, Prof." as a greeting in a chance meeting with an instructor. Such informality was "not quite courteous to one of such position." "A prompt, noiseless entrance and courteous attention to the program" was advised for chapel, and, lest anyone treat that time as a study hall, the guide counsels, "The time is too limited for effective studying." Since the library "isn't really a social hall . . . telling the latest jokes and making dates should be cared for outside."

Many students may have had limited exposure to the finer points of public dining before entering college. Thus, the book reminds everyone that " a gentleman seats the lady to his right" and

that "silverware is placed in order of use from the outside in." In an effort to encourage conversational intercourse, *It's Being Done* states that it is a "duty to talk to one's neighbors at the table. . . . When there are strangers present, it is many times helpful to get a few topics in mind beforehand."

Sartorial charts reduced the anxiety of wardrobe selection. Thus, we learn that cords, sweaters, and sport suits were expected of men in the classroom, with the exception that freshmen "were forbidden to wear cords." Classroom options for women varied; sweaters, skirts, wool dresses, sport suits, sport silks, and cotton prints were sanctioned. Chapel mandated more formal dress. Adding a hat seemed to suffice for women, while etiquette required suits of the men.

The dating section, presented as "tips to the men from the West side of the Quad," contains such handy advice as not waiting until the last minute to ask a "girl" out, the proper phrasing of an invitation, and a reminder to stand when the girl enters the room. Speaking of time, escorting one's beau back to the dormitory before curfew indicated one's gentility. Flustered by the pressure of choosing the right corsage to match the color of a date's dress? *It's Being Done* could make any formal occasion perfect with its handy corsage guide, pairing eight types of flowers with various colors.

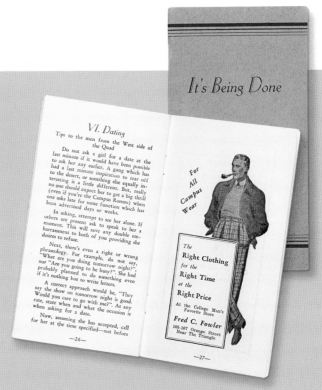

Incoming women learned that courtesy required accepting or declining a date at the time "one is asked. . . . Otherwise, the impression is, 'I'll be glad to go provided nothing better turns up in the meantime.'" When the moment arrives, the young woman should "look as attractive as possible." Because "Redlands isn't noted for its moneyed men," the coed should "not expect the fellow to spend lots of money." A more ambiguous piece of advice suggests she "be a good sport about everything," One trusts that both sides understood that advice to have limits! The section concludes with this cautionary statement, addressed "to the campus": "Three consecutive dates does not mean a couple is going 'steady'!" Some things, at least, never change. — JDM

had been roused from his slumber, the callers professed to have erred—they really wanted someone else. Soon, they had gone through most of the dorm roster. In retaliation, the men arranged to have an insider cut the power to Grossmont one evening. Just before plunging the hall into darkness, the Melrose men released goats, "borrowed" from a nearby farm, via a fire escape onto the second-floor landing. Coeds, startled from their rooms by the sudden loss of light (including some who had been showering) encountered the bleating animals in the hall. No less frightened than the students were the con-fused goats, and pandemonium ensued.

The goat-herders had the misfortune to encounter a "campus cop [who] caught the culprits." That misfortune inevitably brought them to the attention of Dean of Men Herbert Marsh, whose job it was to dole out discipline. Ironically, the dean apologized to the miscreants for the necessity of punishing them, which prompted Oliver to remark decades later that he, "felt like a heel" in the face of Marsh's graciousness.

That same night, by coincidence, two students managed to get a cow to climb to the third-floor office of Professor George Foust in the Hall of Letters. Confronted by Marsh, they had to

BELOW: *The Feathered Serpent* was the extravaganza for the Zanja Fiesta of 1934. Its authorship by local resident Bruce McDaniel illustrates how the fiesta evolved into a true town and gown event. Benjamin E. Smith '37, who performed in the musical, recorded the following impressions in his diary: "The evening was perfect. The play sure did go over swell. We made lots of mistakes but the audience didn't see them." According to Smith, an audience of two thousand saw the show each night.

confess: one received probation, but "stonewalling" resulted in a one-year suspension for the other. As for the poor cow, the city fire department had to tie the beast to a board and carry it downstairs before it could reunited with its owner.

The Depression had little impact on Bulldog athletics. Across Colton Avenue to the north of Currier Gym lay the football and track fields and the baseball diamond. One of Oliver's favorite stories involved football coach Cecil Cushman. The team traveled to Los Angeles to take on heavily favored Loyola and radio announcers talked with Cushman before the contest. The interview was piped into the visitors' locker room, and the Bulldog players heard their coach assess their chances in the face of unusual weather conditions. The announcer asked, "'Cush,' do you think this low fog tonight will interfere with your team's razzle-dazzle passing attack?' 'Cush' replied, 'Nope. My boys are in a fog most of the time!'" The coach's deadpan analysis broke the tension in the locker room, and his players took to the field laughing. Although Loyola had been favored by six touchdowns, the Bulldogs triumphed with a 19–18 score.

The football team topped the conference every year from 1930 to 1934, led by Donald W. Baum '34, Theodore Schmidtmann '34, W. Earl Bandy '35, Archie J. Cochrane '35, and Reinold A. "Swede" Peterson '36. Following an undefeated season in 1933, the gridders achieved the same in 1934. Their championship was one of several attained that year. The cross-country men posted an undefeated season, attaining their fifth consecutive title. The tennis team also broke into the championship ranks for the first time in 1934, led by Captain J. Overton Pratt '34. The Bulldog basketball and track teams enjoyed successful seasons, and the baseball squad took third in the league. Freshmen teams, harbingers of a bright future, were first in every sport except track. The former athlete Thurber expressed great satisfaction.

The matriculating class in the fall of 1937 was the largest in seven years, a sign that the financial ravages of the Depression were easing. The campus newspaper welcoming the freshmen to campus sported a new moniker on its mast, as *The Bulldog*

replaced *Campus* as the paper's name. The editors explained that the shift resulted from "much thought." "Because many schools and colleges have titled their papers *Campus*, a name was chosen that would be individual and better suited to our University."

In 1937 the Associated Students of the University of Redlands (ASUR) urged an honor code for students during examinations. But one year later, student leaders changed their minds and opted for a faculty proctor system. They concluded that the watchful eye of a professor would be more effective. This indicated the strong sense of community that existed between students and teachers. Some students who were short of funds received loans or cash gifts from thoughtful instructors. Students were invited to professors' homes to share a meal. All student groups had faculty advisors. At a faculty meeting, Professor Nelson reported that Yasuo Kubota '33 needed help to return home. He noted, "Individual members of the faculty might be approached . . . for assistance in securing him the passage necessary."

Twenty-five years of scholastic achievements were highlighted in the 1934 *La Letra* with a survey from the beginning of classes in 1909 to the present. Citing the "romance and color" in building the University, the literary magazine *Spectrum* featured block prints and etchings by students of "spots near the campus."

Students were proud of the college chorus when it joined with Pomona's choir to present Giuseppe's Verdi's *Requiem* during

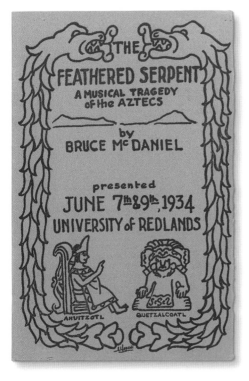

Dusky Day

In 1933 a popular novel aimed at "girls of junior high and high-school age" featured a thinly disguised University of Redlands as its setting. Penned by Florence Crannell Means, *Dusky Day: A College Story* was one of at least fourteen novels Crannell wrote for children and teenagers, including *The Moved Outers* (1945), about a Japanese-American family ousted from their California community in the opening days of World War II. *Dusky Day* and its sequel, *The Singing Wood: A College Story*, were set at the University, where Means's daughter, Eleanor C. Means '32, was a student.

Now largely forgotten, the novel sold moderately well in the 1930s. It provides an insider's account of the Redlands campus from a student's perspective. The heroine of *Dusky Day* is a coed named Lodsuska Day—Dusky to her friends. Dusky enrolls at a college called "Highland University," in Southern California. (The town of Highland is actually adjacent to Redlands.)

The resemblance of Highland to dear old U of R can hardly be mistaken. Eucalyptus trees dot the campus, which features a "chapel at the end of the quad." Other geographic markers heighten the resemblance, including a certain creek that flows through campus. "Who wants to go down to the Zanja with me and study?," Dusky asks at one point. Even the local corruption of the Zanja's name makes it into the story. When Dusky searches for a friend who is distraught over her rejection by the "Kappa" sorority, our heroine suddenly realizes just where her missing friend may have gone for solace. "She'd go toward the Sankey. I know she'd go toward the Sankey."

The students of fictional Highland University also share with their real-life Redlands counterparts a cherished—and uniquely local—tradition: the Pajamarino. Descriptions of nightshirts and colorful bedclothes enliven the scene in the book, which ends at the local town's bowl (yet another parallel), where prizes are handed out. The story even reflects the town and gown nature of the Pajamarino, as downtown "turned itself inside out to do honor to the student body." After the festivities conclude, students return to campus for a bonfire—to build morale prior to the next day's big Bulldog football game. The opposing Citrus team, bedecked in orange and black, calls to mind Redlands's traditional archrival, Occidental.

While soap-opera elements characterize the story—for example, as Dusky's days at Highland draw to a close, she discovers her birth mother, the plot's culminating event. Nevertheless, *Dusky Day* evokes a tender nostalgia. Perhaps her fondness is expressed best in a passage in which she expresses a desire "to live in an orange grove with the Zanja flowing through my front yard." What Redlands alumnus or alumna could not relate to that? — **LEB** and **JDM**

"Passion Week." The A Cappella Choir sang for the Pilgrim Congregational Church in Pomona and for the Easter Sunrise Service in Palm Springs. The Men's Glee Club sang in San Francisco, while the Women's Glee Club performed throughout Southern California. The ubiquitous band played at Homecoming, the San Bernardino Mardi Gras Parade, an Armistice Day commemoration, and Lincoln's birthday event at the Lincoln Memorial Shrine in Redlands; it made a special appearance at the Redlands Community Music Association's summer concert series at the Redlands Bowl. The editor of the 1935 *La Letra* voiced delight in hearing "music coming from Fine Arts" and in seeing the "expertise on the tennis court." All of the campus activities, he concluded, bore witness to "students growing up to living." In assessing student experience, historian Earl Cranston concluded, "Individual activities are not ends in themselves, nor do they stand in disconnected isolation . . . only as they are interpreted together by each student into consistent and creative daily life."

Emphasis on independent study and on Duke's legacy of asking students "to become largely what you will" were accelerated concepts during the Thurber years. Students welcomed these changes. In adopting the program, the faculty, in Thurber's view, had placed Redlands "abreast with the foremost institutions of the nation." Oliver remembered that "President Thurber made significant and valuable changes during his four-year tenure, introducing an honors program of individualized study. [For example,] a European history course had just one student, who got reading assignments, and lectured to the professor for an hour each week, earning 12 credits for the year. Seminars conducted by students, under professional guidance, typified other courses."

Other initiatives intended to strengthen academic life required students to take classes in related topics from a wide selection of disciplines rather than focusing on a single field "to accomplish what major and minor have failed to accomplish." As may be imagined, debate focused on the merits of change versus the status quo. The faculty were not immune to change. Thurber requested that each member endeavor to prepare at least one article a year for publication in a magazine or newspaper.

Following the Lynn and Roberts contretemps, Thurber began to feel the heat. Ironically, enrollment statistics helped erode his position further. While more than half the entering students were now from the upper twenty percent of their classes, freshman enrollment numbers dropped from 143 to 103, while other Southern California private schools were experiencing growth. The situation had both academic and budgetary implications for Redlands.

One reason for the decrease in enrollment was that the proportion of Baptists in the student body had steadily decreased since 1930; critics latched onto this, pointing to Thurber's leadership as the cause. Of the six hundred and two students in the autumn of 1931, twenty-six denominations were represented. There were two hundred fifty-two Baptists, ninety-eight Methodists, sixty-four Presbyterians, twenty-nine Congregationalists, twenty-one Disciples of Christ, one hundred twenty-one Episcopalians, and ten Roman Catholics. Only nine students stated no preference, with seventy-seven others adhering to no specific denomination. This growing diversity had been addressed in the past by the trustees in their annual affirmation of the founders' principles and of the tenets of Baptist belief. Though the trend to recruit more Baptist students yielded some results by 1936, this happened too late to help Thurber.

THE PRESIDENCY MISCAST

The deaths of some of the old-guard trustees, founding members of the board such as Katherine (Mrs. Martin) Bekins and Judge J. H. Merriam, occurred during Thurber's presidency. This proved to be unhelpful to

Thurber, as students and faculty continued to question his imperiousness.

Sensing a sea change, many trustees voiced their views about the University's mission. Intense discussions focused on academic freedom in relationship to maintaining good relations with the Baptists. It was inevitable that the influence of Baptist creeds would wane at Redlands, although this would be a slow process. The board would reach a consensus ten years later under a new president who made changes that sought to balance the secular and the sectarian.

The tension must have been palpable at the February 22, 1936, trustee meeting, attended by a formidable delegation of twenty-six of Redlands's leading citizens: among them, Republican State Senator Lyman King, owner of the *Redlands Daily Facts*; C. M. Brown, President Franklin D. Roosevelt's right-hand man in Southern California and a leading citrus grower; and Robert Watchorn, philanthropist and recipient of an honorary degree from the University. The group also included John Marvin Dean, Jr. '32, president of the Alumni Association, and Malcolm M. Rink '38, student-body president, who bore a petition signed by 175 students. Thurber's future ranked number one on their agenda.

King, acting as spokesman, expressed his dismay at reports about Thurber's possible dismissal. "So I come today bearing an expression of the highest good will from the people who live in the area surrounding the University. I feel that whatever degree of material prosperity has been given both the University and community will suffer a body blow if the word shall be said which will send Dr. Thurber away." Adding to these remarks, Brown declared "his belief that the entire community, except for the Baptists, . . . [supports] the president." Calling Thurber "honest, upright and a man to be proud of," Watchorn urged the president's retention.

The trustees listened respectfully to the presentations on behalf of Thurber. They then took up a lengthy list of business items and called in the president to address them, after which they adjourned to executive session.

At issue was the recent granting of railroad passes to Thurber by the Southern Pacific Company at his request. This became the center of discussion and justification for board action. After a dinner break, the trustees again asked the president to address material "relative to his administration." They returned to executive session, with the full board reconvening at 9:10 p.m.

It was a long day and night. The Executive Committee concluded that the acceptance and use of railroad passes were contrary to the law. Both the president and the board regretted it; and the trustees were ready to reimburse the railroad company.

In His Own Words: One Man's U of R

Diaries do not always make riveting reading, since they mostly record the mundane happenings of everyday existence. On the other hand, for the historian trying to reconstruct the rhythms of student life seven decades ago, the very ordinariness of the entries becomes invaluable. Benjamin E. Smith '37 was a dedicated diarist during his four years at Redlands. Coauthor of the campus fight song and student-body president, Smith played an active role on campus. His notes about day-to-day engagements provide priceless glimpses into the personalities and events that shaped the Redlands of his era. The first excerpted entries hint at some of the turmoil surrounding President Thurber. The last entries are from Smith's final week as a student—and from what turned out to be Thurber's final days as well. Smith died in 2003.

TUESDAY, FEBRUARY 11, 1936: We presented Roberts with his copy of the petition. This aft[er] he went before the Board—they withdrew all previous charges, but gave him an immediate sabbatical leave, and so that is that. We're losing a fine man. 3 Trustees met with the student Council.

WEDNESDAY, FEBRUARY 12, 1936: Professor Roberts wasn't in his classes today.

TUESDAY, FEBRUARY 9, 1937: The Board met today—but did not discuss the Prexy's standing. It was all a good pep talk for Thurber. I guess, however, that he's on his last legs.

WEDNESDAY, FEBRUARY 10, 1937: Breakfast for a change. Cinnamon rolls. Didn't have S. B. [Student Body] mtg. tonight. Board hasn't considered retention of Thurber yet. Went to see Del and had a peach of a time.

WEDNESDAY, JUNE 2, 1937: Breakfast this morning. Dashed about. Chapel. Thurber talked. O, my! Oh, my! What a storm!

MONDAY, JUNE 7, 1937: I got Mom and Dad at 10:00 and we went to Class Day Exercises. They were swell.... Prexy's reception with Mom and Dad and dinner after at Grossmont. Procession-Graduation with Honors—Recession to Ad Bldg., Alma Mater, Lights in Chapel—It's over—all over—it has been just as I dreamed it would. So full of memories—so full of life. Took Del home. Got my graduation kiss—and a lot more like it. She is the next big project, though she'd resent the reference taken literally.

WEDNESDAY, JUNE 9, 1937: Del and I went for a walk up the

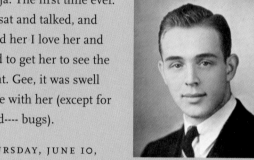

Zanja. The first time ever. We sat and talked, and I told her I love her and tried to get her to see the point. Gee, it was swell there with her (except for the d---- bugs).

THURSDAY, JUNE 10, 1937: Rose at 9. Gave Jimmy my report, checked out. Cleaned room and helped Berg move. Called Del at noon. Took her to Scripps to stay with Mad Wynne.... Home with Berg to Glendale, home—and to bed. Darn, I'm missing the place already—and Del—.

Well, Life, Here I come, ready or not. What's ahead? ? Quien sabe? Just God. **– Ed., JDM**

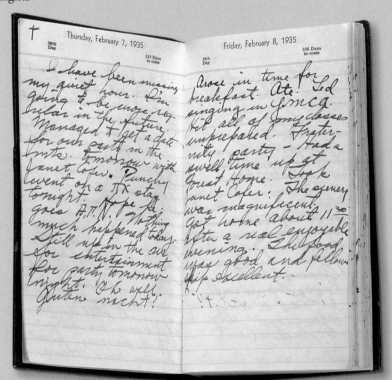

BELOW: Rivalry and hazing marked
class relationships well into the 1930s.
This poster from 1931 is a general warning
to the "frosh" from the "omnipotent"
sophomore class of 1934.

Sophomore Proclamation!

Heralding the insipid influx of neophites which have invaded our beautiful and undefiled campus, we the OMNIPOTENT AND ALL-POWERFUL CLASS OF '34 do hereby issue the following proclamation to those lowest of mammal species—the frosh. Be it known to these benign children that neglecting to strictly adhere to the forthcoming annotations will be classed as criminal insubordination. Be it further known that benumbed frosh who have the audacity and insanity to fail in keeping the following commandments will receive a call from the imperial CLASS of '34, who, as their guardians, will attend to them eagerly. Read the proclamation and endeavor to comprehend as much as possible with your limited capacity. Even the heart of a sophomore is almost touched at the thought of the poor, unfortunate class of '35

THOU SHALT

1. Cap the northern extremity of the vertbrae column with the ensignia of submission to the sophomores to wit—the beanie. This sign shall be worn from sun up until sun down every day except Sunday. The skies of the innocent flock shall adorn their tawdy dresses with a like sign of servitude—a large pin and green ribbon. On Wednesday they shall wear conspicuously in their tawdy tresses a green ribbon.

2. Memorize immediately, (if luckily thou findest thyself capable of such application) all songs and yells of the university which is thy Alma Mater.

3. Always be in readiness to repeat to the best of thy meager ability at the request of any of thy superiors, which includes everyone, the Och Tamale.

4. Drop everything and respectfully touch thy thumbs to the button of thy beanie at the command of "Button, frosh."

5. Always be in readiness to do the menial labor when upper classmen lower themselves to give thee an opportunity.

6. Remember that thou art the lowest of animals and that thy color is green.

7. Hang this in a prominent place in the room and keep it for daily reference lest thou annoy thy superiors.

Ordered and signed, September, 1931

THOU SHALT NOT

1. Permit thy poor bewildered mind to think this place is thine because thou didst come three days early.

2. Tread upon the quadrangle from this time forth until next year for this ground is holy and for students only. However if the Bulldog Varsity triumphs over the Pomona Sagehens on the gridiron thou, too, may cross the quadrangle.

3. Under any circumstances be seen in cords or Sophomore Blues. Nor shall any frosh attempt to wear a moustache or sideburns. Failures always hurt one's reputation.

4. Be seen "Queening". For your enlightenment this is being with or talking to any member of the opposite sex while in any building on the campus. Further thou shalt not permit thyself the company of the opposite sex to any place of solitude or amusement until the second week in October. It is hoped that by then thy choice will be improved.

5. Forget to remember that thou hast been forced upon us and that thy superiors will tolerate thee only so long as thou remainest in thy proper low place in the college. Thou art a handicap and not an asset to the school.

The Omnipotent Class of '34

To be signed by all frosh

I, a lowly and ignorant frosh, groping in the dark, have read the above proclamation issued by my betters and superiors, the OMNIPOTENT SOPHOMORES, and will try in my own poor way to follow its commands and restrictions. Further, at all times I will be at the service of any of my numerous superiors, realizing my ignoble station at the University of Redlands.

PRICE 50 CENTS   Signed _____

For decades many well-connected citizens had customarily accepted preferred railroad passes for free or discounted travel. That the trustees focused on this issue rather than on Thurber's performance reveals their desire to create a reason to fire him.

Thurber agreed to resign as of June 30, 1937. He was granted sabbatical leave, which allowed him to remain in the President's Mansion until August 1. Further motions expressed appreciation for the president's cooperation and for what he had done for the University. Nonetheless, the cloud under which he left took its toll on his career, and he never fully recovered his equilibrium.

Professor of History Earl Cranston, a friend of the Thurbers, awaited the news outside the deliberation room. When he heard the decision, he took a rose to Mrs. Thurber, who was sitting under a trellis on the walk leading to the President's Mansion. When she saw the flower, she said, "He's leaving, isn't he?" "Yes," replied a teary Cranston. Cranston always believed that, despite Thurber's admitted shortcomings, it was his liberalism that did in his presidency.

Although he continued to attend trustee meetings until June 30, Thurber's era was over. Over, except in the hearts of the citizens of Redlands. Early in May, one hundred influential townspeople gathered at the Wissahikkon Inn "to honor the Thurbers and present them with gifts in token of their esteem, and to hear their spokesmen characterize the couple's contributions to the community during their four years here."

In setting the tone for his departure, Thurber chose to take the high road. His farewell salute in the 1937 *La Letra* was emotional and gracious: "May the joyous memories of happy college days and loyal friendships be inextricably intertwined with the choicest fruits of your college years; nobility of character, refined and gentle manners, courtesy of expression, and an unyielding pursuit of the good, the beautiful, and the true in these hectic days of flux and instability. Aloha oe."

Following Thurber's "resignation," the faculty invited a local Congregational minister, Dr. Herbert C. Ide, to participate in a dialogue. How could they better cooperate with the City of Redlands? What did the residents think of them and why? What did the residents want of them? To the first question, Ide responded that the community had only the highest praise for the University. No town and gown function had ever gone wrong. Relationships were cordial and supportive. He pointed to the donations from several local residents and their participation on the board itself.

Ide reminded the faculty that it was their duty to lead, to provide light rather than heat. Redlanders, he averred, wanted faculty to further public understanding of intellectual and moral values, spread knowledge, help create tolerance, stimulate intellectual interest, and raise cultural awareness.

> My first and earnest request is that you do not lower your real standards in the hope of currying favor with any group. We, who care for the highest interests of this town, hope you will keep uncontaminated our academic freedom, and set the pace, rather than follow. We hope you continue to stand for free opinion and free speech . . . which is so vital to our democracy and so essential to any real progress.

> I am one of a large and by no means influential company, who are proud of you for your independence of judgment and your tolerance of opinion, whether our conclusions always match yours or not. And we shall be glad to pledge you our support . . . [for] teaching what you believe is true, and . . . giving your students a chance to know all the truth and adjust their lives to it.

Ide then turned to the issue of "propaganda," which he believed had become a science. This was not far from the mark, considering current unfolding events in Germany. Ide urged the faculty not to let propaganda of any type take "control. If you are to continue to abet intellectual leaders, you must justify those claims by your freedom to explore all sides of all questions. 'Radicalism,' according to its root meaning, means going to the root of things. We honor . . . that sort of attitude, and will stand by you in it to the end of the chapter."

Ide urged that the school community maintain a good temper, noting that a closed mind turns democracy into autocracy. Dissent must be permitted. Concluding, he acknowledged the controversy around religion professor Robert H. Lynn by noting, "We are grateful and proud of the position your administration has taken on this, and we assure you of the support of the

Redlands and Bacone: An Enduring Legacy

For many decades, the University of Redlands has enjoyed a close relationship with Bacone College in Muskogee, Oklahoma. Named for an American Baptist missionary to a Cherokee mission who began the Baptists' first college-level instruction in 1880 with three students, Bacone serves both Indian and non-Indian students. Beginning in the 1930s, Redlands made a concerted effort to recruit Bacone students after their first or second year at the Oklahoma college. Over the years, a number of Redlands faculty taught at Bacone, further strengthening ties. Mary S. McLendon '25, taught at Bacone from 1927 to 1935. As a Redlands student, McLendon, who was Native American, majored in philosophy and plunged into the thick of campus activities, joining the Life Service League, Poetry Club, Philomeia Choirs (which she served as manager), and Alpha Theta Phi. After graduate work, performing under her Indian name, "Ataloa," McLendon presented musical programs interpreting the life of her culture to audiences from Carnegie Hall to the Redlands Bowl.

Two Paths: Emmett Oliver's Revolution in Indian Education (1996) by Benjamin E. Smith '36, chronicles the life of a Bacone student who graduated from Redlands. In this biography, Emmett S. "Punchy" Oliver '36 is quoted extensively on his life at the University. "Humanities, music, and spiritual life at Redlands were a natural extension of Bacone, but academic competition was more intense. That was offset by the big place Redlands had in its heart for the Indians from Bacone." Seniors Newton Rose '35 and James T. Trentham '35 helped ease Oliver into campus life. He took to football and greatly admired Coach Cecil Cushman, delighting in "Cush's" malapropisms: "Boys, that's a football. . . . I can tell you a little about the game and give you some plays, but when you get out there on the field, you have to do it. Y'know, you can drive a horse to drink, but you can't make him water!" Oliver acknowledged that Professors S. Guy Jones and Harold Woodrow "helped make me a better teacher." Upon returning to Bacone to teach, he declared: "Redlands goes with me wherever I am. Through Redlands I came to understand universal love . . . love for all people everywhere. . . . If it is caught, it stays with a person, and he or she can apply it to all people."

Three decades after Oliver's experience at Redlands, W. Richard West '65 and James L. West '68, brothers whose father taught art at Bacone, came to Redlands. Members of the Cheyenne and Arapaho tribes of Oklahoma, the siblings distinguished themselves at the University. Richard graduated magna cum laude with a major in American history. A lawyer, he has served as counsel to numerous Indian tribes and organizations. He became the founding director of the National Museum of the American Indian, which opened on the Mall in Washington, D.C. in September 2004. Jim heads Futures for Children, an organization dedicated to helping American Indian communities improve the quality of life for future generations, and he founded and led one of the nation's first Indian-owned securities companies. A nationally recognized expert on economic and business development, he has written extensively on Indian history and spirituality.

people in this community who really count, in your following of this course. We hope you will never weaken. We believe you are in position to render us unexcelled service along this line." Ide's position lay in stark contrast to that of Lynn's critics and some community leaders in a town that had voted overwhelmingly for Alf Landon over Franklin D. Roosevelt in 1936.

Professor W. Edward Raffety, who had served as acting president following President Duke's death, agreed to attend trustee meetings early in March, and by July was being referred to as "President Raffety," causing speculation that the appointment would become permanent. If the reappointment of Raffety seemed like déjà vu to the community, the acting president may have felt the same—many of the issues on the presidential plate during his first stint were still there during his second. James L. Norwood, Jr. '38, president of ASUR, presented a petition from the students regarding dancing. Board Chairman Jones called for a special committee on student life to consider the matter in February 1938. But the trustees stalled, waiting until their June meeting—when students were conveniently absent from campus for the summer—to approve a resolution branding as "contrary to the wishes of the constituency" any social function sponsored by the University that included dances. Furthermore, they passed the buck to the new president by mandating the formation of committee on extra-curricular activities as one of his assignments. Raffety doubtlessly felt no small measure of relief that this apparently eternal conflict would be the new president's problem.

The acting president would never know how the issue resolved itself. An untimely automobile accident claimed his life just two weeks into the fall semester of 1937. Benumbed, the board tapped Professor Herbert E. Marsh to replace Raffety as acting president. The shock to the University community over Thurber's sudden departure and Raffety's death led Chairman Jones to appear before a faculty meeting. He invited the group to share individually with him "ideas concerning the qualifications desired in a new president." Unaccustomed to such

overtures from the board on executive personnel matters, a stunned faculty sent the trustees a letter of appreciation at being included in the process.

The lines of communication between the institution's governors and its faculty helped to ensure that Thurber's successor was a better fit for both groups. It was clear that Thurber had pushed too far, too fast. Had his presidency occurred a decade or two later, the climate would have been more favorable to his presidential style. His urbane manner drew the intellectual and social elite of the city to him, but for many of the University's trustees, these traits seemed too liberal, too urbane. They wanted greater orthodoxy.

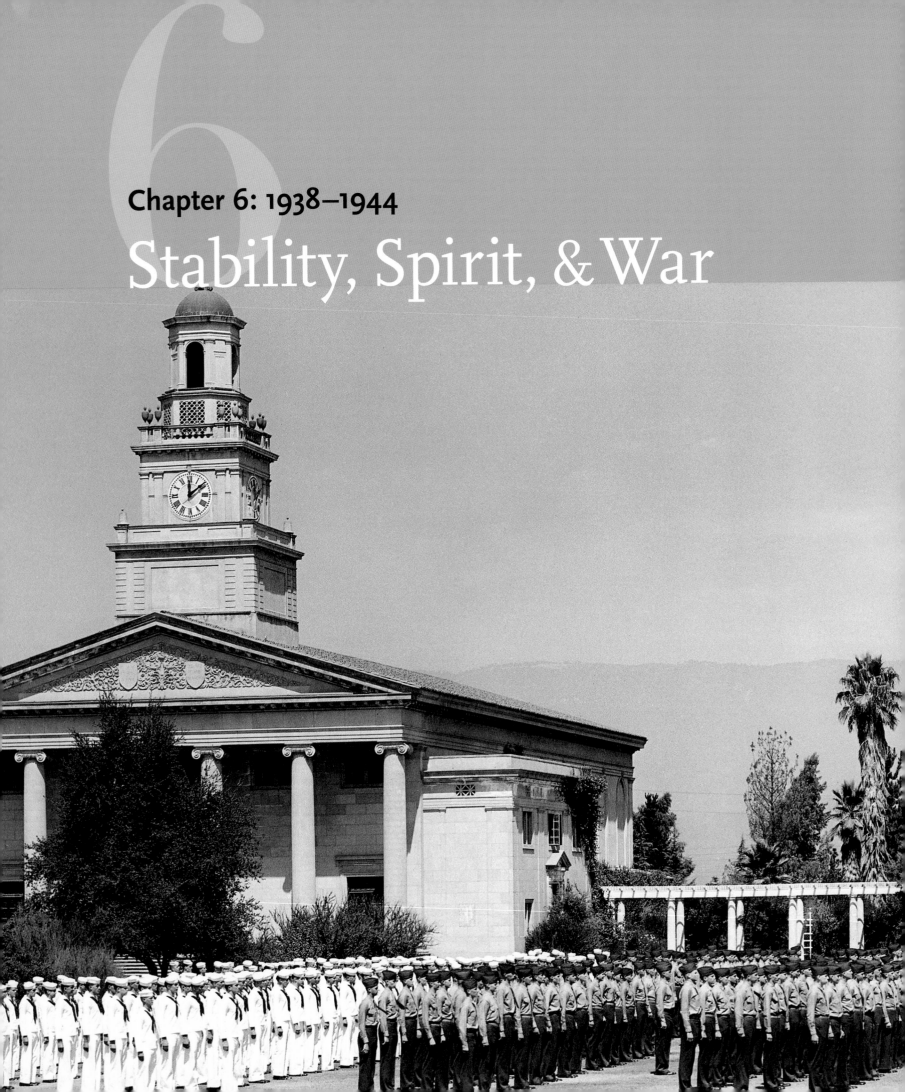

Stability, Spirit, & War

World War II—"These terrible and significant days."

—COLENA (MRS. ELAM J.) ANDERSON, 1943

THE PRESIDENCY RECAST

In the wake of the failed flirtation with a "liberal" president, the ensuing presidential search contained a whiff of rancor. When Clarence Howe Thurber resigned, the alumni for the first time spoke as a group about the selection of a new president. They circulated a questionnaire concerning the qualities they desired in a leader. As Redlands historian Lawrence E. Nelson pointed out:

> This had greater than surface significance. For a decade, becoming more numerous and better established in life, [alumni] had been growing increasingly restive. Were they an integral part of the University or not? They had built the outdoor theatre; it was largely unused. They had urged initiation of Founders' Day, with but meager results. They had suggested recognition of the twenty-fifth anniversary; a committee had been appointed to prepare a historical brochure. No brochure appeared. Of the ninety-four trustees thus far, only eight had been alumni. They felt ignored, and took action.

The questionnaire results were telling. Should the new president be primarily an outstanding educator with a religious interest, or an outstanding religious leader with an educational interest? Alumni voted eight to one for the former. They voted three to one that he need not be a Baptist. Seventy-three percent wanted a theologically open-minded president. Nine percent wished him to be theologically fundamental, while seventeen percent wanted him to be liberal. On social and economic questions, six percent preferred a conservative, fourteen percent a liberal; seventy-nine percent were open minded. The Baptist-dominated board's insistence on strict adherence by faculty and administrators to the 1926 creed created a chasm with middle-of-the-road alumni: religiously, socially, and economically, they had little interest in denominational labels. They exhibited a "militant insistence that the college be primarily an educational institution, not a quasi-church masquerading as a college."

Desiring a *bona fide* fundamentalist, some trustees objected to the qualifications of several candidates. Sensing potential conflict, another prospective candidate cautioned the board not to hire him if their charge would be to create a second Wheaton College, with its orthodox focus. In a letter, Elam J. Anderson assured Chairman of the Board Mattison B. Jones that while he respected his fundamentalist brethren, "I have felt that such a labeling has done more harm than good. My first loyalty is to Jesus Christ and my second to the Baptist denomination." Anderson's thoughtfulness must have impressed the search committee, for they recommended to the full board on April 1, 1938, that he be named the University of Redlands's fourth president.

In newly appointed President Anderson, the University community got a Baptist and a Ph.D. from the University of Chicago. He had taught speech, played the piano, authored books, taught at the University of Shanghai, and for six years had been president of Linfield College in Oregon. As shall be seen, his Shanghai experience would serve him well during the trials of World War II. When considering Redlands, he asked for a meeting with the faculty.

It was a stormy and dangerous night when he journeyed to Redlands. At the end of the interview, he asked, "Do you think I am the man for the job?" He wanted an honest, blunt answer. His decision depended on it. The reply was "Yes." In accepting, Anderson agreed to raise funds and cultivate donors and accept outside speaking duties; in return he was granted permission to travel "to the Orient on alternative summers at his own expense." With many ties and academic interests in Asia, Anderson was deeply attached to the area. A new era began on an imperative to mend relations with the town and to assert the University's hegemony among private colleges and among the Baptist constituency.

By October's 1937 Executive Committee meeting, Anderson reported the largest enrollment in the University's history—seven hundred students—an increase of ninety-eight over the previous year, including fifty graduate students. This led to a thorough discussion of how many more students the physical plant and faculty could accommodate, as well as the scholarship standards "to be maintained or attained" at the University. Anderson wasted no time in implementing both small and large changes. In September 1938, he asked for direction markers to be placed outside faculty office doors and classrooms, and directories at the entrance of each building. Also, faculty minutes began to list those absent from the meetings, revealing something about Anderson's management style.

Yet, unlike Thurber, who sought to impose his vision immediately, Anderson took a year to study the University's "landscape" and made changes only where he could. In his second year, he was ready to push for substantial alterations, including a new numbering system for courses: 1–49, no prerequisite; 50–99, prerequisite required; 101–49, upper division; and 150–99, advanced. These actions forced departments to reassess existing courses and how they should be sequenced. Faculty reorganization took place. The responsibility and authority for faculty committees constituted in the Faculty Council were restructured. The council was chaired by the president.

In 1939 the trustees made a major shift in the procedures for nominating and electing trustees. In an effort to broaden the board's base but still keep the selection largely from among Baptist constituents, they amended the by-laws to create a nominating committee of seven board members. The committee consisted of three trustees representing the Southern California Baptist Convention; one each representing the Arizona Baptist Convention, Northern California Baptist Convention, and the Alumni Association; and one at-large board member. While this kept the Baptists in control of who would be elected to the board, it also recognized the emerging alumni voice.

Upon accepting the presidency, Anderson addressed the Southern California Baptist Convention, where he reminded his listeners that the "Baptist denomination . . . has insisted that each person has the right to think for himself . . . we are different and must continue to be so." In 1943 he asserted his stand in his report to the board: "It was one of the hopes of this board in calling me to the presidency that I might be able to 'bridge the growing gap' between the churches and the University. It was one of the fears of faculty and students that I would succeed in this realm at the cost of honesty and integrity of faculty and a sacrifice of freedom of instruction and expression." Such expression was the result of hard experience.

Attempting to bridge the gap, Anderson actively sought off-campus speaking engagements. In his first month, he made thirty speeches; in his first year, he made two hundred. By the third, he limited himself, under trustee pressure, to one hundred. He sent a letter to 200 Baptist pastors pointing out that only 247 of 749 students were Baptist. He urged the clergy to raise the percentage by encouraging eligible congregants to consider Redlands. The letter offended the University's more than five hundred non-Baptist students. Their displeasure was exacerbated by eight hundred Baptist high school students who swamped the campus during Thanksgiving vacation for an admissions promotion and left many dormitory rooms in

Founders' Day

The Alumni Association joined forces with the students in 1925 in agitating for a Founders' Day. The University's trustees and administration acceded, and the first observance took place on December 7, 1925. Founding President Jasper Newton Field offered a prayer and land donor Karl C. Wells and others addressed the assembly. By 1930 the occasion had become controversial and that July the *Alumnus* magazine contained a petition signed by ASUR President R. H. Edwin Espy '30, Norman W. Taylor '30, John M. Dean, Jr. '32, Ruth Percival Ikerman '31, Alumni Association President Roger W. Truesdail '21, and alumni committee members Arthur D. Jacobsen '17, Paul L. Bruington '23, Norman W. Taylor '30, and Catherine H. Mitchell '24. They took the University to task for "misunderstanding their intent." Homecoming and Founders' Day should be two "distinctly different" events. Holding them at the same time forced an impossible combination of intellectual appreciation with the emotions around a football game and a crowded good-fellowship dinner. They suggested that Charter Day, or Founders' Day, be held in April, perhaps on the 19th, when ground was broken for the campus's first edifice, the Administration Building. In 1932 the association approved a permanent yearly event in April. That tradition continued until the academic calendar changed in 2003 and the event was moved to May. However, the Founders' role was dropped in the early 1990s, when it became Alumni Day.

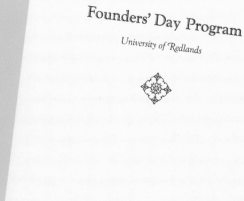

Founders' Day Program
University of Redlands

MEMORIAL CHAPEL
EVENING, DECEMBER 14, 1930
7:00 o'Clock

BELOW: The 1940 football team defeated Cal Tech 40–0 to win the SCIAC championship. Back row (left to right): Knox M. Cologne Jr. '41 (manager), Theodore R. McKinney '42, Eugene K. Burson '42, Herbert E. Morrelli '41, Robert J. Bierschbach '43, Eldon Roy Miller '40, Austin O. Ellerman '43, William G. Burrows '42, James M. Eacutt '42, Percy H. Burrows '42, and Cecil Cushman (coach).

Middle row: Joseph Ikeguchi '47*, Loren A. Beckley '43, Bruce T. Jewell '41, Doug A. Brown '43, John R. Hoffman '48*, Donald W. Gallup '43, Joseph F. Doyal '42, Robert G. Bartlett Sr. '41, Franklin B. Craven '41, and Harold F. "Popeye" Rowe '48.

Front row: Grover H. Clem '42, Robert G. Campbell Jr. '43, John C. Fawcett '41, Alvin K. Chang '42, William J. Settle '41, James R. Edwards '42, DeJack Williams '41, and Jack Solomon Maloof '47*. Not pictured: Herbert J. Ford '42, George R. McGregor '44 (manager), and William W. Cook '43.
*Indicates they finished their degree after World War II.

disorder. The students developed the chant "kneel and pray with Elam J." Irritated, they sent the president a mock petition complaining of abuse to their rooms. He delivered a tongue-in-cheek reply, taking the humor given with humor returned. He addressed the heart of the matter by emphasizing that "no denominational distinctions as to scholarship honors, student aid, work, or tuition reduction to sons and daughters of ministers or missionaries have ever been made." He allowed that since coming to Redlands he took pride in the large number of non-Baptist students as evidence of the high standing of the University and of its friendly atmosphere. Further, he declared that in the offending letter he meant to convey to Baptist clergy that the University only wanted more Baptist students, not fewer Methodists, Presbyterians, and so forth. "Joke or nor joke, we are glad you had the good sense to select the U of R."

Little did students and most alumni know then what Anderson had to endure in dealing with the issue of the University's

denominational ties. A minister from the Eleventh Street Baptist Church of Los Angeles wrote Anderson, questioning the "doctrinal soundness and spiritual tone of Redlands." He asserted that the faith of some students had been "undermined or wrecked at Redlands. . . ." He charged, "By contrast, I cannot recall having heard of a single student from Bethel, Wheaton or Westmont whose faith in the fundamental doctrines of Christianity had been undermined by the teaching of those colleges."

The reverend further asserted that the University, while formally adhering to the historic Baptist position, actually "must be taking a middle-of-the-road policy which destroys its effectiveness from a conservative point of view. Liberalism and conservatism are irreconcilable, making a midway position untenable." "At Wheaton College," the clergyman concluded, "God's presence so manifested itself so mightily that classes and meals were forgotten while students and faculty members sought the Lord

through confession and prayer. My sincere prayer for Redlands is that something comparable may be its experience."

President Anderson had to answer dozens and dozens of such ministerial lectures. While admitting that some students may have graduated "with their faith weakened," he attested that far more moved on with strengthened faith. He dismissed the liberal versus conservative argument, declaring that the " most important thing is that of being true to the Scriptures and true in one faith and willingness to Jesus Christ. . . ."

This litany of ecclesiastical complaints focused once again on religion professor Robert H. Lynn, whose right to academic freedom had been championed years before by President Clarence Howe Thurber, himself a Sunday-school-teaching Baptist layman. "How deep can Professor Lynn's convictions be?," intoned one critic. He then answered his own question: "Can he face misguided youth without giving a positive personal testimony concerning Christ?" No support would come from Baptists in Tucson, Arizona, warned one minister, unless "assurance that the Word of God is being exalted in the classroom." In the face of veiled and direct financial threats, Trustee Joy Jameson acknowledged that these exchanges were "doing no good but I hate to see this kind of critical attitude continue." If Redlands wanted to stabilize its budget and construct new buildings, it had to balance strong feelings on the part of certain influential Baptist clergy against dancing and "liberalism." Such religious and political pressure weighed heavily upon Anderson. His own view is best presented in his response to one ministerial critic:

> I am sorry that you lack faith and willingness to support the University. If the only kind of university you are willing to support is one which proclaims that it is a fundamentalist university, then I am quite ready to agree that under my leadership it does not have that particular label. On the other hand, it does not ask for and does not deserve the label of liberal university, for actually the institution is Baptist in the sense that it serves all of

the Baptists of our territory and not just one group. The very fact that liberal people in our convention speak of it as conservative, and they do, and conservative people speak of it as liberal, may indicate that it is doing what it ought to do—including all Baptist young people in its ministry rather than just one group.

A measure of relief was afforded the University in the mid-1940s when a militant wing of the conservatives left the Northern Baptist Convention and organized their own mission societies, seminaries, and colleges. Under pressure from the Southern Baptists, the branch that had split off during the Civil War with headquarters in the Confederacy, the conservatives, eschewing the "liberal" tendency of the University of Redlands, ultimately created their own university, California Baptist, in Riverside in the early 1950s. The issues of academic freedom and religious orthodoxy that bedeviled Anderson thus left Redlands's academic program less accountable to strict denominational interpretation.

Academic learning in the classroom and the student experience in the dormitory—the heart and rhythm of campus life—

continued in familiar patterns during the early Anderson years, only slightly altered by the Depression and the administrative travails with the University's critics. Students played on the athletic fields, planned dorm parties and activities, and sometimes joined faculty who hosted at-home dinners. An enterprising group in the basement of California Hall figured out a way to use the steam and distillate from the hot-water pipes in the boiler room to install a still and produce a potent alcohol. The liquid was then dispensed to eagerly awaiting student customers who, for a small price, carried off the elixir in containers ranging from empty Listerine bottles to flasks.

As always, a youthful sense of frolic prevailed that tested the patience and the mettle of the president and the administration. President Thurber was once visited in his office by a cow; he led it back down the stairs, having tied a bandana around its eyes—a trick he had learned from his farm days. President Victor L. Duke had also experienced a cow-in-the-office incident in 1920. Anderson must have been stumped by a mysterious occurrence at the Memorial Chapel, only

explained in 2005. After the death of Broadway musical star John E. Raitt '39, a superb athlete in javelin, shot put, discus, and football who possessed an "amazing physique," his roommate Dan L. Carmichael '39 recalled a day when he and Raitt were walking past the Chapel. He asked the athlete, "You think you can throw a rock over the steeple?" Raitt, knowing he could, "picked up a good size rock and launched it," Carmichael explained. "Son-of-a-gun if it didn't hit the face of the

clock and knock it down, I don't know—some glass and some of its workings. We immediately disappeared. I don't know if they every figured out who did it."

WAR'S CHALLENGE

The United States late in 1939 was ambivalent about the war raging in Europe. Certainly there were leaders who advocated vigilance and protective armament. Others believed in centrality and urged non-involvement. On December 5, 1939, the faculty decided to draft a letter to President Franklin D. Roosevelt, to be signed voluntarily, decrying recent increases in military spending. The letter cited reputable sources within the military who swore that no European power could possibly attack the United States "within the next twenty or thirty years" and urged the president to keep out of the war.

The last of the University's founding generation passed from the scene in 1941. The institution's first chairman, Mattison B. Jones, ended a thirty-four year term of leadership that year, having earned an emeritus title from his colleagues. He died soon thereafter. As significant as Jones's departure was to the University's internal affairs, the most significant transition that year came from the outside world.

World War II was the primary agent of change in the academic and social structure of the University in the first half of its life. "Out of the brushings and bludgeoning of the Thirties and Forties Redlands emerged with a clearer self-knowledge," observed Nelson. This period also marked a more influential role for the alumni in college affairs and a closer draw to the town by the gown.

With the bombing of Pearl Harbor on December 7, 1941, a variety of problems and challenges beset all Americans, with serious consequences for higher education. Conscription notices depleted the male student population nationwide. Redlands responded by providing classes for more than one hundred soldiers stationed near Riverside and at Camp Hahn, west of March Field. The summer session was accelerated to

BELOW TOP: World War II brought many changes to campus, but this invitation to the 1943 Alumni-Parent Conference illustrates that some events continued as they always had, even if the war effort was never far from mind.

BELOW BOTTOM: After World War II ended, campus social life quickly picked up its pace, as this 1945 invitation to the PanHellenic teas attests.

twelve weeks to enable entering freshmen to graduate in three years. The January 15, 1942, issue of *The Bulldog* summarized the intense work of only one month:

> We have already added special defense courses . . .
> in such subjects as mathematics for prospective army
> and navy officers, chemistry for nurses, meteorol-
> ogy and astronomy for pilots and navigators, applied
> engineering and radio, first aid, bacteriology for sanitary
> engineers, and foreign languages for Foreign Service.
> Courses in economics and history have been adapted to
> provide a study of the background and for the war, and
> a series of six to ten chapel addresses have already been
> scheduled to provide a more intelligent understanding
> of the causes.

Physical-education classes were increased from twice to five times a week. Blackout drills, incendiary defense, and Red Cross service training all marked the preparations for "the worst" on campus. More than one-third of the students volunteered as messengers if telephone service became crippled by enemy attack. Students declared such skills as fire control (seven), plumbing (sixteen), electrical work (twenty-four), switchboard operation (thirty-eight), and semaphore (twenty-one). They also reported that they could muster up fifty-seven bicycles, one hundred twenty-eight cars, seven trucks, one motorcycle, and one station wagon. Practice drills became the order of the day. An emergency control center was set up in the basement of California Hall, where the students once ran the still that had supplied much of the campus with alcohol during the 1930s.

As we have seen, the faculty suffered from salary cuts during the Big Freeze of 1913, and again during the Great Depression of the 1930s; World War II proved no different. Enrollment and college income dropped; prices soared, wreaking havoc with faculty wages. Since 1930 the faculty had been working on a minimum salary basis. The University's bottom line, ever tenuous, was the cause. Two increases in tuition and board costs had not resulted in higher compensation, which was

especially hard on young faculty with tenure. In addition, taxes were raised to support the war. Anderson presented a sober account to the trustees on February 10, 1942:

> That in order to emerge from the war with educational
> services, faculty and student, morale, and equipment
> unimpaired as far as possible, it becomes the policy of
> this board for the duration of the war to maintain our
> program at its accustomed level of efficiency by provid-
> ing necessary financial support to the limit of our ability
> to do so. . . . That in the event conditions of war make it
> impossible to provide such support through the ordinary
> channels of income or other war-time channels which

may be opened, this board proposes to explore every possible source of support including the feasibility of borrowing against the capital resources of the University in order to meet any deficit that may arise from the economical administration of an efficient educational program and the maintenance of efficient faculty personnel.

The president believed that faculty salaries were a top priority: "We dare no longer delay restudying their program, now made more critical by the heavy tax burden and rising cost of living." In anticipation of increased military commitments, he advised the trustees to make sure that faculty remuneration was "in proportion to the increase of the [work] load."

How the wizard of finance and fundraising did it is anyone's guess, but Business Manager George Cortner announced within the year of Anderson's recommendation that the University "for the first time" was completely "out of debt." This included modest faculty raises.

By the autumn of 1942, nearly three hundred alumni and former students were in the military, and by 1943, two hundred students were in the service; five of them died in the line of duty. Army, Navy, Marine Corps, and Coast Guard recruiters regularly visited the campus even as the government urged male students to remain in school until called to active duty. Redlands was one of the first Southern California colleges to receive funding for a government program that paid tuition for courses in physics and chemistry.

President Anderson's love of Asia and the dreadful casualties there often were the subjects of his chapel addresses. According to Nelson, he did not hesitate to describe the horrors of the war. Students complained to him in *The Bulldog*, avowing that they were going to "the service not to be corpses, but to get to Tokyo, Berlin, Rome where the brute force and treachery are forced upon us as the order of the day." Furthermore, they asked, "Will you try to appreciate our attitude on this question? Let us have some affirmative talk, send us from this easy life

with an urge to protect those who remain, rather than misgivings and fear of what destiny has forced us to do." Anderson was taken aback. He mistakenly thought his November 11, 1942, Armistice Day address made clear his firm belief in the imperative of military victory over Japan and Germany. As a result, he revamped his chapel-service messages.

Not surprisingly, Anderson focused his attention on the Japanese-American population concentrated on the West Coast. Old anti-Asian prejudices intensified and public opinion became further inflamed by newspaper columnists and radio commentators who advocated that Japanese-Americans be removed from California and that the Nisei (American born, second-generation Japanese) be stripped of their citizenship. In February 1942, news came that President Roosevelt had signed Executive Order 9066 allowing the Army to remove "alien or citizen" from military areas if necessary. By March the relocation centers were authorized and internment of Japanese-Americans began.

These anti-Japanese sentiments troubled Anderson deeply. In January 1943, he wrote Roosevelt a letter of support and offered to meet with those of his assistants who had the responsibility "of dealing with the deeply troubling problem of racial tolerance and justice, whether in regard to the negro or this one now acute on the Pacific Coast, the Japanese." Though he did not include the following in his history of the

University, Nelson recalled an emotional meeting with his student Yoshiko Nagamatsu '51, who had received notice that as a Japanese-American she would be sent to a relocation camp. "I called Yo into my office" he wrote, "and, with tears in my eyes, tried to tell her how terrible we all felt about this unbelievably unfair order. I told her to take any of my books that she wanted, but she was allowed so little baggage that she politely refused. I hugged her and told her we wanted her to return as soon as possible." Indeed, Nagamatsu graduated from Redlands in 1951 and went on to a career in office management in Michigan.

Writing to President Anderson from a "relocation camp" in Poston, Arizona, another student, Toshio Yatsushiro '43, related his feelings and detailed conditions at the camp. "Redlands seems so distant yet the friends I made seem so near to me. . . . Through letters, *The Bulldog*, and visiting friends my bond with the University seems to be increasing in strength. All too often in my tranquil moments I relive the happy and unforgettable experience I experienced at 'dear ole U of R.'" He provided a detailed account of a strike that "prevailed at one of the three camps in Poston, a deep-seated reaction to living conditions, poor clothing, food conditions, and delay in pay checks. It was such an explosion of all these complaints harbored within the hearts of the people. . . . " Yatsuhiro continued his studies through the University of Chicago extension program. With three years completed at Redlands, he was able to obtain a Redlands degree. The response by Anderson to such letters reveals a depth of care and concern and, more importantly, support. He provided testaments of character, recommendations for employment, and endorsements for the release process from camps.

Bulldogs in the military received much attention from President Anderson. He counseled soldiers, "You must not forget that if you are tempted to wrong doing there are many others like you have had less privilege of Christian nurture than you." Describing life in North Africa, Lt. Henry Romo, Jr. '40 asked the president to give "all the professors and students my

sincerest regards and tell them there's lots of us over here that still remember that Dear old U of R." Anderson responded, "Now that you men from the University of Redlands are participating actively in this struggle . . . we realize that we are at war. . . . We hope that you feel our support, for we think of you and remember you constantly. . . . "

When Annie Jane Newland '42 applied for the WAVES (Women Accepted for Volunteer Emergency Service) Officer Training School, Anderson provided a strong written endorsement. He did his best to "shake hands" with every student who left school for military service. Sometimes, he read excerpts of letters at chapel, hoping to inspire students and bolster their faith.

THE V-12: UNEXPECTED DIRECTIONS

In March 1943, Anderson wrote one Bulldog soldier, "You will be pleased to learn this morning we have had confirmation of our selection as a Navy training unit. This unit will begin on July 1st and of course we are all very happy about it."

Navy v-12, a nationwide program that ultimately provided more than 60,000 Navy and Marine Corps officers with college education, brought 631 men to the University through Anderson's assiduous efforts. According to V-12 historians, the number of military trained in the program "exceeded the output of the Naval Academy, Navy ROTC, and other pre-V-12 programs combined." In addition, the "unprecedented democratic nature of the selection process for V-12 trainees opened the door of educational opportunity to many young men."

Each participating school selected its own textbooks, determined course content, and established academic levels for achievement to remain in the program, which was offered in sixteen-week terms. At Redlands registration for 1943–44, in addition to the above-mentioned males, included 473 women and 110 men, for a record total of 1,214. Subsequently, with more civilian enrollments, the school registered a new high of 1,360. The influence of the V-12 program on the University of Redlands was attested to by the school's physical fitness perfor-

In Their Own Words: The V-12 on Campus

Why settle for the historian's voice when the historical actors can speak for themselves?

The following account first appeared in The Redlands Report *in the spring of 1985. Because the tale recounts a signal moment in the history of the V-12 on campus, we reproduce, with slight editorial modification, some of its highlights here. The witty and charming words flowed from the pen of John Scott Davenport x'46.*

On the marines' participation in campus life:
During their 16 months on campus, their number shrank from 198 to 54 . . . , but during that time if you followed UR athletics, its stars were usually marines; if you looked at student government, marines were in key roles; the weekly *Bulldog* was edited by marines; fraternity life, again the marines; and who were the BMOCs squiring around the cream of the coed crop? Why, the marines, of course.

On the marines' cultural fit at a Baptist University:
A confrontation of opposing cultures forced the University of Redlands to recognize the existence of the twentieth century. . . . To understand this crisis point, a brief review of what the University then stood for is appropriate: no alcoholic consumption on campus (or elsewhere if the University administration could reach), no smoking, no card playing, no holding hands in public, [and] . . . all coeds locked up by dark . . . ! Then there was mandatory chapel and an overly oppressive (from the marine point of view) religiosity that just begged to be twitted.

On the marines' respect for Baptist policies:
Mind you, there was always at least one poker game going on during off-duty hours. . . . Pipes, cigars, and cigarettes abounded. There was a beer route established by the fifth month—into the back of Grossmont after dark.

On the marines' revels of New Year's Eve 1943:
Victorian morals, coupled with a stern disciplinary code, met their Waterloo on New Year's Eve 1943 on the steps of Memorial Chapel. . . . Denied an official opportunity to celebrate the advent of 1944, the Redlands marines pulled out all the stops. For starters, they wired the tower of Memorial Chapel with loudspeakers connected to a record player, then passed the word to key coeds. That evening, between hourly musters, there was a gala dance on the steps of the University's holy of holies. Glenn Miller's "Jersey Bounce" could be heard all over Redlands and halfway to Colton. There was a particularly melancholy recording of "Wait for Me, Mary" that reduced even the sober ones to tears. Alas, "demon rum" was there, too: valiant coeds provided a steady stream of beer and more devilish concoctions. Hand-holding was rampant. At the 11 o'clock muster there were three stone-sober marines: two dozen or so semi-sobers. The rest were three-sheets-to-the-wind and listing-to-starboard. The coeds, to their credit, had departed by this time—matters were getting out of hand. There was no midnight muster. Chaos had taken over. . . . All of Redlands was surely aroused . . . but no gendarmes appeared. **– Ed., JDM**

mance. Scoring 16 on Navy strength tests, Redlands almost tied with UCLA, which placed first at 16.2. Following them were the University of New Mexico with 12.3, California Institute of Technology with 12.3, Arizona State Teachers College with 11.4, USC with 10.4, and Occidental with 6.2.

twenty-nine hours a week, including gymnasium and laboratory periods; they also performed pre-breakfast drills and marching during the day. Athletics and fraternity life could be added if the student was "found feasible" for such involvement.

The presence of the V-12, along with a collective student desire for changes in the campus's social life, led to new challenges

When natural calamity occurred, the V-12 men obeyed orders to help out. Across America—at Colgate, Cornell, Middlebury, and North Dakota State Teachers College—marines helped to save local crops. "When the freeze warning went out to the Orange growers around Redlands . . . an appeal was sent to the V-12 . . . to set up smudge pots to ward off the cold. Although it was billed as voluntary duty, one trainee said 'Volunteer, my foot!'"

Intellectually, the University's marines constituted a formidable presence. On campus were Warren M. Christopher x'46, future secretary of state; John Scott Davenport x'46, future executive of Bonneville International; Harry R. Haldeman x'45, future assistant to President Richard M. Nixon; Van A. Harvey x'45, who later headed Stanford's department of religion; and Chester McCorkle, future executive vice president of the University of California system. These men and hundreds of others were not all involved in the social changes occuring at Redlands, but their caliber was repeated tenfold among the ranks.

The University of Redlands now engaged in year-round teaching, six days a week. An already over-loaded faculty in education, English, German, philosophy, and physical education were asked to provide compensated extra instruction in math-ematics and physics. V-12 students were in class

for the administration and trustees. The Pajamarino became an unintended temporary casualty of war because "only civilian men might wear such informal garments in public." It was against military regulations for University students in uniform to do so.

Student hijinks and horseplay, cherished traditions dating back to medieval colleges, saw no lessening during the grim World War II years. Just as President Duke had found himself the target of an injured student and his litigious parents, the result of the hazing of freshmen, so too did President Anderson have his travails.

Hazing was and continues to be a problem for college administrators, especially in the face of angry parents, uncompromising demands of lawyers, and insurance companies. What students view as harmless pranks, an ancient form of "unity building," administrators see as potentially harmful actions. Anderson in many ways was more fortunate than his successors, because *in loco parentis* still reigned as the law of the day. In the 1980s, national legislation guaranteeing eighteen-year-olds legal autonomy and the right to vote made it even more complex to deal with confidentiality about student behavior and disciplinary proceedings.

In March 1943, Anderson received a letter from the father of a male student expressing his horror at having entrusted first-born son to Redlands only to find out that the lad's hazing had involved "cutting full locks of hair from the center of the head down to the scalp." "It will no doubt take six months or more

for the hair to grow out," expressed the outraged father. In reply Anderson explained the haircut was part of an approved "plan of initiation." Even so, many senior males had donned such a cranial arrangement, and Anderson suggested it all may be part of a fad. He noted that his own son had received such a coif as a freshman. The president lamented that such hazing likely would never go away. After five years as president, he concluded that the freshmen "are almost unanimously opposed" to eliminating hazing, "insisting that it makes them happier to be introduced into freshman life by some such foolish ritual." Despite his dudgeon, the father replied that he wanted the matter kept entirely confidential, lest his son "know I had written you."

As students and enrollees in the armed forces contemplated the serious issues of war and especially of life and death, the seemingly archaic regulations prohibiting dancing came into question. "The University of Redlands, a traditional Baptist College, was never quite the same after its encounter with the sailors and marines of the V-12 program," concluded author James G. Schneider in *The Navy V-12 Program: Leadership for a Lifetime.*

Off-campus dances sponsored by student organizations had taken place for many years, to the dismay of the trustees and some in the administration. Six months after the arrival of the V-12, things began to change. Redlands was not unique. The president of Berea College in Kentucky personally favored letting trainees dance, but Schneider wrote, "he feared the reaction of his trustees. He broadly hinted that if the Navy were to recommend such

a course of action as good for morale, he thought that trustees would find it palatable." On one college campus, a coed was expelled for dancing, but her marine date was not because he was beyond the authority of college disciplinary procedures.

As early as 1939, Anderson reminded the trustees that dancing was permitted at off-campus class parties, with other forms of entertainment provided to non-dancing students. At Redlands the marines chafed at the unbending administration.

One University requirement, chapel attendance, became a marine target. Since chapel was a religious service, the Navy was sensitive to criticism for its men's poor attendance record. In one incident, marines returning from weekend visits to Los Angeles gin mills stopped at the front yards of the president and the several deans singing lusty verses of "Onward Christian Soldiers." They also gathered up every liquor bottle they could, and the night before trash pickup, divided the collection between the garbage cans of the president and the deans.

Schneider, citing John Scott Davenport's x'46 previously published article in *The Redlands Report*, stated: "The marines' most spectacular performance at Redlands came on New Year's Eve in 1943 when they were restricted to campus because of previous wrongdoing. They had orders to muster every hour, on the hour, until midnight. Suddenly on the Chapel steps it happened. Glenn Miller's 'Jersey Bounce' could be heard all over Redlands and halfway to Colton." Complicit coeds streamed out from the shelter of their dorm rooms, dancing between musters "on the steps of the University's holy of holies." No police arrived. The statement had been made, or "the tide had been irreversibly turned."

Presidential condemnation soon followed, and resentful students sent a message in response. Leaving for his office from the President's Mansion, Anderson saw blood dripping from above the doors of the first floor. Suspended to the door jams were chicken parts (perpetrators had taken

terminally ill chickens from a nearby chicken ranch), and references to the anti-dancing promulgations were written in blood on the sidewalk. Word spread fast; student-body officers knew who had planned "the stunt," and there were rumblings of a crackdown. But the crackdown never came, because the administration and the trustees recognized that the war had forever altered priorities in every context.

Within two months, the University administration agreed to permit dances on campus, provided they were held in the Commons, which had been leased to the Navy. The trustees and president reasoned that the Navy had exclusive use of the building, so it therefore was not technically part of the campus. The military held a jubilant student-body dance on Saturday, February 19, 1944.

Nevertheless, on June 13, 1944, the board inexplicably sent a survey to the constituency about dancing. An overwhelming majority of parents, including Baptists, turned out to favor dancing on campus. The trustees relented. Trustees and students had sparred about dancing for thirty-four years. It took a world war and the V-12 to resolve the matter.

TRANSITIONS

For six years, Anderson had used his prodigious energy to expand the circle of supporters of the University, seeking to "give the institution a place both in the hearts and in the respect of the people." A gregarious man with strong principles and religious convictions, he exuded a genuineness that won friends. He was civically engaged, having agreed to chair the Chamber of Commerce committee on post-war planning. Save for the occasional protest, the President's Mansion hummed with social

activities throughout the war. Anderson reported that in 1943–44 he and his wife entertained 1,600 individuals at receptions and teas, while 450 friends of the University were guests around their dinner table.

The University's official notification on August 15, 1944, from the Servicemen's Readjustment Act (known as the G. I. Bill), of Redlands' acceptance into the program was received with joy. "We are very pleased the University of Redlands has been approved for this training, and hope that we may begin the training of Veterans on an increasingly larger scale," Anderson enthused.

Anderson, when he assumed office, realized the need to increase the University's enrollment. In 1944 the student body had grown twenty-five percent since 1941. He pointed out to the trustees that in the 1942–44 classes, the freshmen tested in the upper third of freshmen all over the United States. He noted that more faculty had earned doctorates and were undertaking many research and teaching initiatives. The School of Music had received accreditation for the first time.

Anderson also backed academic boldness. Historian Earl Cranston and philosopher Philip Merlan had urged a two-year cooperative interdepartmental course in the humanities, later called the history of civilization, intended to bring together all freshmen and sophomores to study developmental aspects of world cultures. The course represented a major commitment to the centrality of the liberal arts at Redlands. For two years, they and their faculty colleagues labored and readied the project for launching, but with the outbreak of war in 1941, the relative importance of the project came into question. Should the whole concept be shelved until after the war? Should such a bold required course wait until the University's commitments were less stretched? Faculty and staff said no. Thus began one of the University's major curricular changes.

In February 1944, Anderson reported to the trustees:

First Dance On Campus To Be Military Ball

History will be made this weekend on the campus of the University of Redlands when students gather at the Commons building for a formal military ball, the first dance ever to be held on the university grounds.

Presiding over the occasion will be a queen, to be chosen from one of four candidates and crowned Saturday evening by Commander Carlisle Thompson, captain of the university naval V-12 unit. Identity of the queen will be a secret until the moment of crowning, although the election will take place tomorrow.

The four candidates are Barbara Newton, Jean Hentschke, Martha Lou Rollins and Fern Martin. Even they will not know the winner until the last moment.

Gene Molle and his band will provide dance music from 8:20 to 11:30 o'clock. General chairmen of the affair are Jeanne Crider and Pvt. Edwin Scotcher.

Other committee members include Queen committee, Don Mansell, Ed Scotcher and Carolyn Siebell; refreshments, Glen Martin and Warren Christopher; refreshments, Kay Wilson and John Burch; invitations, Peaches Arthur and Betty Schwing; publicity, John Davenport.

I am unwilling to lose this opportunity to express my personal pride in this striking evidence of faculty initiative and enthusiastic devotion to the liberal arts function of the University. I believe we are making history and striking out toward new frontiers of learning at a period when marking time would be fully justified. Nowhere else in the United States so far as I know are college students being provided with such a unique opportunity. . . . To begin this project in the midst of our unique program and to do so with syllabi, tests, and equipment more detailed and complete than in most established courses is an outstanding achievement.

WAR'S UNLIKELY VICTIM

Slowed by fatigued, Anderson sought to pace his involvement and initiatives. As he readied himself for work on Wednesday morning, August 17, 1944, he felt unwell and was in considerable pain. Minutes later he lay dead. The University population was stunned and the town in shock.

Five days later, the town and gown packed the Chapel for a memorial service. Speaking on behalf of the board for both the University and the Southern California Baptist Convention, Trustee Ralph Jensen praised Anderson as an innovator during a time of war and as an "outstanding Christian." President Remsen Bird of Occidental College focused on his unique knowledge of Anderson's wise counsel in the American Association of Colleges, noting that his colleague was accepted "as one of the leaders in the educational work of our country."

Faculty member Lawrence E. Nelson paid an outstanding tribute to the late president for "his unfailing courtesy, for his quick mind . . . for his discipline of himself . . . for his wholesome outlook on life, his sincerity" and concluded by noting that "he arrived always where he was going regardless of the difficulties, fresh, vigorous and ready for action."

Nearly forty years later, Anderson's wife, Colena, reflected on the essential nature of her husband's commitment to his presidency in a letter written to President Douglas Moore during the University's seventy-fifth anniversary in 1982. She expressed her regret at being unable to attend the events, but noted that the "six years when Elam was president were full of many happy days and satisfactions for the family. For Elam, there were many challenges. I trust the record shows he met them with courage, giving mind and heart. Were he here on earth, no one would be more enthusiastic over this Jubilee than he. Only just: 'Would be'? No. I have it in my faith to say, 'No one will be.'"

Elam J. Anderson had arrived at Redlands at a time when local community relations needed mending and healing. Indeed, he succeeded. The *Redlands Daily Facts*, recounting the president's life, declared, "Mr. Anderson demonstrated an amazing ability as an executive, accomplishing a series of objectives that only a man possessing his vision and vigor would have undertaken."

In countless ways across the globe, World War II proved to be a catalyst for fundamental change, and the world-shaking conflict even wrought its transformative power upon a tiny Baptist University in an out-of-the-way corner of Southern California. Wartime social upheaval challenged dogmatic governance of student life according to the Baptist creed. In more placid days, such upheaval might have meant the loss of many core donors. But wartime government aid to higher education ensured no deleterious effect to the institution's bottom line. The exigencies of war thus afforded to Redlands's president the freedom to embrace new directions. Anderson's tenure distanced the University from its Baptist progenitors but left the institution on better footing financially and educationally.

Change, Growth, & Protest

REDLANDS

JOHN YEOMANS   JACK PARHAM   JOE LYNN   PETE GREGO...

CAPTAIN

UNIVERSITY OF REDLANDS

"Any President coming to Redlands in the autumn of 1945 was coming virtually blindfolded, so many and so unprecedented were the problems. . . ."—LAWRENCE E. NELSON, 1959

POST-WAR MAN ON A POST-WAR CAMPUS

At its executive session on June 5, 1945, the University's Board of Trustees extended an invitation to forty-year-old George Henry Armacost to become president. A graduate of Dickinson College in Pennsylvania, with a major in chemistry and minors in physics, history, and social science, he had taught and served as a principal in high schools. In 1940 he earned a Ph.D. from Columbia University, and became an assistant professor of education at the College of William and Mary, Williamsburg, Virginia. There he would assume many administrative positions, ranging from academic affairs to student life.

To her role as first lady, Verda Armacost, whom George had married in 1933, brought exceptionally good judgment, strong academic grounding, and a legendary memory for names. Having completed her coursework for a graduate degree in education from Columbia University, she would become an important ambassador for Redlands, speaking before diverse audiences and constituencies.

Late in the evening of September 13, 1945, the Armacosts arrived on campus with their four young children in tow and

settled into the President's Mansion. Despite the hour, they found the residence stocked with food and supplies, lights blazing, and beds ready for tired occupants—all the handiwork of the ubiquitous Business Manager George Cortner.

The new president outlined his immediate goals in his inaugural address in November: adherence to Christian principles and academic excellence; character development "on par" with academic excellence and material success; commitment to a free flow of ideas and information; and the necessity of adequate faculty salaries for outstanding scholarship. He concluded by emphasizing the importance at a small college of personal attention to the needs of individual students. Accordingly,

increasing faculty ranks became an early priority. Soon, the faculty-student ratio dropped from 1 to 18 to 1 to 14.

The management of the University's business affairs changed greatly with the retirement of George Cortner in June 1946 after thirty-one years of service. Charles O. Pierpoint was selected to succeed Cortner. Armacost paid high tribute to Cortner at a retirement ceremony: "Few colleges had been blessed with so capable and so versatile a business manager, with ability to erect buildings, manage investments, gain gifts for endowments, and handle myriad complex employee relationships. . . . We hate to think of the time when we shall not have his wise and friendly counsel." Cortner agreed to stay on as a consultant.

But this did not occur. The day after the June Trustee meeting, his last, Cortner died of a heart attack at home. Shocked and saddened, the trustees passed a resolution declaring that he "gave the best years of his life to the efficient management and promotion of the University of Redlands." They noted that he was "a faithful servant and friend," the "very symbol of integrity, high character and trustworthiness," and a man who led "an honest life of service not only to the University but to neighboring cities and counties."

Cortner's personal touch was captured by Allen B. "Curley" Griffin '34. Griffin remembered that he was toiling shirtless on his father's cotton farm in the oppressive heat of California's Imperial Valley, when he saw an automobile driving down a long, dusty road. A man leaned out of the window and asked if he were Allen Griffin. Griffin said, "Yes." "Good," said Cortner, "I am here to offer you a place as a student at the University of Redlands." Griffin, stunned, replied that it was the middle of the Depression and his family had no money for college." "That's all right, I'll find it, if you find the way to study and become a credit to your community." He remained deeply grateful to Cortner for giving him a chance, "taking the risk on a young guy

with average grades and as yet few accomplishments. His faith in me changed my life."

Recognizing the need to reorganize the business operation for the post-Cortner era, Armacost had the trustees vest in him the rights and the powers of business manager, in addition to those powers being vested in the business-manager position itself. Armacost began to restructure the University in line with the modern practices he had observed in the East.

Ever more complex and sophisticated, the University's fund-raising became the domain of trained professionals. Their new approaches would prove instrumental in planning for the 1959 Golden Jubilee, which sparked a major campaign for both annual giving and the endowment. Armacost engineered another important innovation in fundraising with the creation of a new support group, the Fellows. Based on similar organizations at the California Institute of Technology, Dennison University, and Pomona College, the Fellows focused on the annual fund. Their ranks comprised an influential group of donors harvested from among trustees, administrators, faculty,

alumni, parents of students, and interested friends throughout
Southern California.

Another administrative area requiring a fresh philosophical
approach was admissions, which underwent an organiza-
tional overhaul. Previously, admissions had been coordinated
by faculty and administrative committees, the president, and
even George Cortner. All served as "admissions officers."
Canvassing regional Baptist churches, mining alumni con-
nections, and spreading the news by word of mouth among
parents and students had always served as the bedrock of
enrollment. The post-World War II era demanded greater
sophistication: the University had to market itself. Throughout
the 1950s and 1960s, the baby boomers flooded the nation's
education systems, prompting the founding of numerous new
institutions of higher education. The California state university system added campuses in Fullerton, Long Beach, Los
Angeles, Northridge, San Bernardino, and San Diego, while the
University of California opened sites in Irvine, Riverside, and
San Diego. Armacost appointed Louise Jennings, a professor of
history at Redlands, as the University's first director of admis-

sions. At the same moment, some faculty received release
time to recruit and read over applications. By 1951 alumnus F.
Byrns Fagerburg '46 was hired, and Kenton W. Corwin '48 came
aboard in 1954. The admissions staff could tout Redlands's
ongoing commitment to a liberal arts curriculum and residential campus environment. Redlands and its sister institutions at
Claremont, Whittier, LaVerne, and Occidental continued to offer
small classes with low teacher-student ratios and a nurturing
residential environment, as an alternative to the larger state
educational enterprises.

In 1945 admissions visited more than three hundred California
and Arizona high schools, as well as institutions in Hawaii,

Chicago, Washington, D.C., and New York. The formal involvement of alumni in the admissions process, starting in 1955, helped Redlands evolve from a largely regional institution to one of a broader national makeup.

Establishing national standing first required enhancing the University's reputation in Southern California. The admissions staff strove to increase the percentage of students selected from the top quartile of high school graduating classes in the overall admissions pool. Improving the quality of students soon paid another dividend, as the University secured chapters of the academic honor society Mortar Board and of the leadership society Omicron Delta Kappa. (Phi Beta Kappa, the oldest and most prestigious academic honor society in the United States, remained an illusive quest.) Redlands's academic excellence in those days was pared against Bates, Bucknell, Carleton, Denison, Dickinson, Oberlin, Occidental, Pomona, and Wabash.

Nonetheless, enrollment levels continued to be uncertain during the 1950s and 1960s. In addition, because of increasing competition for students, the University's decision not to participate in ROTC programs foreclosed the possibility of attracting new students from a government-subsidized pool. Those who did

choose Redlands demonstrated an ever-growing need for financial aid. This taxed the annual budget, which became increasingly dependent on tuition, with serious consequences in the late 1970s and early 1980s.

Academic life at the University changed significantly after the war. Spurred on by the G. I. Bill, veterans of World War II and later of the Korean War swelled enrollment figures. To accommodate the influx, the University hired many new instructors and added summer-school sessions. The additional faculty also allowed departments to offer more upper-division courses. As faculty recruitment was still the sole province of the University president, Armacost informed the trustees that he sought candidates who possessed "the doctor's degree from accredited universities . . . [and] who choose to be active churchmen in the denominations of their preference." In order to boost faculty morale, he announced a plan to restore sabbaticals, and in 1946 he secured a five-percent raise in salaries below $5,000, followed by a second raise a few months later.

In order to improve the curriculum, faculty were asked to emphasize the quality of instruction. Supplementary reading assignments became standard, research papers became routine, able students were encouraged to undertake independent study, and graduation requirements were toughened. Teachers were expected to prepare a syllabus for each offering and were also asked to gear courses to students preparing for entry into graduate school. All these changes reflected the belief that a liberal arts education should demand both breadth and depth.

Christian principles continued to affect departments across the board. In presenting comprehensive and specific academic aims, the faculty in a 1949 report to the trustees advocated a liberal arts curriculum that embraced Christian values. The report clearly illustrated how mid-century faculty applied religious practices to academics. Among the specifics: use of oral and written English so students might "accumulate a knowledge and appreciation of the riches of our Christian culture in literature, art, music, and in the meaning and method of science"; understanding of society, its history, and its institutions, which would permit students to comprehend Christian values for "correctly" judging contemporary issues and responsible citizenship; managing mind and body to live and work effectively not just for oneself but for family and others; experience of "belief in the Christian faith, as a generative power in personal living, as a dynamic in social change, and as a cohesive force in the brotherhood of man"; and the acquisition of a superior knowledge of principle and practices in one or more areas of learning appropriate for instruction in a "Christian college" to

prepare for one's life work. Within ten years, a consultant group was able to compliment the University for being "eminently successful in the religious education of its students."

Another area into which Armacost injected new thinking was the recruitment of trustees. In the University's seventy-fifth anniversary book, *Whose Emblem Shines Afar*, Armacost, Professor Emeritus Ralph E. Hone, and retired Registrar Esther Mertins detailed a central dilemma facing the new president:

> The University of Redlands was still considered a Baptist school. From the twenties on, fundamentalist pressure had been exerted from various quarters to restrict the University to policies and performance of narrow doctrinal position. The University's selection of faculty and administration was avowedly Christian. It created a faculty that largely adhered to Baptist honored traditions that it not be sectarian in admitting students. All in all it became unacceptable to the fundamentalists and unintelligible to secular humanists. There had even been attempts by fundamentalist forces within and without to purge the faculty; the attacks on Professor Robert Lynn were evidence.

Baptist trustees remained involved and influential, they no longer wielded the doctrinal clout of the past.

Armacost wasted no time applying his views to student recruitment. Having analyzed student demographics in 1946 and finding a wide mix—one hundred ninety-four Baptist students, one hundred twenty-three Methodists, eighty Presbyterians, fifty Episcopalians, and one hundred ninety-nine "others"—the president realized the makeup of the student body no longer reflected the school's Baptist origins. Thereafter, he determined to go after quality first and denominational affiliation second.

MEETING THE BABY BOOM WITH A BUILDING BOOM

The University constructed new dormitories, science facilities, arts buildings, and a library during Armacost's tenure. Not since the 1920s had so much capital expansion occurred. The influx of veterans taking advantage of the G. I. Bill taxed the University's limited housing supply. Fortunately, in the warm afterglow of the victorious war effort, Uncle Sam was in a giving mood. By a special Act of Congress, the federal government authorized housing for veterans, and Redlands received fifty war-surplus housing units transplanted from a military facility

From the beginning, it was clear that George Armacost had a global view of higher education, and he recognized the need for trustees who shared his approach. Reflecting on his presidency after he retired, Armacost observed, "One of the first things I had to do was root out the old line Baptists from the Board." In that, he was to be eminently successful; yet he still managed to retain ties to the Baptist constituency. The men and women he recruited valued the principles of Christian citizenship, but they also represented secular business outlooks and material success. While trustees often sought out board candidates, their respect for Armacost's judgment led to the acceptance of many individuals he nominated. The influx of new thinking on the Board of Trustees extinguished the last gasp of Baptist hegemony. While

in Washington State. These structures, located on Brockton Avenue, were quickly dubbed Vets Village.

This gift proved fortuitous at a time when enrollment reached a new peak: 442 men and 481 women in 1947. With the dorms overwhelmed, the University sought to accommodate the overflow in private homes in town. Additional relief came in 1949 when Cortner Hall became the new dormitory on the men's side of the Quad. The women gained Anderson Hall in 1955, while Cal-Founders completed the residence-hall configuration on the Quad in 1957. In 1958 North Hall became the first dormitory on the north end of campus fronting Brockton Avenue. To this location Merriam Hall and the Johnston campus, to the east, were added in the 1960s.

A chapel brought from the Santa Ana airbase saw new service as the "Little Theatre by the Zanja" from 1947 until 1969, when it was replaced by Glenn Wallichs Theatre. Now renamed and refurbished, it is known as the Gannett Center and houses academic offices.

By the early 1950s, the Administration Building had also become overcrowded. To free up more space for administrators, the University built a new complex to house student activities, which had been located in the basement of the Administration Building. The Dog House (as it was called) served as the student union and included the student store and meeting areas. For over four decades, the Dog House served as the social hub of student life until Hunsaker Center assumed those functions in 1994.

Two academic buildings—Watchorn Hall and Hornby Hall—were constructed in the first half of Armacost's tenure. Watchorn originated in a deal struck by President Elam J. Anderson on a golf course with the noted philanthropist Robert Watchorn, who wintered in Redlands. Located on the original site of Fine Arts West next to the Chapel, Watchorn Hall became headquarters to the School of Music in 1952. Meanwhile, the sciences continued to demand updated

Pajamarino

Traditions have always flavored student life at the University of Redlands. Annual rituals observed and perpetuated by students and faculty members have included the Zanja Fiesta, Senior Ditch Day, and the Whiskerino, for which male students grew beards. Many of these now-forgotten events originated as tools to acquaint freshmen with school traditions or to rally school spirit. Soon they numbered among the institution's most hallowed customs. Perhaps the most unique of these fun-filled activities was the "Pajama Parade," or the Pajamarino.

Occurring sometime before the first conference football game of the year, the Pajamarino typically kicked off around 7:30 p.m. with a bonfire at the north end of campus. Then male students frolicked down Colton Avenue toward the business district clad only in nighttime apparel! The men boisterously performed the "Pajama Top Hop"—a street dance sponsored by the Yeomen—which both stopped traffic and vexed local residents. As it made its way downtown, the unruly group also indulged in the nasty habit of "hijacking" trolley cars. The parade often paused for rallies at the Casa Loma Hotel (University Hall) and at the corner of Orange and State Streets, where Redlands's rivals were burned in effigy.

According to Professor of English Ralph Hone, "The students marched/cavorted gaily, no doubt unaware, for the most part, of their similarity to [participants in] ancient Bacchanalian processions." After a brief rally at the Fox Theatre, the crowd convened at the Redlands Bowl, where prizes were awarded to those with the best costumes.

While the Pajamarino enjoyed huge success for over half a century, not everyone was enthusiastic to take part in the merriment. Navy and marine cadets in the V-12 Program were willing to participate, but were compelled to wear military-regulation undergarments. Filipino students at the University, indifferent to western costume styles, wore kimonos.

The first annual Pajamarino took place on October 6, 1911. Prior to the event, Professor Don José Rodriguez treated all sixty-three students to tasty delicacies at Hutchins' Confectionery Parlor. Those who did not attend the ceremony did so under the penalty of "tubbing," which included being dunked in the murky waters of the Zanja or the Smiley Park fish pond. While initially an all-male activity, from 1925 on women as well as local residents were included in the celebration.

Ultimately, the Pajamarino fell victim to modern society. Officials of town and gown found reason to discourage the tradition. Population growth meant increased traffic, so that the parade's progress down city streets became more annoying and dangerous. The relaxation over time of students' sense of modesty, and occasional outbreaks of disorder, gave pause both to the town and gown authorities. The Pajamarino final run occurred in the mid-1970s. While it lasted, though, the event bridged gaps between Redlands and the University. It was a unique tradition, one remembered by generations of students with a deep fondness for their class and their alma mater.

facilities to accommodate progress. Located south of Duke Hall, in what had evolved into the University's first science hub, Hornby Hall opened in 1958 with state-of-the-art labs and classrooms for geology and biology.

A new addition to the music program began in 1950. Professor Edward Tritt asked a group of local music lovers, faculty, and students to consider creating a symphony orchestra. The Redlands University Community Symphony Orchestra showcased the talents of the School of Music faculty and students, who played alongside professional musicians recruited from the Redlands area. The orchestra continued under Tritt's direction until his retirement in 1975.

An unbroken Redlands tradition, the Feast of Lights (a Christmas program), was conceived by Professor J. William Jones and first presented in 1947. The event has attracted thousands of spectators each year and is known in the area as one of Southern California's great holiday musical extravaganzas.

STUDENT LIFE IN FLUX

Outside the classroom, Redlands students displayed their debate skills by scoring sweepstake honors at the Pi Kappa Delta National Annual Debate in 1947, 1948, 1949, 1951,

and 1952. In 1951 and 1952, the Redlands team of Holt V. Spicer '52 and James Q. Wilson '52 won the National Debate Championships.

In the sports' arena, Redland's football team triumphed as conference champions in 1945, 1946, and 1947. This led to an invitation to play the University of Hawaii in the Pineapple Bowl on January 1, 1948. Alas, in the last few minutes of a nail-biter, Hawaii scored two points to win, 33–32. In tennis too the men's team began a long succession of championships. The men's

students to question these beliefs. Many viewed the University's denominational ties as "too conservative, too religious, and too Baptist."

Tensions surfaced as the 1950s fundamentalists in Southern California's Baptist community admonished President Armacost regarding the University's direction. As he recalled, their anxieties were addressed in a number of questions: "Does the University teach 'good old Baptist distinctives'? Is the faith of students being destroyed by 'modernistic teachings'? Why are students allowed to dance, smoke, and use alcohol? Why are so few Baptist ministers invited to speak to students in Chapel?" This struggle, an ongoing one as we have seen, presaged growing student resentment regarding the tight control the institution exercised over student social and residential life. The principle *in loco parentis* had served Redlands, indeed all of the nation's liberal arts colleges, for the better part of the twentieth century. (It would be rendered null and void by congressional action insuring student privacy—the Buckley Act—in the 1980s). Casting the institution in the role of the parent, the

basketball team won the conference championship in 1950.

The Los Angeles Rams professional football team rolled into Redlands in the summer of 1949 to establish their annual training camp at the University. Suddenly, the campus became a hub of famous big-time football players. The University accorded the team red-carpet treatment, and the players were appreciative and friendly. An annual scrimmage to benefit University scholarships drew large crowds. Redlanders, both town and gown, became Rams fans, making trips to Los Angeles for the games. In all, the Rams remained thirteen years.

During the first fifteen years of Armacost's reign, students went about their business largely unmindful of the contradictions inherent in college life that would, in another decade, fracture the structure of higher education across America. What student discontent there was in the 1950s tended to focus on areas in which University governance reflected Baptist mores. Baptist notions regarding chapel attendance—which was encouraged—and drinking, smoking, and card playing—which was discouraged—had always shaped campus life, but now the reality of the student body's religious diversity led some

Pineapple Bowl

After a triumphant season, the 1947 Redlands football team was selected to compete against the "Roaring Rainbows" of the University of Hawaii in the 1948 New Year's Day Pineapple Bowl. When asked about the team's chances of having their bid for the game accepted, Coach Cecil Cushman told a San Bernardino newspaper that he believed that there were two conditions working in the University's favor: 1) The strong presence of its alumni on the island of Oahu; 2) its willingness to send its team for less money than other competitors. Moreover, the team had gained fame for its "aerial attack" play and the powerhouse "Little All-American Duo," Stanley J. Flowers '49 and Ted C. Runner '48.

On December 29, the thirty-member team, Cushman, Coach James E. Verdieck, President George H. Armacost, and Homecoming Queen Norma Christopher took off for Honolulu. As part of the festivities, the host school dispatched the Pineapple Bowl Queen to accompany the Redlanders on the long, trans-oceanic flight. Before they left, Shirley Moss, the University of Hawaii student who won the honor that year, participated in pre-game festivities in Redlands. A highlight of the flight were servings of ice cream in the University's colors—maroon and gray. Alumni and local fans with banners greeted the team

in Honolulu, and players and officials soon found themselves bedecked in leis. The Redlands mascot, then named Deacon, even met a dubious cousin, a sheep whose wool had been dyed maroon and gray for the occasion.

For several days prior to the main event, the football team toured the island, visited with Hawaiian alumni, and met local football fans. President Armacost took the opportunity to spend time with the mayor of Honolulu, exchanging gifts of Hawaiian pineapples and Redlands oranges, speaking with local radio personalities, and seeing the island through the eyes of thirty strapping young athletes.

When New Year's Day arrived, the Bulldogs took to the field, eager to prove to everyone that they did not deserve to be the underdogs. Under the guidance of Coaches Cushman and Verdieck, the team held off the aggressive offense of

the Rainbows, until the final thirty seconds of the game, when a "fluke play" allowed Honolulu to score the final winning points. Redlands's only bowl game ended with a score of 33–32.

Despite the loss, the troop came home to the cheers and greetings of several hundred proud fans. The Pineapple Bowl Queen returned with the team and made some radio and television appearances. Even the players themselves seemed to overlook the loss, and focus on the island adventures they had. McDaniel "Mack" Hammond '49 told the student newspaper that Hawaii was "almost as fine as Texas," while other boys were eager to make plans to go back. Many seemed to share this sentiment, and there was talk of making the game an annual event. Though this never happened, the University of Redlands's participation in the Pineapple Bowl helped to strengthen good relations between Hawaiian alumni, university administrators, and future students. — VJW

BELOW LEFT: Bulldog cheerleaders fluff their pom poms at a football tilt. Left to right: Barbara J. Powers '59, Donna van Osdel '59, Jan F. Pellegrin Duggan '59, Molly A. Hubbell '59, and Sally Jo High '59.

BOTTOM LEFT: The 1966 Homecoming parade included this Chi Sigma Chi float of a Roman chariot pulled by pledges.

BOTTOM RIGHT: Elaborate floats by Greek organizations and campus clubs were the highlight of the annual Homecoming parade. This 1966 entry with a replica of the Chapel alludes to the vineyard that once occupied the University's land.

BELOW RIGHT: Four women play a doubles match on the old tennis courts west of Currier Gym.

concept justified restrictive policies governing student behavior, including curfews and visiting hours in residence halls. The decline of *in loco parentis* in the 1950s was the result not of a concentrated, coordinated assault by students, but rather a slow, persistent questioning of a plethora of little policies. Collectively, they would spell the end of this governing tenet. Shifting student attitudes made obsolete many formerly hallowed collegiate customs, such as glee clubs, bonfires, and impromptu skits. This included one of the University of Redlands's most cherished traditions, the Zanja Fiesta. Always dependent for its success on the contributions and guidance of students, it was briefly run by the faculty before they too allowed it to wither. The last Zanja Fiesta was held in 1956.

While polls at the time indicated that a majority of students supported established rules and regulations, a concerted minority effort clamored for change. A clear demarcation existed between the many

ex-military (and often married) students, who were more accepting of regulations often created for life-and-death situations, than civilian students, who chafed at rules they thought invasive of their privacy. In the 1950s, male students were granted the right to smoke in their dormitory rooms. Women received reluctant approval to do the same by 1960. This small victory owed less to shifting social mores than

to the sight of Bulldog coeds standing curbside on Colton Avenue languorously puffing their cigs outside University Hall. Armacost associated such scenes with those of ladies of doubtful virtue soliciting customers on street corners.

The increasing legal and managerial complexity of a residential campus led to the professionalization of overseeing student life in the 1950s. Much to their relief, faculty no longer had to police student affairs. The University faced challenges regarding student behavior. Assuming his duties in 1951, the first dean of students, Clifford Holmes, arrived none too soon, as the student atmosphere was becoming increasingly charged.

Despite the rumblings about religious practices, many student traditions endured. Students made their annual march into downtown Redlands dressed in nightwear into the mid-1970s. Freshmen maintained the "R," which was lit for Homecoming until the Forest Service ended the practice in the early 1960s. Fraternities and sororities conducted pinnings and rushes. The annual water fights soaked the Quad (and coeds). Beneath the seeming quietude of the Fifties, the winds of change were gathering force. As the University prepared for its golden jubilee in 1959, few would have guessed that what lay ahead would make the second fifty years a dramatic departure from the experience of the first fifty.

BELOW RIGHT: In more innocent days, hazing freshmen was a venerated rite of passage, and not just for the men. Seen here rubbing Zippy-brand starch into the hair of their frosh victim are (left to right) Marjorie A. Johnson '58, Catherine Suzanne "Suzy" Owsley x'58, Joan M. Morrison x'58, Jacqueline Banning '58, and Sandra J. Reese '58.

BELOW LEFT: Shaving cream, a blindfold, and a polka-dot nightshirt. Oh, the humanity!

BOTTOM, LEFT TO RIGHT: A typical dinner scene in the Commons in 1965.

Mary Emma Wright's '50 1950 Food Service card. Don't leave home without it!

A letter from Dean of Women Martha Gannaway illustrates the perils of rebelling against social norms during the age of *in loco parentis*.

THE UNIVERSITY AT FIFTY

The University's fiftieth anniversary was celebrated in 1959. Unlike the half-measures taken during the twenty-fifth Silver Jubilee in 1934, planners chose to celebrate the golden anniversary in a series of memorable occasions. One highlight was a symposium featuring outstanding alumni: Fred D. Fagg, Jr. '20, president of the University of Southern California; Fred Drexler '36, insurance executive; Ralph M. Johnson '34, American Baptist Convention; and Robert C. Pierpoint '47, CBS broadcaster. Special features enhanced annual events such as Homecoming, Parents Day, and Founders' Day. Planners programmed off-campus functions in regions with strong alumni presence. Back home the Redlands Chamber of Commerce coordinated a "Salute to the University of Redlands," and the *Los Angeles Times* published a special editorial and news feature praising the University.

With the fiftieth anniversary serving as impetus, the trustees in 1957 undertook a daunting, long-range fundraising goal: $8 million by 1970, $5 million of which was designated for the endowment and the balance for capital improvements. The campaign elevated University fundraising to a new level and provided a solid financial foundation for the future. It also helped to broaden the base of alumni donors. Beyond that, for the first time Armacost and the trustees established important ties with fundraising and investment organizations.

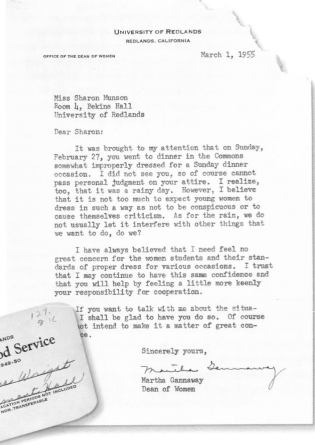

UNIVERSITY OF REDLANDS
REDLANDS, CALIFORNIA

OFFICE OF THE DEAN OF WOMEN   March 1, 1955

Miss Sharon Munson
Room 4, Bekins Hall
University of Redlands

Dear Sharon:

It was brought to my attention that on Sunday, February 27, you went to dinner in the Commons somewhat improperly dressed for a Sunday dinner occasion. I did not see you, so of course cannot pass personal judgment on your attire. I realize, too, that it was a rainy day. However, I believe that it is not too much to expect young women to dress in such a way as not to be conspicuous or to cause themselves criticism. As for the rain, we do not usually let it interfere with other things that we want to do, do we?

I have always believed that I need feel no great concern for the women students and their standards of proper dress for various occasions. I trust that I may continue to have this same confidence and that you will help by feeling a little more keenly your responsibility for cooperation.

If you want to talk with me about the situation, I shall be glad to have you do so. Of course I do not intend to make it a matter of great concern.

Sincerely yours,

Martha Gannaway
Dean of Women

EXPIRES JUNE 13, 1950
UNIVERSITY OF REDLANDS
"Commons" Food Service
SPRING SEMESTER 1949-50
SIGNATURE Mary Emma Wright
LOCAL ADDRESS Brussmont Hall
SCHEDULED VACATION PERIODS NOT INCLUDED
NON-TRANSFERABLE
2025

A restructured alumni office also resulted from the Jubilee initiatives. From its beginning in 1912, the Alumni Association had been independent of the University, while effectively working with and for it. For many years, Ruth Jacobsen, wife of Professor Arthur D. Jacobsen, served as executive director and editor of the *Alumnus*. Gradually, the association came under more direct University control. The first step, in 1948, was the addition of an alumni director, Larry H. Hendon '47, whose salary was paid by the University, the result of a joint alumni-administrative committee regarding alumni relations. Thereafter, a professional team handled the alumni program. An alumni board initiative resulted in seats for three of its members on the Board of Trustees in sequential terms. At this time, the alumni program assumed new responsibilities in the area of student recruitment and fundraising.

NEW BUILDINGS FOR NEW NEEDS

The 1960s brought unparalleled financial and grant opportunities for higher education in the United States. Among the most important windfalls for Redlands came with the announcement by the Ford Foundation that it would make $260 million available to strengthen selected independent liberal arts colleges. In

supported by a team of effective administrators, trustees, and alumni. During his last four years in office (1967–70), the University received more than $15 million.

With funds in hand, the building boom of the 1950s continued into the 1960s. The ever-increasing student body, now approaching 1,600, required two more residence halls: Bekins-Holt, housing women, was completed in 1965 across Colton Avenue from the library; and Merriam Hall for men opened in 1964 south of North Hall. Not far from these buildings, the trustees elected to construct a new collateral college, which included two residence halls and a separate student center.

So too did the Greek organizations join in the building boom. The Pi Chi house constructed a decade earlier along the Zanja east of the Alumni Greek Theatre, was now on fraternity row, along with houses for Alpha Gamma Nu, Kappa Sigma Sigma, and Chi Sigma Chi.

June 1966, Ford announced that the University of Redlands had been awarded $2 million, the only grant given that year to a West Coast school and the largest Redlands had ever received.

The addition of academic buildings especially benefited the arts. A gift from Tom and Ann Peppers led to the completion in 1963 of an eponymous headquarters for the art department, located at the foot of Ad Hill on the site of an orange grove that was razed for its construction. Not surprisingly, the structure's location and design generated both detractors and admirers. Nevertheless, it was a much-needed expansion, with classrooms, studios, and a gallery. Another boost for the arts resulted from the generosity of Trustee Glenn E. Wallichs, who provided funds for a new performance theater, built along University Avenue south of the Zanja. Opening in 1969, it adjoined, through a common courtyard, the recently completed Truesdail Speech Center, which was ready for use in 1966.

One of the conditions of the grant was that the University raise three dollars for every one promised by Ford. This challenge was met through the concentrated efforts of a committee of national figures and local alumni. James Graham Johnston served as honorary chairman, likely because of his impending gift for a new collateral college. He was joined by Trustees Dwayne Orton '26, Earnest R. Larsen '23, Roger W. Truesdail '21, Omer E. Robbins, and Glenn E. Wallichs. Hundreds of donors contributed. In three years, the campaign raised $7,581,248, exceeding the goal by $1,581,240. President Armacost merits credit for the campaign's success. His own fundraising abilities were greatly respected, and he was

Rounding out construction in the 1960s was a library, which would become the largest academic building on campus. The relocation of the football stadium north of Brockton Avenue created a prime location in the center of campus for the new structure. The need for this facility attested to the tremendous growth of the previous twenty-five years and anticipated an increase in future enrollments as well as the proposed new collateral college. With George Armacost set to retire shortly after the building's completion, the trustees opted to honor the first family by naming it the George and Verda Armacost Library.

CURRICULAR INNOVATIONS

As early as 1930, the trustees, recognizing the importance of the radio and the messages it carried, authorized the administration to pursue a campus radio station. The effort took twenty-five years. KUOR, housed on the second floor of the Hall of Letters, began transmitting at 7:00 p.m. on June 12, 1955. At first limited by the Federal Communications Commission

to the dormitories, the student-run and faculty-advised station operated from Sunday through Friday, 7:00–11:00 p.m. The relationship between KUOR and the University was always uneasy. There never appeared to be a clear understanding or articulation of the station's mission or of its role in the overall curriculum. Yet over

the years it prospered, and its coverage stretched to most of San Bernardino and Riverside counties, as well as portions of Orange and Los Angeles counties. By 1982, under a pay-as-you-go management contract, it offered music and University sports selections. A budget shortfall in 2000 forced the administration to scrutinize anew the role of KUOR. The development office, which oversaw the operation, recommended terminating the staff and student volunteers, keeping the license and transmitters, and leasing the operation to an Orange County radio station. Curiously, given that the voice of the student on the

airwaves was to be silenced, the decision aroused little controversy, and the Board of Trustees ratified the strategy.

Among the many new opportunities for students was off-campus study, which was initiated in 1953. Redlands students could spend a semester in Washington, D.C. This opportunity opened many doors, since a number of alumni were highly placed in government circles and provided access to offices and federal employees. Professor Robert Morlan coordinated this program until his death in the 1980s.

At the same time, other faculty began to lead study tours to Europe in the summer. These experiences led to the creation in 1959–60 of a semester program in Salzburg, Austria, which in turn inspired similar programs at other institutions. Victor Clark Kerr, president of the University of California, acknowledged that Berkeley, the flagship campus of the University of California, modeled its own overseas study course after the Salzburg program. The Salzburg semester was endowed in 2005, with funds largely contributed by alumni of the program who believed in its importance to the curriculum and to the lives of students. Funds were even received from individuals who had "experienced" Salzburg vicariously through roommates or as parents but never actually participated in the program.

Across America in the 1960s, colleges introduced the pass-fail grading system. The innovation permitted students under a set criterion to take a course and receive a "pass" or "fail" instead of the traditional letter or numeric grade. Inaugurated at Redlands in 1967, the system encouraged students "to

explore areas where they feel insecure" without jeopardizing their grade-point average. Although one could take only a few classes on a pass-fail basis, both students and faculty benefited. While some faculty became convinced it decreased student participation in the classroom, the pass-fail option has become an academic staple over the decades.

An important curricular and calendar change took place in 1968, when the month of January was designated as an interim term. This allowed students to concentrate on a single subject for four weeks and faculty to teach courses that would not otherwise fit into the traditional semester. Offerings ranged from concentrated academic fare to independent study. But experimental and unusual topics were also included: mathematical theories of gambling, the ethos of fly fishing, the complexity of wine tasting, and hands-on internship experiences and community-service projects. Some courses, such as theater in London, could be conducted entirely at locations throughout the world. Students could also attend interim terms at other schools on the same schedule, including the University of Puget Sound in Washington, and Gustavus Adolphus and Carleton colleges in Minnesota. The initiative drew faculty and students even closer together, with daily contact and subjects that often required new ways of learning.

In 1969 at Redlands two hundred enthusiastic students signed up for and accepted responsibility for enrolling, attending classes, and helping to establish the criteria of evaluation of the course work for the "Free University." Sired "by protest as much as by idealism," the Free University movement—a national trend—responded to dissatisfaction with formal, credentialed, and institutionalized higher education, and embraced the time-honored concept that all vital education is achieved by sustained personal motivation of the purest sort. Grade averages, prerequisites, even professional requirements were eschewed in favor of courses offered without cost or grades. This concept became fashionable at schools across the country.

A push for curricular change that emerged near the end of Armacost's presidency attests to his willingness to respond to the times and to community concerns. During his last two years, students sympathetic to these goals advocated change through orderly marches and other protests. Student unrest and administrative progressivism combined to produce an important addition to the curriculum. Minority students nationwide complained bitterly that the traditional disciplines failed to include their experience or to reflect their cultural legacy. In response, universities instituted black, Chicano, American Indian, and women's studies programs in various guises.

Redlands instituted a minor in ethnic studies in June 1969. Designed to "provide a greater opportunity for both white and minority students to become better informed on contributions of minority groups to the American way of life. . . ," the program became a legacy of Sixties' student activism that has endured. Within the new department, students could concentrate in either black or Chicano

studies. Selling the idea to the trustees, President Armacost observed that the "program recognizes the needs of minority people to understand their history and culture and to prepare for leadership in society." The board unanimously endorsed this addition to the curriculum.

The new ethnic studies program also contained a community-service component. In 1969 the California Coordinating Council for Higher Education awarded $16,000 to the University—the only small, private university to receive a grant—to focus on minority participation in community service. The goal was to redress the lack of minority representation in traditional curricular offerings by creating an ethnically diverse community board

within the School of Education to address the need for more "Mexican-American and Black citizens as participants in a democratic society." A major in minority studies was proposed by Armacost's academic team in June 4, 1969. This curricular innovation, designed to serve the University's traditional mission of producing alumni engaged with society, belies any notion that the president was out of touch with student sensibilities of the Vietnam War era.

A LANDSCAPE OF PROTEST

No one could have predicted the intersections of the civil rights movement, women's rights, and the Vietnam War, nor the political assassinations that began with that of President John F. Kennedy and ended with those of Robert Kennedy and Martin Luther King, and the impact these forces would have on colleges across America. The University of Redlands was not immune.

Seeds of discontent and change are always present in the soil of a university's life. Occasionally, an issue blossoms forth here and there and sometimes even bears fruit. More often than not, however, chary administrators cut off student protest at the roots, treating discontent like an impudent weed that has invaded an ordered garden.

A casualty during these years was compulsory chapel. Once the mainstay of most church-related liberal arts undergraduate institutions, the practice had slowly but surely given way. In 1965 permission was granted to students to take part in various cultural programs in lieu of non-sectarian convocations. One year later, required chapel attendance was reduced to six times per semester. By 1968 one convocation per week became the rule. With less than one hundred people regularly attending, compulsory chapel ended at Redlands, as it already had at La Verne, Occidental, Pomona, and Whittier. Even venerable Oxford University had abandoned its five-hundred-year-old tradition of compulsory chapel. Attendance became voluntary in 1968.

Student hijinks got out of control during one particular incident in 1960. For many years, the men's and women's dorms had staged an annual water fight in May. The battle raged across the Quad, drenching participants and innocent bystanders alike, and no doubt dousing buildings through open windows. In 1960 the rivalry turned into a melee.

It began as a spontaneous water fight on the Quad in 100-degree weather. It ended when one student suffered a serious eye injury and had to be hospitalized. "The massed forces of the Redlands police and fire department fell into conflict with the students," reported the *Redlands Daily Facts*. Students were sprayed with fire hoses, there was a false alarm at the home of the dean of students, and the skirts of three palm trees behind Bekins Hall were set afire. Concluded the newspaper: "It was quite a night."

The whole fiasco resulted from an anonymous telephone call to the police department intended to spread false information about the water fight. The officers who answered the call did not take lightly being doused with water. Shouting "Go home!," a group of exuberant young men rushed the firemen, who had turned the fire hoses on the crowd in an attempt to restore order. Then the youths formed a huddle and playfully rushed the authorities, dowsing them with water. Ultimately, calm prevailed by 9:00 p.m. Three of the male students were issued citations but none was booked. Instead they were turned over to the dean of men for possible disciplinary action. Writing in the *Redlands Daily Facts*, editor Frank E. Moore '34 concluded, "The crowd psychology prevalent insulated them [the students] from sensitivity to the attitudes of the police and firemen." Indeed, during a lull in the action, students eagerly took up the challenge of a peer who raised his arms and led the boisterous, good-humored mob in the "Och Tamale"!

On another front, the humor expressed in the student publication *The Fireplug*, which administrators often criticized for its questionable taste, resulted in controversy that led to its discontinuation. That action raised howls of anger over censorship. Another contretemps with students over censorship occurred when the University suspended *The Bulldog* in May 1962 over criticism of the administration's attempt to regulate the newspaper's contents. A joint announcement by the editors and the Student Council declared an impasse with the administration. The statement urged new policies that "neither violate administrative authority nor sacrifice student freedom." Freedom and responsibility are inexorably linked, proclaimed President Armacost in removing one of the faculty advisors. The students refused to retreat from "freedom of the press," and the struggle continued for the rest of Armacost's administration.

THE GREAT DEBATE - 1965
Brown vs. Armacost

University policy regarding outside speakers also riled student sensibilities. Once again, the younger generation viewed their elders as censorious. Students often sought to bring outside speakers to the University on their own initiative, but standing policy—established by trustees in 1963, at the height of the Cold War—required pre-approval of such guests from the administration. While acknowledging that studying communist ideas had a place in the classroom, the University expressly denied students and faculty the right to bring speakers to campus who might advocate such ideals. One must remember that this was an era when loyalty oaths were required for employment, and that federal funding, on which the institution was mightily dependent, could be jeopardized. However, such restrictive policies ran athwart the burgeoning Free Speech Movement, spawned at the University of California, Berkeley, that swept college campuses across the nation, including Redlands.

The Bulldog latched on to this "cause" and by the mid-1960s the newspaper had become the chief vehicle for student protest of this and other campus issues. Ultimately, students asked for a meeting with the trustees to argue for the freedom to invite whomever they wished, even communists, to campus. A meeting took place, but no policy change resulted, in spite of strong faculty support for the student position.

A fateful confrontation brought the issue to a head on April 6, 1967. Twenty-three student leaders had asked Berkeley student

BELOW LEFT: The body language in this photograph of University students encountering an older Redlands citizen at a protest downtown demonstrates the generational division that fueled the acrimony of the Vietnam War era.

BELOW RIGHT: The Quad served as the site for a teach-in during the October 15, 1969, moratorium.

Bettina Aptheker to speak at the Student Union. An activist and an avowed communist, Aptheker was already on campus when the administration got wind of her presence. President Armacost now faced a choice: he could summon the police to disband the unauthorized assembly or he could ignore it. Armacost wisely allowed the talk to proceed. The well-attended event proved to be orderly. Students stoked by their challenge to the policy found the occasion itself anti-climactic, with a standard presentation followed by a question-and-answer session. Once Aptheker had departed, however, the other shoe dropped. The president declared that those who had issued the invitation to her without prior approval would be subject to discipline.

A five-week suspension resulted for the student leaders following several rounds of discussion among faculty and administrators. Although the students were allowed to complete assignments (thus enabling the seniors to graduate), peer reaction to the sentence proved divisive. Students from other colleges offered to send buses of protesters to campus. Student leaders thanked them for the offer but said this was a Redlands issue and would be solved by Redlands people. Two and one-half weeks later, determining that their point had been made, administration officials lifted the suspension and invited the students to return.

Now all sides focused their attention on the policy. Discussions occurred among trustees, alumni, parents, students, and many others. With the specter of the Free Speech Movement, the board saw little to gain in not yielding some ground. It subsequently approved the principles of the American Association of University Professors (AAUP), which had outlined ideas governing academic freedom. In contrast to similar battles on other campuses, the University of Redlands resolved the issue without recourse to violence, picketing, or marches. Several weeks of earnest, sometimes heated, dialogue, brought

about a better way of dealing with outside speakers and a more flexible policy that fell just short of allowing communist party-affiliated speakers.

The Aptheker incident clearly illustrated that student politicization at Redlands had dovetailed with the mood of college students nationwide. The month of October 1969 showcased how differing views and generations could address complex issues in parallel. Early in the month, a new drama theater had opened, named for Glenn E. Wallichs, a founder of Capitol Records and parent of two alumnae daughters. Wallichs's remarks at the opening reflected the growing anti-war sentiment, then pervading America's academic institutions. "I am pro young people, pro our education system, pro America, and anti war," he said. Just two weeks later, in a spirit of cooperation, the administration, faculty, and students planned to join a nationwide Vietnam event slated for October 15. An instrumental figure in organizing the event was Sam W. Brown, Jr. '65, a former student-body president who had struggled with President Armacost over *The Bulldog*'s censorship and over speaker policies. Now a fellow at Harvard's Institute of Politics, Brown had taken his activism to a national stage. Locally, the moratorium was originally planned to include a boycott of classes, but then evolved into a campus-wide forum for discussion, debate, and teach-ins. City residents also participated in the planning.

The event offered a broad spectrum of viewpoints, including that of the featured speaker, civil rights leader Reverend Ralph Abernathy. From Washington, local Republican Congressman Jerry Pettus spoke via telephone hook-up. That same day, nearly seven hundred students marched quietly into downtown, together with faculty from the University. Students from Redlands High School also joined the throng. Local business people reacted largely with disapproval, and yet expressed appreciation for the lack of disruption. The *Redlands Daily Facts* noted that many community members took strong issue with the young marchers, but added, "It takes personal courage to stand up . . . and be counted."

Despite the peaceful nature of the moratorium, Redlands's immunity from the violence of the time did not last. On April 22, 1970, two Molotov cocktails jolted the campus. One caused minor damage to a restroom in the Hall of Letters, but the other inflicted $50,000 in damage to the Administration Building. Quick action by Redlands firemen at 3:30 a.m. prevented the destruction of the sixty-one-year-old Administration Building. Originating in the Dean of Men's Office, the conflagration spread to the second story. The firebombs destroyed irreplaceable student records.

The attacks generated much anxiety both on campus and in the community. No motive emerged, and no one claimed responsibility. At the time, police dismissed them as a "random incident." Eighteen months later, the case was solved. Interviewing a police recruit, they inadvertently elicited a confession from the man, an alumnus. The former student described how he and eight other minority students prepared and threw the firebombs "in retaliation for disciplinary actions taken by the Dean of Students for a 'food riot' in University Commons." The dining-hall incident had had racial overtones. With this knowledge coming so long after the fact and a new president having by this time replaced George Armacost, the University declined to prosecute. Instead, the new administration of Eugene E. Dawson focused on healing racial and ethnic wounds and providing a better educational and living environment for minority students on campus.

Like other 1960s disruptions to campus, the firebombings and their link to racial and ethnic unrest mirrored concerns confronted nationwide by college administrators. On April 17, 1970, a few days before the attacks, President Armacost had called for a committee to investigate institutional racism at the University of Redlands. A faculty-chaired committee comprising diverse university community members was charged to identify areas of concern, determine how to better sensitize the campus community, and propose a plan of action. The committee's final recommendations called for greater diversity in the student body, on the Board of Trustees, in the faculty, and in the administration. Progress toward these admirable goals was made over the following decades in the student population and, to a lesser extent, in faculty appointments. With universities throughout the country taking similar stances, the competition for teachers and scholars from minority backgrounds created a highly competitive market, hampering the effort to achieve the goals quickly. The University of Redlands, quite frankly, was outbid more often than not.

In George Armacost's final year on the job, 1969–70, the mood of students across the nation worsened as the national and international picture became gloomier. At Redlands students staged additional protests over the widening of the Vietnam War into Cambodia. Teach-ins focused on the history, politics, and culture of Southeast Asia. One forum lasted three days, with attendees varying from two hundred to five hundred students. The dialogues resulted in greater student understanding about the issues.

By decade's end, the phrase "Don't Trust Anyone over Thirty" had become a cherished part of the argot for all students. At the University of Redlands, Armacost and other administrators strove to communicate with the students to ameliorate cross-generational tension. Noting in a September 1969 speech that no one could predict whether there would be "a decline in violence or confrontation or whether there will be a continuation. . . ," the president helped to form the Campus Community Council and the University Community Council. The two bodies brought "students, faculty, administrators, trustees, alumni, parents, friends and donors together" for the purpose of developing understanding and consensus where possible. Their mandate covered issues of the day and addressed the University's future direction.

Acknowledging the existence of a "generation gap" and a divergence in lifestyles preferred by many people under thirty, Armacost stated that members of the younger generation "exemplify . . . personal freedom in the midst of squalor [which] is more liberating than social conformity with trappings of wealth." He concluded, "It is obvious that their statement expresses an idea which creates a gap of acceptance with many adults, but rather than accept it at face value, there should be a communication between people of different generations to understand why such an attitude is expressed and how we can harmonize different concepts of freedom and responsibility. . . ."

These various initiatives and approaches explain why Redlands managed to escape the sit-ins and violent protests that plagued other campuses. In the wake of the massacre of students at Ohio's Kent State University in May 1970, when many other universities and colleges sent their students home early, President Armacost and the trustees chose to keep the campus open and operating.

ASSESSING THE ARMACOST LEGACY

At the end of 1969–70, George Henry Armacost became the first University of Redlands president to retire on his own terms. His tenure, spanning twenty-five pivotal years in the history of both nation and institution, represents the end of an era. For most of the twentieth century, the University's presidents wielded tremendous personal control over faculty matters. They hired and fired professors, chaired faculty meetings, weighed in on sabbatical requests, and acted as an intermediary between trustees and faculty, representing each group to

the other. "George Armacost ran the entire University in a way that a president can no longer do," recalled Professor Emeritus Robert Stuart in 2004. "In those days, by the way, I do not think any member of the faculty would have dared called the president 'George.'"

Armacost was part of a small group of the old-style, "imperial" presidents in Southern California liberal arts institutions, leaders who had served a quarter of a century or more. Armacost's contemporaries included Lee Dubridge at the California Institute of Technology, E. Wilson Lyon at Pomona, Paul Smith at Whittier, Arthur Coons at Occidental, and George C. S. Benson at Claremont Men's (later, Claremont McKenna). All their tenures were marked by innovation and financial achievement and each brought prestige and academic excellence to his institution. The traditional model of the dominant president began to decline nationally during the 1960s in favor

of faculty self-governance and departmental control over hiring and curriculum.

At Armacost's retirement celebration in 1970, Alumni Director Jack B. Cummings '50 captured the essence of the president's strong will and expectations of his colleagues. According to Cummings, some criticized Armacost "for bottlenecking decisions and limiting extremely the delegation of authority." Yet Cummings, whose grandfather Selden Cummings had chaired a joint Baptist clergy-University of Redlands trustee committee on financial support in 1915, noted that "none could fault him because he worked longer hours than anyone else, and the burdens he carried were heavier. He had the difficult task of trying to please a predominantly conservative constituency while at the same time keeping the college moving in the company of other leading liberal arts institutions."

Reflecting shortly after his retirement on the various presidents under whom he had served, Professor Emeritus Stuart characterized Armacost's managerial style as firm yet institutionally minded. "However questionable his compelling control, President Armacost was motivated at heart, I believe, by the sincere desire to build a community of shared values. His hirings, however heavy-handed, did result in bringing together a faculty that identified strongly with key aspects of the University's mission, not only with their individual areas of professional interest and expertise."

As the Sixties gave way to the Seventies, no more would the University of Redlands comprise a single undergraduate college. Significant changes in the University led to the abandonment of a long-cherished curriculum. The civil rights era ushered in new thinking about race and gender both inside and outside the classroom. Even the very corporate structures of America's colleges and universities were transformed.

Despite Armacost's many and obvious achievements, his departure evoked a bittersweet aura. Intense troubles hung over the nation. During his last few years on the job, the increasingly strident voices of people with causes took its toll. In a private conversation with this author shortly before he retired, Armacost voiced his weariness. "Frankly, the last two years have been difficult for both Verda and me. I think I should have retired sooner."

"Prexy" need not have fretted about his legacy, which attests to substantial growth across every facet of the institution. The physical changes to the campus are especially notable. During his presidency, twenty-one buildings were constructed. Much of this expansion testifies to Armacost's skill as a fundraiser and to the development staff he assembled. By the end of his term, he and his team had managed to raise $10 million toward a ten-year, $30 million campaign begun in 1967.

Over his tenure, Armacost naturally experienced criticism from those who felt he favored particular disciplines or professors.

Sometimes perceived as autocratic, the president manifested a shrewd sense of when to listen to his constituency. Knowledge that the president kept a list of faculty who consumed alcoholic beverages and who smoked rankled faculty sensibilities, but the list never came into play for promotions. He managed to make faculty salaries, after years of penury, more competitive with comparable institutions. While championing AAUP wage ratings in order to wrest raises from the trustees for his faculty, Armacost believed that every worker must "earn" his or her pay, and that classroom teaching remained the core of the faculty's professional duties.

Fostering community was another hallmark of the Armacost years. The president belonged to numerous regional, state, and national organizations, both secular and sectarian. He also valued participation in the local community. As a citizen of the City of Redlands, he served on the governing boards of A. K. Smiley Public Library, the Lincoln Memorial Shrine Association, the Chamber of Commerce, the YMCA, and the First Baptist Church. He was the first chairman of the Redlands United Way fund drive.

The Redlands community, town and gown together, bid the Armacosts farewell at a party on May 30, 1970, that filled every seat in Memorial Chapel. Feted with accolades, humor, and applause, George and Verda Armacost beamed their appreciation, as a genuine outpouring of warmth enveloped the crowd. Speaker after speaker extolled the president's many achievements. The highlight of the evening was the presentation to the retiring couple of a gift from grateful alumni, guests, and trustees. Upon exiting, the astonished couple found a new Lincoln Continental sitting on the lawn at the foot of the Chapel steps. For once, even George Armacost was momentarily speechless.

After a two-year teaching and consulting sojourn at Anderson Broaddus College in West Virginia, the Armacosts returned to Redlands. Both resumed their active participation in community organizations and were fixtures at University events. As the years unfolded, George Armacost watched with interest the twists of fate that challenged his successors.

Those '70s Blues

"I know there were the usual concerns, apprehensions, and some reservations because of problems we were told we would be confronting. . . . [We] had been introduced to Redlands some years prior to becoming President and we held the institution in high esteem."

— EUGENE E. DAWSON, NOVEMBER 25, 1971

A CALM BEFORE THE STORM

Eugene E. Dawson began his presidency on August 1, 1970. A Baptist with a degree in theology, Dawson earned a Ph.D. in psychology and taught at Temple Buell College (formerly Colorado College of Women) in Denver, where he also served as president. A member of several national educational commissions and a consultant to more than thirty colleges and universities, he appeared to the trustees as the ideal man to succeed George H. Armacost and chart the University's future.

Dawson's academic record as professor, director of religious activities, and dean of students at Kansas State Teachers College stood him in good stead with the Redlands presidential search committee. At Temple Buell, where Dawson spent thirteen years, he had succeeded in doubling enrollment, been a vigorous fundraiser, and transformed the institution from a two-year to a four-year school. In Denver he served as president of the influential Rotary Club, was a member of the mayor's commission on community relations, and sat on the board of the Denver Symphony and Goodwill. He enjoyed bicycling and golfing. His wife, Arlene, was equally engaged in civic affairs, especially in opera and symphony groups.

Upon his arrival at Redlands, President Dawson's plate of challenges was piled near to overflowing. One of his sons had attended Redlands, as would another, so the new president was familiar with the campus milieu and its setting. He was enthusiastic about the advantages of small, independent colleges and universities. Such institutions offered, he declared, "a special concern for students, an emphasis on teaching, and the development of a unique sense of community. It should prove exciting and rewarding to be associated with further expansion planned at Redlands." Recalled Professor Emeritus Robert L. Stuart, "The choice of Eugene Dawson to succeed President Armacost seemed promising, [as did] the appointment of several young faculty to key administrative positions. . . . "

Dawson took the helm of a school that, since 1945, had increased its undergraduate enrollment from 1,120 to 1,732, its operating budget from $664,617 to $6 million, and its assets from $5,377,836 to $28 million. Charting how such optimism soured and such potential was not realized requires inquiry and reveals a poignant narrative.

From the beginning, Dawson had two goals that inflected his style and tenure. First, he was determined to build on the University's recent strides toward change, "while holding on to the best of the institution's heritage." Second, he advocated "shared responsibility" and "team management for the operation of the school among trustees, faculty, staff and students."

Dawson's candor was laudable, but not all of the Redlands constituency appreciated it. In response to a question at an open meeting regarding the University's ties to the Baptist denomination, Dawson observed that he could advocate the dissolution of relations he considered nominal and of little significance, "in view of the fact that the University is not meaningfully functionally related to the Baptists anyway." This sentiment delighted some but distressed others. Disillusioned, some of the old-guard Baptist constituents transferred their financial allegiance elsewhere. Replacing this lost donor pool became a great challenge, especially when the federal government reduced support of higher education in the early 1970s.

The new president spent his first five months in office studying the administrative lay of the land. He then determined to make changes and imprint his own style. For example, he moved the president's office, traditionally on the second floor of the Administration Building, to the third floor. Longtime academic administrators either resigned or found themselves reassigned to new duties, with faculty members elevated to replace them. The changes affected the highest echelon of administrators. Three of four vice presidents departed in 1971: the vice president for student affairs, the vice president for financial affairs and the vice president for development. Other administrators followed suit, and by 1974 all but two of Armacost's lieutenants had been replaced. In fact, by the end of Dawson's tenure in 1977, seventeen administrators had come and gone. However appropriate these moves may have been, concern soon arose both within and without the University regarding its future. The revolving door created instability and confusion. Clouding issues further was a financial quagmire. "The Dawson years

were stormy," Stuart recounted. "Gene Dawson was brought here with the expectation of considerable fundraising expertise. Once here, however, he did not manage to produce a cornucopia of financial gifts for our benefit. To some measure in his defense, the University was in weaker shape financially by the time he got here than was generally recognized."

Before his forced resignation in 1971, Vice President of Financial Affairs Larry Hendon had handed the trustees and president a sobering outlook of the University's economic picture. Higher-education institutions across the land, including Columbia and Stanford universities, were experiencing major budget cuts and a declining donor pool, the result of student unrest and profound educational shifts. Fiscal strain was to become a constant during the Dawson presidency. In the final year of Armacost's tenure, a small but telling deficit had developed. National economic pressures, unexpected expenses from previously approved curricular enhancements, and student recruiting challenges all led to a tenuous budget environment. Headlines in the local press helped little by calling attention to shortfalls in 1974 and 1975. Stuart described the sobering picture: "Budget deficits skyrocketed, business managers came and went, and eventually the board put much of the management of the University into the hands of its attorney. . . . We were in fiscal crisis, and, among other emergency measures, some real estate was sold in an attempt to generate cash." He was referring to valuable assets meant for quasi-endowment, or "rainy days," to meet the annual budget when necessary. Clearly, it had begun to rain.

At the core of Dawson's mid-1970s financial travails lay a decision made in the mid-1960s by Armacost and the trustees to found a new college. While the plan was a testament to their faith in the University's mission and future, it proved to be overly ambitious. The commitment of resources required to achieve this goal outweighed the benefits that could be gleaned from a distinctive academic program. The University plunged into the capital construction necessary to undertake

a project of this magnitude, relying upon rosy financial projections and exuberant faith in the brightening of the nation's economy.

The timing could not have been worse: just months ahead lay a recession, soon followed by the first oil embargo, which resulted in long, contentious, and dispiriting lines at filling stations. The economic juggernaut failed to materialize, dooming the University's grand ambition. While neither Armacost nor the trustees could have anticipated in 1966 how future blows to the national economy would affect the fortunes of their new college, they also could not envision how its development would elude their control. Thus, President Dawson faced not only a financial crisis, but an administrative one. Here then is that story from the beginning.

BIRTH OF JOHNSTON COLLEGE

The fateful and eventful decision to found a new college was rooted in the student unrest of the 1960s. Concerned over reports and perceptions that linked the impetus for many protests with the sheer size of many colleges and universities—and the ensuing depersonalization felt by many—the University's trustees elected to cap the student body at a maximum of 1,500. They also determined that a collateral college would solve the dilemma of absorbing future growth. This second institution, with its own faculty, would preserve the University's cherished low student-faculty ratio and assure

its continued commitment to excellence. Other models for the multicollege format abounded: the Claremont Colleges, the University of the Pacific, Hamilton College, and Hampshire College. In 1967 more than thirty-two institutions across the country announced intentions to grow by establishing clusters of collateral schools. Not unexpectedly, the curriculum of some of the new institutions reflected a spirit of experimentation.

The pages of the University's seventy-fifth anniversary book, *Whose Emblem Shines Afar*, review the collateral college's origins. Approving the creation of such an entity, after much committee study, the Board of Trustees began planning on February 8, 1966. The new entity was to be characterized by the same sense of purpose and identity as the University, "that is, it would be a collateral Christian liberal arts college, and both schools would employ the structure and services of the Business Office, the Student Personnel Office, the Registrar, athletic program, and (with separate facilities) the same food supplier."

The new school's academic mission would focus on government, international relations, and public administration. In charge would be a chancellor who reported directly to the president. The faculty would be freed from the University's traditional curricular and degree requirements. A fifteen-member Board of Overseers would provide consultation and guidance on the curriculum and graduation requirements, with final approval coming from the Board of Trustees and the president

of the University. Joint-use policies would be regulated by formal agreement.

The great champion on the Board of Trustees for a new college was Dwayne Orton '26. He had utilized his Redlands education to rise through the ranks at IBM, becoming editor of the company's magazine, *Think*. Prior to the 1966 announcement of a new school, Orton indicated to the board that he had a donor in mind, a personal friend who would give a naming grant for the new college. Orton journeyed to the donor's home in Canines, France, carrying renderings and drawings of new buildings.

He returned with a check for $300,000 and a promise from the donor's attorney that outlined a plan to pay an additional $1.2 million. For $1.5 million, James Graham Johnston had purchased the right for his name to adorn the University's new college.

Born in Scotland in 1887, Johnston had immigrated to the United States, gained employment, and eventually worked for the Computing, Tabulating, Recording Co., one of the first experimental laboratories of IBM. There he focused on early mechanized counting devices and became associated with founder Thomas Watson in the formative years of the corporation. Later he served as vice president of IBM World Trade Organization in Europe.

In February 1967, the Armacosts, Jim Fox of the development office and his wife, Martha, and the Ortons flew to France to meet with Johnston. Four months later, Johnston came to Redlands to receive an honorary degree and to see final plans. He was pleased to know that construction would begin in 1968, with the opening of the college planned for 1969.

A college needs buildings, but a leader is required to attract faculty and students. The administration nominated three candidates for the chancellorship of Johnston College. A faculty committee interviewed them and unanimously recommended Pressley C. McCoy. The original plan allowed the chancellor and overseers wide latitude in determining finances and selecting faculty. While the University trustees retained ultimate approval over Johnston's personnel and financial affairs, all parties envisioned the new college as a largely independent entity.

The overseers convened their first meeting at the exclusive California Club in Los Angeles on August 21, 1968, barely two weeks before McCoy assumed his position. Appropriately enough, Orton served as the group's first chairman, with Johnston listed as honorary chairman. The roll also included five members of the University Board of Trustees: H. Park Arnold, John Scott Everton, Turney Fox, C. Herbert Wennerberg, and Frances Wills.

BELOW TOP: With three buildings completed, the University of Redlands opened Johnston College in the fall of 1969. Its campus was expected to expand toward this sign fronting Colton Avenue, but years of tumult and financial shortfalls forced a halt to the plans.

BELOW CENTER: Luminaries gather for the groundbreaking of Johnston College in 1967. They include the Armacosts (left), James Graham Johnston (center), and Edna Olson Orton '27 and Dwayne Orton '26 (right).

The group discussed nuts-and-bolts issues, such as criteria for choosing faculty and additional overseers, but also touched upon the venture's underlying ideals. Most significantly, they agreed that the new college would become an "experimenting unit with educational autonomy." This language, it would soon be clear, invited various interpretations. Alert to the possibility

of a runaway train, Armacost clearly warned all connected with Johnston that "educational autonomy" should not be construed as "independence" from the administration of the University of Redlands concerning finances, student life, administrative policies, salaries and fees, and the offices of the registrar, admissions, business, and student life. To be fair, Armacost's interpretation left little purview to the new college; however, its partisans construed those terms far more broadly than the trustees anticipated.

Undaunted by the president's admonition, Chancellor McCoy, a number of the new faculty, and the charter students quickly stretched the concept of "experimenting" to "complete autonomy." They wanted no assistance from the University in matters of curriculum or campus life. Disputes about the identity of the college would consume much of the University's energy for the next decade. The die was cast, the stage set for struggle.

FROM VISION TO REAL McCOY
The October 3, 1969, issue of *Time* magazine highlighted the state of American higher education. Correspondent Timothy Tyler and his colleagues found "the old hierarchy of formal education to be under attack" at campuses nationwide. Traditionally rigid curricular models were being dropped in favor of "open curriculums" that permitted students to design and experiment with their own course of study. The article utilized a single case study to represent the movement: Johnston College, which had opened its doors scarcely one month earlier.

The selection of Johnston College to represent this national trend indicates just how innovative, daring, and different was the educational agenda set out by Pressley McCoy and his associates during the year preceding the school's opening. The article framed the appointment of *this* chancellor as indisputable evidence regarding the intent of the University of Redlands to participate in this curricular experimentation. "The Trustees . . . hired McCoy to overcome what *he defined* as the two basic problems in education: rigidity in attitude and rigidity in structure." The report included no comments on this subject from either Armacost or the trustees. Quite literally then, the article provides an early indication that the University hierarchy and new chancellor were not on the same page.

McCoy assumed the responsibilities of his new post in September 1968, a full year before Johnston was to open. By November 8, he outlined to the overseers plans for an interpersonal, intercultural, and international focus in the curriculum. An interdisciplinary approach to problem solving became a key component. The chancellor especially advocated community learning, which he believed would enhance the capacities of the individual for personal growth and social fulfillment. McCoy sought to ensure open-mindedness, evaluative awareness, creative sensibility, conflict resolution, philosophical and theological commitment, and, finally, a sensitivity to and concern for public affairs. As if this philosophical approach did not already represent a sharp break from the University's traditional curriculum, the chancellor's plan eschewed the standard grading system. Written evaluations of students' strengths and weaknesses would replace letter grades.

The Johnston curriculum also abandoned the traditional emphasis on sequential courses to complete a program of study. Instead, each student assumed responsibility for negotiating his or her graduation requirements directly.

Seminars, tutorials, and "regular" classes comprised the bulk of classroom learning, but student-suggested and student-taught courses also figured in the mix. A contract delineated the concentration and emphasis of study, and a committee certified progress through a variety of evaluative means: written or oral examination or completion of specific projects being the most common. This committee also determined which needs remained unmet in the four-year contract.

No one should doubt that this radical approach reflected the educational philosophy of Pressley McCoy. Kevin O'Neill, a founding member of the Johnston faculty, recalled that the chancellor envisioned a college in which students would be the "center of the institution and in which learning would be an entirely cooperative, democratic process. [He] also believed that education should honor both the head and the heart. . . ." Interestingly, this statement echoes sentiments voiced by Jasper Newton Field upon the founding of the University of Redlands in 1907.

McCoy spent 1968–69 recruiting Johnston College's first faculty. The chancellor confided to *Time* reporter Tyler that he sought instructors who displayed a capability "for flexibility and [a] willingness to interact with the kids, not preach at them." McCoy strove to employ faculty who shared his goals for higher education. That meant an emphasis on upcoming scholars, in tune with the times. Tyler observed, "Most of his 17 professors are in their 30s, have top credentials — and uncommonly high motivation."

A cosmopolitan flavor figured prominently in the charter faculty's profile. According to O'Neill, "[McCoy's] initial faculty represented a broad and diverse background. He scoured the country for an international, multicultural, interracial and minimally multigendered faculty." The group included a Spanish lawyer, a Swiss business expert, a Japanese anthropologist, and a British historian. A number of Americans on the faculty roster had spent significant parts of their lives in foreign settings — India, Lebanon, and Latin America. Two had

been Rhodes Scholars. An African-American French instructor sang opera and had spent many years working for corporations in Africa. A handful of young faculty from leading American institutions — Berkeley, Columbia, Stanford, UCLA, and Yale — rounded out the company. The contingent included two women; one a radical political scientist from New York who had led antiwar protests; the other the child of missionaries in the Far East. Their combined life experience seemed to represent — inadvertently — the convergence of progressive and conservative values that would soon rend the University community. To this rich mix were added several humanistic psychologists trained in the then-popular encounter-group and psychodrama techniques.

Excitement mounted as the fall of 1969 drew closer. Admissions was actively recruiting charter students. Construction of dedicated facilities was underway — two residence halls and a student center for the exclusive use of Johnston's incipient student body, anticipated to be 240 strong. Despite the optimism, conflicts between the University and Johnston began to emerge over just about everything. McCoy and the overseers concluded much of their planning with little University

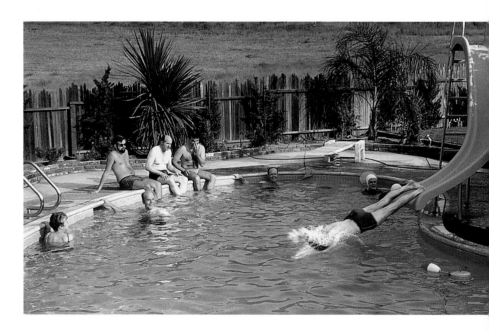

was set to commence instruction. East and West Halls stood ready to house the 180 men and women who comprised the charter class. A commons stood ready to provide food and entertainment space. Administratively, the "euphoria" did not last long.

Any new institution defines its identity through its first actions, whether purposefully or otherwise. McCoy was a purposeful individual, and he hardly intended to leave the college's identity to chance. Given his emphasis on student participation in the democratic exercise of institutional authority — perhaps Johnston's most obvious departure from the prior tradition of governance at the University of Redlands — McCoy sought a format that would best express these ideals. Thus, the entire Johnston community — overseers, administrators, faculty, students, a few outside consultants, and even some parents — decamped for the forested hills of the Pilgrim Pines retreat at Oak Glen, near Yucaipa. At a series of encounter groups over ten days, they shared feelings, hopes, dreams, and visions for their new college.

John R. Watt, professor of international programs, later recalled that encounter groups were central to Johnston's "every social structure, from classes to faculty and community meetings, and even to personal interactions." Watt attributed McCoy's faith in the techniques, which became the focus of the retreat, to the chancellor's unique educational philosophy. "I doubt that anyone who knew McCoy will forget the single-minded determination with which he pursued this goal. McCoy's approach, which can be described as basically Rogerian, was the force which brought about Pilgrim Pines. . . . " The retreat inadvertently exacerbated the infighting between Johnston's leaders and President Armacost. The college's curriculum had already aroused the suspicion of the University hierarchy. At the behest of the chancellor, Watt prepared a course catalogue that would pass muster with Armacost and the trustees. Watt's colleague O'Neill recalled the effort to make Johnston "look something like what Armacost wanted." But the document

oversight; the administration remained blithely unaware how far the college had strayed from the original concept. Not until McCoy ambushed the unwitting Armacost with his unorthodox plans for the college during a live broadcast of the local television news program "On Campus" did the soon-to-retire president begin to comprehend that something different was afoot. (The tape is sometimes played at Johnston reunions, where peals of laughter greet the astonished expression on Armacost's face.)

Johnston's first accreditation report acknowledged, "The birth of Johnston College was not without pain." A conflict of leadership produced that pain — a battle of wills between Armacost and McCoy. As events turned out, "not without pain" was an understatement.

GROWING PAINS

Sixty Septembers after the University of Redlands first opened its doors to students, Johnston College received its first class. Three years had elapsed since the Board of Trustees had initiated the venture. The college's Board of Overseers was ready to preside. Administrators were ready to cogovern. The faculty concealed that McCoy remained determined to forge Johnston not as the collateral college conceived in 1965–66 but as he envisioned it.

Time correspondent Tyler attended the retreat, and his story captures the participants' spirit of cooperation, equality, and adventure. In an interview with the reporter, Watt declared, "I'm a teacher, why should I also be an authority? . . . That's no longer the University's job." An opportunity for the instructor to demonstrate the new world order arose before the reporter had time to reply. "Just then a pretty girl stood up, wrapped her arms around [Watt] and said: 'I don't want to take world religion after all, John. I've already had too much philosophy and religion. More would make me a lopsided person.' Watt beamed at the girl, agreed, and gave her a little hug and she pranced off into the forest to find her new boyfriend." As depicted in a national news magazine, the incident signified the intent of current collegians to retain control over their own educational choices, and the willingness of "new-fangled" institutions to let them.

The encounter-group approach had its limits, however. Tom Greening, one of the outside consultants at the retreat, recalled in 1981 that the constant push for unanimity did not work. While dissidents were thought capable of joining the majority through persistent interactions, in reality, "too often time ran out, leaving behind community fragmentation, individual alienation, and vulnerability to coercive intervention by the University administration."

O'Neill recalled that "good spirits frayed even further" upon Armacost's visit to Pilgrim Pines. Invited by McCoy, the president found himself in the midst of encounter groups under the direction of a dozen licensed psychotherapist trainers. Conventional norms of behavior were discouraged. "Predictably, the scene was marked by shrieks, and other manifestations of intense feelings openly shared," wrote O'Neill. "In the group to which George Armacost was assigned on the first day he visited, students caught up in the egalitarian spirit of the group addressed the bewildered president as 'George' and told him to 'get with it,' among other things." O'Neill noted that, while Armacost was by no means a rigid conservative and had an exemplary record on matters of civil rights, he could not help but bristle at being treated as an equal by long-haired eighteen-year-olds.

Time's piece gleefully recorded the "get with it" incident, reporting that in response Armacost was up "at 4:00 a.m. banging away on his portable typewriter, getting down his reaction to the experience. He didn't quite understand his new college, but it was making him think. Whether his new students will think as deeply as they feel remain to be seen. It should be quite a year." The *Time* reporter could not have known how right he was.

CONSERVATIVE REACTION TO SOCIAL ACTION

Kevin O'Neill described McCoy as a visionary and a "brilliant recruiter," but not "a detail man." Driven by his idealism, McCoy overlooked the inherent conservatism of the town of Redlands and the institutional conservatism of its namesake university. Clashes between such forces were inevitable. A contretemps erupted almost before the denizens of the forest had time to stamp the mud from their shoes. It concerned Professor Jeanne Friedman, one of the most junior members of the Johnston faculty. A political scientist, she had been recruited by McCoy from Stanford while still a graduate student. President

BELOW: Form and elegance in movement constitutes art as much as painting or song, as these members of the interpretive group "Designs in Dance" demonstrated. Pictured (left to right) are Gayle H. Billhardt '73, June K. McKee '71, Deborah L. Wormley '71, and Beverly Lewis '73.

Armacost, who retained final say over Chancellor McCoy's faculty selections, did not know that before she was hired, Friedman had been arrested during an anti-war demonstration. Palo Alto police charged her with inciting a riot. Armacost learned of her status only when he received a phone call from a reporter from the Palo Alto *Times*, who asked the surprised president, "What will the policy of this University be now since yesterday she [Friedman] was convicted on five counts ranging from disturbing the peace to inciting to riot?" *The Bulldog* described Friedman as "an unapologetic radical, the child of old-line socialist/communist parents . . . a person whose worldview was entirely exotic to Armacost and to tell the truth to many of the students and faculty at Johnston as well." In the days before affirmative action and privacy laws, Armacost could—and did—demand Friedman's termination.

McCoy quickly rallied the Johnston faculty to Friedman's defense. On September 5, while still at Pilgrim Pines, they met "until after midnight" to discuss her continued employment—with the young professor present. After a long, tense session, they determined that, if Friedman left, so would they. The coincidental presence of *Time* reporter Tyler, combined with faculty bravado, prompted Armacost to back down, as O'Neill recalled in 2004. "But he did not forget, and a spirit of mutual fear and distrust flourished between the faculty and students at Johnston and Armacost and his administration."

News of Friedman's conviction provoked a flurry of consultations among the Board of Trustees and the University attorney. Alerted by Armacost, the Executive Committee heard a report from Chancellor McCoy. Rather than informing Johnston's Board of Overseers fully about the incident, the University hierarchy chose only to query the overseers regarding their views on faculty participation in demonstrations. Armacost urged Dwayne Orton, chairman of the overseers, to discuss the situation with the entire group as quickly as possible. When the overseers met, they heard from the University attorney and two Johnston faculty members who had journeyed to San José to view evidence and talk with the district attorney. Casting their lot rather pointedly against the conservative reaction of Armacost, the overseers unanimously approved a mission of faculty activism and went so far as to form an ad hoc committee whose purpose was "to consider the enlargement, modification, and application of the University of Redlands policy regarding social action." Their attitude: if Friedman had violated University policy, better to change the policy. University trustees met soon after the Friedman affair at a Los Angeles airport motel together with Orton and McCoy. They appointed a committee, whose members realized an appeal by Friedman could drag on for a long time. While the committee dithered, Friedman continued to teach. She finished the school year and later left Johnston for other employment.

Regrettably, the issue mushroomed once the local press got hold of the story. Residents of Redlands first felt unease and then resentment. In fact, the Friedman affair damaged town and gown relations more profoundly than any incident since the firing of President Clarence Howe Thurber thirty-three years earlier.

At the same time, a number of University students, watching from the sidelines, formed opinions about their Johnston colleagues. Both populations would ultimately benefit from each other's environment, academic offerings, and social traditions, but it took nearly a quarter century for those involved to recognize this fully.

THE JOHNSTONIAN IDENTITY

Johnston College students quickly found ways to make their part of campus uniquely, well, Johnstonian. In the process, a distinct and colorful culture emerged. Johnstonians enriched campus lore by contributing highjinks to rival the illicit still that Depression-era students operated in the basement of California Hall, or the Chapel tower loudspeaker prank perpetuated by World War II-era students with the aid of a Glenn Miller tune. Disgruntled with the mundane names the trustees assigned to their two residences—East Hall and West Hall—the students conjured new ones. They drew four consonants from a hat, added two vowels, and then shuffled the letters into two "names." The buildings became known among students as "T. A. Kofap" and "P. A. Fokat," respectively. The new sobriquets gruntled them enormously.

While the monikers symbolized the college's independence and its students' free-spiritedness, they exacted a price. Because proper Johnstonian pronunciation of "Fokat" evoked phonetic similarity to a common vulgarity, the name seemed calculated to rile those already upset by McCoy's unorthodox curriculum, Pilgrim Pines's "touchy-feely" atmosphere, and the Friedman case's acrimonious denouement. The nicknames seemed yet another example of Johnston students thumbing their noses at the sensibilities of the trustees, administration, town, and students in the University's College of Arts and Sciences.

Thus, Johnston College existed in an uneasy, poorly crafted alliance with its progenitor. As O'Neill saw it, "What began as a noble experiment, a way to put Redlands on the map and increase the academic prestige of the institution," had gone awry. The two institutions hardly seemed to belong together. On one side stood a college that sought to embody the communal and egalitarian ideals of the 1960s, replete with attendant anarchy and disorder. On the other side stood a small, conservative Christian university whose hopes for a college to train diplomats had "evaporated in the cool morning mists of Pilgrim Pines."

DAWSON TAKES COMMAND
President and chancellor continued to spar for the rest of the school year. Issues ranged from the fundamental—Johnston's

refusal to accept the primacy of University policies regarding student life—to the absurd. At one point, Armacost suspended a coed over a pet cat because McCoy refused to enforce the rule forbidding animals in dormitories. A final discussion between the soon-to-retire president and the chancellor in the spring of 1970 featured Armacost lecturing McCoy about the need for accountability to the administration. No gestures of accommodation or friendship were forthcoming. A waiting-and-baiting game had begun. The Johnston community believed that time was on its side, as Armacost was to become emeritus at the end of the year. Settling the governance issues dividing the University and Johnston would become the responsibility of the new president, Eugene E. Dawson. What they had not bargained for was that Dawson would prove to be both a shield and a sword.

Having inherited the ill-will between the University and Johnston, President Dawson found himself on the horns of a dilemma. The board wanted the new president to rein in the tempestuous chancellor. McCoy expected unconditional backing from him. It seemed to many that the board spent "enormous amounts of time debating" Johnston's future. Dawson appeared unable to "make up his mind about its value" and

The announcement of McCoy's firing was accompanied by the news that University professor Eugene G. Ouellette, an expert in communication disorders with a specialty in audiology, would serve as acting chancellor of Johnston College. The circumstances behind Ouellette's appointment were described by Bill McDonald and O'Neill: "The President [Dawson] offered him the job directly, telling Gene he had only five minutes to decide. Ouellette pleaded for a bit more time, called his wife, Anne, thought hard for an hour, then called Dawson back and accepted." Expressing shock, McCoy, in an interview with the *Redlands Daily Facts* on January 14, indicated that he had been close to Dawson since 1954. "It has been most painful to be dealt with in such impersonal terms by one I had long regarded as friend and counselor."

A petition signed by ninety college students and ten faculty protested the firing. In truth, McCoy's administrative style had not won over everyone within the Johnston community, but his firing sent shivers of fear through Johnstonians that the experiment's end might be near. The overseers met and offered a number of possible solutions, one of which envisioned McCoy continuing as chancellor of academic affairs, but the University trustees rejected them. However unpalatable for the college community, his firing was a textbook case of a university president and board exercising their rightful administrative power.

In a state of denial, however, McCoy continued to work at his desk, believing that the decision to fire him would be reversed. Exhibiting great sensitivity and administrative savvy, Ouellette agreed to sit at a desk nearby. Seeing two chancellors working in the same room must have been disconcerting.

McCoy delivered an emotional farewell at a January 22 community meeting in the student center. There, in a stinging denunciation of the trustees, president, and governance of the University, he offered to lead the community to another location. "If you choose to remain here," he declared, "so be it. This statement has been motivated by hope, promise and a vision of

contact between the faculties and students of the parent university and Johnston "was minimal," Stuart recalled. On January 6, 1971, McCoy was summoned to the office of board chairman Fred Llewellyn at Forest Lawn Memorial Park (founded by Llewellyn's father-in-law, Hubert Eaton). Llewellyn got right to the point, informing the chancellor that the Executive Committee of the trustees had agreed to terminate his contract in June. Secretly, this decision had been taken at a November 1969 meeting. Between November and December 1969, Dawson nonetheless met with McCoy five times. On January 12, 1971, Llewellyn and Dawson decided to place McCoy on terminal leave, effective immediately.

Dawson and the trustees acted without consulting the Johnston overseers. The omission is a glaring statement of how far the internal governance issue had deteriorated. Although the trustees apologized to the overseers on January 21, the damage had been done. Johnston's autonomy had suffered serious erosion in only its second year.

things to come. This has been a wonderful learning experience
for me at Johnston College, probably the greatest of my life."

A standing ovation with cheers and tears followed. A series
of meetings ensued. Faculty were conflicted about leaving
Redlands for Lone Mountain College in San Francisco, where
McCoy had made an arrangement. Orton favored remaining
at Redlands, a decision that effectively separated him from
McCoy. By March the ardor for a move had cooled, and
President Dawson affirmed his and the trustees' support for
Johnston College. Even during his final days as president,
Dawson vigorously continued to defend the college to the
board, stressing the need to retain key faculty, some of whom
left for new pastures and others who questioned the new order.
The trustees' response was tepid. Although McCoy was gone,
Johnston College's students, faculty, and curriculum retained
the maverick spirit he had instilled.

RED INK FLOWS

After a year as acting chancellor, Gene Ouellette assumed
the position permanently. While he never asserted the sort of
administrative autonomy advocated by his predecessor, neither
did he modify Johnston's curricular distinctiveness. For several

years, the University and
college learned to coexist and
the intellectual life of both
prospered.

From 1970 to 1976, Johnston
inaugurated a series of
innovations and academic
initiatives. A community-
insight program housed
students with families of
various cultural backgrounds.
Johnstonians also instituted
a creative playschool for
preschoolers. Located in the
1950s-era University Village
on Colton Avenue, the enterprise provided early child-
hood education to forty-five
youngsters. Still in its infancy,
Johnston received glowing
accreditation reports from

the Western Association of Schools and Colleges. This era also
witnessed increasing numbers of Johnston students registering for classes at the University, and vice-versa. This interaction
indicates that Arts and Sciences students had discovered some
advantages in the Johnston curriculum, and is a testament to
the intellectual richness a collateral college system can bestow
upon a university.

Unfortunately, the University continued to hemorrhage red
ink in the mid-1970s, and many pegged the start-up college as
the primary culprit. Gift and tuition income constitute life-
blood in higher education; no institution can long endure, let
alone thrive, without a steady, reliable supply of both. Despite
the exuberance Johnstonians displayed for their school's free-
spirited offerings and self-sufficiency, the college faced the
same practicalities of business as any other kind of educational

enterprise: namely, the need to attract donors and students. These challenges continued to vex Johnston College.

For infusions of cash, most institutions depend upon their alumni to share their wealth as they age and become more prosperous. Because it was new, Johnston lacked a readymade donor pool. And outside gifts proved hard to come by. No doubt the turmoil surrounding the college's first years discouraged some potential sources. Moreover, President Dawson's unrelated reorganization of the Development Office created a leadership vacuum and sapped initiative from that department. What gifts Development did generate may have succored the educational mission of one institution, but could not suffice for two. Of course, Johnston competed for resources with the University's College of Arts and Sciences. In some quarters,

this created a perception that the start-up school was siphoning money from the University's mainline program.

Declining attendance also bedeviled Johnston, which proved unable to stem the student attrition rate. By the time Ouellette resigned in 1975 to take a position on the East Coast, Johnston enrollment had plummeted from 280 to 212 students. Attrition also decimated the Board of Overseers, where frustration mounted regarding further compromise of the college's founding vision. Several members resigned in February 1976, shortly after Ouellette's departure. Into these already tenuous circumstances, the trustees injected additional uncertainty when they constituted a committee to study the entire University program later that spring. At that year's regular June meeting of the trustees, the committee presented its conclusions regarding

BOTTOM: The Phi Chis form a
human pyramid in their front yard in
the early 1970s.

BELOW: Students impatient with a
backlog on the conveyor belt left
their empty meal trays on the floor in
the mid-1970s.

the future. The benefit of hindsight makes clear that their recommendations marked the beginning of the process by which
Johnston ceased to exist as an independent college.

Cancellation of separate dining privileges at Orton Center
became the first casualty. (When Dwayne Orton died in 1971,
gifts from friends and his widow, who donated $100,000, led to
the naming of the Johnston College's student center after him.)
Henceforth, students of both colleges dined at the Commons,
a measure that allowed consolidation of food services. The
University's decision to reallocate West Hall to a newly established division, Whitehead College, whose inception is discussed below, constituted an even greater indignity. Shrinking
enrollment meant that Johnston needed only one dormitory.
"Fokat" Hall was no more, and a much-beloved sobriquet disappeared with it.

Citing precarious finances, the Select Committee highlighted
a case for university-wide reorganization, strong administrative
in-house governance, and greater exercise of fiscal control and
responsibility. Dawson responded to these recommendations
with three specific proposals whose implementation would
scale back, if not gut entirely, the Johnston College experiment.
First, he advocated reductions to the college's administrative
and staff positions—a measure to contain runaway expenses.
Second, he hamstrung the Board of Overseers with a recommendation that Johnston's chancellor report solely to the
University president and Board of Trustees—a measure to
curtail the college's troublesome independent streak. Lastly,
he suggested the transfer of Johnston's external degree
program to Whitehead—a measure that reflected awareness
of the growing demand in higher education for programs
targeted to adults. This increasingly lucrative niche market
emphasized quick, flexible degree programs frequently taught
at off-campus locations.

For the moment, Johnston College survived, its independence
relatively intact; however, the changes advocated by Dawson
made its demise as a separate college inevitable. Absorption of

the external degree pro-
gram by Whitehead College
would siphon off additional
enrollment. For example,
Johnston's newly established
master's degree in human-
istic and transpersonal
psychology was reassigned
to the new entity. Dawson's
plan envisioned Whitehead
College as a cash cow whose
profits would buttress
Johnston and the College
of Liberal Arts and Sciences
alike. This third college,
however, would not prove
to be an elixir for University
finances as hoped. Just as
the fiscal expectations of
Armacost and an earlier Board of Trustees regarding the founding of Johnston had fallen short, so too those of Dawson and
the current board would turn out to be too optimistic. When the

trustees formally established the third college in August 1976, optimism was all they had.

THE INCEPTION OF WHITEHEAD COLLEGE

The trustees' approval of a third collateral college was based on the proven history of successful special programs and the emerging market of returning students between the ages of twenty-eight and forty.

The concept for such a college at Redlands can be traced as far back as President Elam J. Anderson's era. In 1943 Karl C. Wells, the donor of the University's original acreage, suggested that if Redlands faced financial difficulty, the campus might seek to enroll local adults who "have never had the advantage of higher education." While the president effectively shelved the suggestion, the concept proved to be thirty years ahead of its time.

The University welcomed a tireless advocate for adult education when it hired Gordon C. Atkins '38 to head its special programs. With a master's degree from Stanford and a doctorate from the University of Southern California, he joined the

faculty of San Bernardino Valley College in 1946. Twenty years later, Atkins returned to Redlands as a professor of philosophy and humanities. After three years, he left, to become founding president of the new Crafton Community College in Yucaipa. Having shepherded the new institution through its birth and to the point where it had become a successful operation, Atkins accepted in 1971 the invitation of Dawson to return to Redlands and direct summer and foreign programs. Special programs, a new initiative in professional training, were added to his portfolio in 1972–73. Soon classes were being offered from Chula Vista to Sacramento, in such areas as nursing training and liberal studies. This program attracted a different demographic groups than that of the traditional undergraduate. By 1976 baccalaureate degrees had been awarded to 843 students averaging thirty-seven years of age. Seventy-five percent of them were women.

By 1976 it seemed obvious that a distinct mission of a third institution should be to meet the needs of older, non-traditional students who, for the most part, continue their college studies on a part-time basis. The concept of elevating the adult program into a college was approved in August 1976. Atkins, appointed provost, advanced the name Alfred North Whitehead College, after the English philosopher-mathematician, a personal favorite of his. Whitehead strongly advocated technical education that was liberal and liberal education that was technical. He wrote, "Education should turn out the pupil with something he knows well and something he can do well. This intimate union of practice and theory aids both. The intellect does not work best in a vacuum." The University, cash-starved and faced with mounting red ink, eagerly embraced Atkins's initiatives.

It was hoped the new college would improve prospects for the University's cash flow. The formal dedication took place amid much festivity on October 3. The first graduating class, of 1977, appeared to augur well for the enterprise and the potential to tap the lucrative adult market. To Atkins's way of thinking,

special programs created an opportunity for the University to generate a new source of tuition income by providing a means by which employed adults might complete their bachelor's degree.

The program, however, did not inspire enthusiastic applause from the undergraduate residential faculty. When the Dawson administration first announced the new college, Professor Rob Stuart recalled that "the administration misled the faculty, at a meeting at which I was present, about how far along the organization of the college had come, and the discovery of that deceit poisoned the relationship of many faculty with the new program. Whitehead became a 'cash cow' for the rest of the institution and, in my judgment, was not given adequate resources for its own development." But he added, "In principle it was a noble effort, and many benefited from it."

While several faculty members taught in the program on and off campus, others expressed disdain for the older students. Issues of quality control and the usurping of scarce faculty time became strong points of contention. Soon adjunct instructors came to carry the load to meet the increasing enrollments. While this exacerbated doubts among some of the already discontented faculty, it also brought excellent additional resources to the mix. In certain fields, adjuncts later converted to full-time, permanent positions.

When Atkins assumed the title of provost of Whitehead College, the growth of returning adult student enrollment increased dramatically. The University offered six degree programs ranging from liberal studies to public service management and a master of arts in management. By 1977, 1,005 degrees had been awarded to 842 undergraduate and 163 graduate students. In 1979, 859 undergraduate and 230 graduate degrees were conferred.

Regrettably, Atkins's tenure proved all too short, for he died in 1978 following a brief illness. Fortuitously, the University had an able replacement already on campus in Donald C. Kleckner, who had come to the University two years earlier as director of Proposal Preparation and Major Gifts in the Development Office. Prior tenures as president of Elmhurst (Illinois) College and Chapman College in Orange, California, more than qualified him to lead Alfred North Whitehead College. He shared Atkins's faith in adult education, and his administrative savvy would keep Whitehead prosperous until 1985, when competition in the adult market became fierce. So esteemed were Kleckner's qualifications that the trustees would ask him to step in as acting president of the University within a year, as Dawson's era waned.

PRIDE, PROTEST, AND PENURY

The Dawson years witnessed many structural changes in faculty governance, departmental organization, and student life. Continuing budget deficits, cash-flow issues, debt, enrollment worries, and increased student-aid costs plagued the president. In addition, student unrest during the early 1970s enervated college and university campuses nationwide. The annals of American higher education contain no analogue to this period of student activism, alienation, and acrimony. The animosity between older and younger generations seemed to bewilder those charged with the governance of the country's boiling campuses, and sheer mistrust predominated on all sides. The

A Legacy of Service

For more than half a century, students of the University of Redlands have provided a wealth of services for both the institution and the community. Two sophomore service clubs, SPURS and Yeomen, exist for no other purpose. The underlying role of these organizations is to uphold the traditions of the University while promoting school spirit, sponsoring school functions, and fostering a general feeling of loyalty and kindness among the student body. Members serve as official hosts of the University, greeting visitors and ushering at special functions.

SPURS, a National Women's Honorary Service Organization, was founded on February 14, 1922, by members of the Cap and Gown Society (predecessors of Mortar Board) at Montana State College at Bozeman. The original SPURS settled on the emblem of the "Spur" to signify their organization. The shank stands for union, the shield represents defense, the chain represents a living "chain" of SPURS, and the rowel stands for continuing duty to service. The term SPURS stands for Service, Patriotism, Understanding, Responsibility, and Sacrifice. The yellow chrysanthemum was chosen as the SPURS flower to signal unwavering assistance to the community. The group's motto is "At Your Service."

On March 15, 1933, the University of Redlands became the fourteenth institution in the country to install a chapter of SPURS. All coeds at the University with a 2.5 grade-point average or higher during the fall semester of their freshman year qualify for SPURS. SPURS hopefuls are elected in the spring of their freshman year, based on their activities, citizenship, and character—the group selects only thirty members. SPURS members year-long duties include ushering at convocation, organizing the SPURS Lantern parade, and offering assistance to incoming freshmen. The most celebrated SPURS function at Redlands, the SPURS Spring Spree in April, is the largest formal dance of the year. While the national organization dissolved in 2005, the tradition continues at many colleges, including the University of Redlands.

In contrast to SPURS, the Yeomen Sophomore Service Club is a purely Redlands phenomenon. It was established on September 23, 1937, with

Mervyn R. Voth '40 as the first president. The organization, one of the oldest on campus, selects its members according to their participation in school activities, athletics, character, and scholarship of their freshman year. By definition, the "Yeoman" is a freeholder of a lower status than a gentleman who cultivates his own land. In medieval England, the "Yeoman of the Guard" served to protect the king and his functionaries. For their logo, the Yeomen chose the archer, symbolizing strength and service to humanity. Yeomen was initially an all-male organization at the University of Redlands until it became coed in 1979. As their motto, Yeomen took a passage from the Bible, "He that is greatest among you shall be your servant." Among their list of annual duties to the University are sponsoring the Freshman Square Dance in front of the Chapel, setting up the luminarias for the Feast of Lights, and decorating the football field. — BJG '04

degree of severity of the generational divide stands out, but nevertheless it did not differ in kind from age-old conflicts. As historian Dexter Perkins observed about young Kaiser Wilhelm II and old Bismarck: the latter always addressed the former "in the imperial tones of condescension which have always irked the spirit of youth."

Armacost presided over the beginning of this period, but retirement spared him the full brunt of student fury. Although Dawson rode the wave of animosity at its crest, Armacost understood the stakes all too well. In the following passage from *Whose Emblem Shines Afar*, he and coauthors Ralph E. Hone and Esther Mertins summarized the psychic health of the United States during the first term of Richard Nixon's presidency and assessed its impact on the nation's institutions of higher education:

> The conflict in Vietnam was distressing enough. When the unauthorized invasions of Cambodia and Laos occurred, indignation — especially of students — soared.

A severe recession occurred. Inflation began to mount cruelly, and the President's wage-freeze only increased wide anxiety. There was also gathering discontent with Nixon's racial policies. There was even more pronounced disgust with Vice President Spiro Agnew (forced to resign in 1973): Agnew's tough stand on law and order, his attack on opponents of the Vietnam War as disloyal, and his criticism of intellectuals and college students stood forth as the grossest hypocrisy when his own political career was brought to light. Even though Nixon achieved a phased withdrawal of American troops from Southeast Asia, there was no escaping broad disillusionment with government. And, of course, the media helped to publicize scandal at home and in Vietnam.

With such a periphery, it was hard for the University to pursue business as usual. . . . Students began to view the liberal arts as embroidery. . . .

The students of the University of Redlands, both at Johnston and the College of Arts and Sciences, hardly proved immune to their generation's zeitgeist. And the University responded to the times. The reforms, some quite substantive, echoed similar measures taken at colleges across the land. At Redlands Dawson appointed a long-range planning committee to explore student life, curriculum and instruction, faculty and staff, organization and structure, and resources and finance. In short, student unrest helped fuel a massive overhaul of campus operations.

Some of the most noticeable reforms occurred in the area of student life. Among the earliest measures was the creation in 1971 of "correlative" dormitories. Ardently sought by students, the new residence halls housed men and women on different floors. Johnston College integrated its two dormitories easily enough, while a vanguard of women crossing the Quad's east side later made Cortner Hall the first coed residence among the older dorms. Students also received support from the president's office to serve on more than twenty-two committees governing campus life. To improve communication between the student body and the administration, Dawson launched Round Table meetings, at which he hosted open forums.

In addition to coed dormitories, other outcomes of the long-range planning committee's work included implementation of a commission on human relations, a commission on the status of women, a new freshman exploratory program, changes in faculty governance, and a consolidation of academic divisions. By 1972 the accreditation team for Western Schools and Colleges would praise the changes, commending especially broad participation by all segments and members of the University community in determining new policies and directions.

The two commissions reflected the local manifestation of another nationwide phenomenon: activism and unrest among coeds and students of color. The commissions addressed their concerns regarding campus climate and faculty and curricular inclusiveness. Change did not always occur quickly or easily. As had their counterparts at other schools, minority students at Redlands felt compelled to force administrators' hands. The issue came to a head during the winter and spring of 1974, when someone painted racial slurs and obscenities in Johnston College's West Hall, which housed about one-fifth of the campus's black students.

Here was one issue about which both Johnston and Arts and Sciences students could readily agree: something had to be done. One March afternoon, reported the *Redlands Daily Facts*, about "60 black students . . . gathered on the steps of the administration building at about 5:00 p.m." A spokesman for the students read a statement calling "the University a racist institution." He cited intense pressure upon black students, especially during the previous six weeks when many received threatening, anonymous notes. Dawson attempted to read a statement expressing concern about "the deplorable acts," but the students walked away before he could finish.

Anger and frustration had simmered too long for a mere presidential statement to ameliorate the situation. One protester urged the group to relocate the rally to the Commons, then packed with students eating dinner. About half the demonstrators entered the building and invited the diners to depart. They then began to upend tables and garbage cans. Fortunately, the only casualties were some broken dishes.

The event served as a vent for anger, fear, and frustration. Many of the black students stayed behind to clean up, expressing regret. In perhaps his finest performance as president of the University, Dawson acted quickly and decisively to ratchet down the racial tension. A statement to the University community denounced the anonymous threats and promised prosecution of those responsible. Lest anyone dismiss this statement as hollow posturing, he summoned the FBI to handle the criminal investigation. The president also calmed fears by hiring additional security guards, confiscating a few guns and ammunition found in dormitory rooms, and narrowing the list of suspects to five.

The University community might have dismissed the threatening notes and inflammatory graffiti as the work of one or two racist individuals. Instead, it chose to gauge its own complicity. Dawson constituted a special committee on institutional racism. Composed of faculty and admin-

istrators, the body heard from over 150 black and Chicano students. With some parents present, the group cataloged the grievances. Collectively, the list suggested that the institution had engaged in active discrimination. Heated discussion produced charges of prejudicial practices in admissions, financial aid, classroom interaction, and hiring policies. Sub-committees researched the charges. Quite understandably, some parents expressed concern for their children's safety. They stressed that the issue of racism had non-academic elements and asked the University for emotional support as well.

One week later, Dawson received the committee's report and responded by announcing major policy changes, which included methods to encourage sensitivity to minority-student issues. The report also advocated increasing minority representation in personnel and allowing greater student "input into University policy making decisions." Reporting on the recommendations, the *Redlands Daily Facts* found both progress and a "considerably softened mood" among minority coeds on campus. Some black students appeared skeptical but hopeful. The

Office of Student Life announced a dozen "black, oriental, and Spanish surnamed students" had been appointed as resident assistants in the dorms. Such language sounds biased today, but this initiative did result in new campus leadership, one of the protestors' demands. The committee also envisioned curricular reform. So, too, the library announced a plan to increase its holdings of books on minorities and ethnic studies.

Despite the prompt response by the University, the rancor did not die out immediately. On March 25, about forty black students staged a sit-down protest from 8:00 a.m. to 5:00 p.m. at the entrance to the Administration Building. Protestors carried signs demanding implementation of the Special Committee's recommendations and condemning continuing racism on campus. Unwilling to cross the picket line to enter the University, employees circulated a petition to verify that they had tried to go to work. Some animosity still lingered three years later. In May 1978, the Dawson administration confronted a list of demands from "Mexican-American students [who] have been allotted a 15 minute portion of the University of Redlands Board of Trustees meeting. . . . " These demands included regular review of student reports at trustee meetings (already granted); funds to hire bilingual professors and a bilingual cultural officer to recruit Chicano students; and the establishment of a Chicano studies department and an outreach program to neighboring inland communities.

Amid the hullabaloo surrounding Johnston, financial

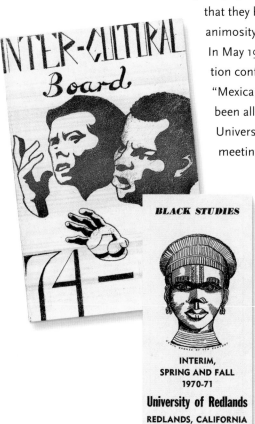

distress, and student unrest, it is easy to overlook the many achievements of the 1970s. Innovations occurred in the classroom, in foreign programs, in performance, and on the playing field. A living and learning center to accommodate visiting artists and writers was created in Anderson Hall. The Humanities Division sponsored annual career days. The School of Music presented a diverse range of performances. Old standbys such as Student Government Day, University Day, Parents' Day, Founders' Day, Homecoming, and Alumni Day drew many through the introduction of innovative programming.

An anonymous gift announced in January 1974 supplied a new carillon in the tower of the Memorial Chapel. It provided the tonal equivalent of 79,462 pounds of cast bells.

A singular honor recognizing the University's academic excellence occurred in 1976, when at long last the University of Redlands was granted a chapter of Phi Beta Kappa. The chapter

BOTTOM: A long-sought goal was realized on April 24, 1977, when the University's first Phi Beta Kappa chapter was sworn in. Those inducted were Robyn A. Birnbaum '77, Carol A. Bjorklund '77, Hilary A. Bray '77, Susan P. Christensen '77, James H. Elliott '77, David O. Hall '77, Barbara A. Hrivnak '77, Dennis B. Jenkins '77, Gary E. Kasler '77, Nancy J. Kleidon '77, Gregory D. Langworthy '77, Martin A. Lewis '77, Joseph P. Skorupa '77, Julia A. Spain '77, Stephanie I. Splane '77, Nora L. Vitz '77, Rebecca Wilson '77, and Daniel P. Whitmore '77.

BELOW: The 1973 Interim class taught by Professor of History Richard Andrews sponsored a well-attended sock-hop in Currier Gymnasium.

installed its first members in 1977, finally realizing a dream first pursued by President Victor L. Duke in the 1920s. The charter group inducted that spring included eighteen students and sixteen faculty. Alumni members added in later years enriched the mix.

When Dawson assumed the presidency in 1970, the University was preparing to matriculate the largest group of new students in its sixty-three year history. Both the College of Arts and Sciences and Johnston College exceeded enrollment predictions, in spite of fewer applications, and, as Dean of Admissions Kenton W. Corwin pointed out, the "increasingly competitive and challenging" world of recruitment.

An effort to make Redlands home to one of the premier alumni programs among colleges in the United States was born with the arrival of Merilyn H. Bonney as alumni director in January 1977. Bonney was the recipient of awards from CASE, the professional higher-education fundraising and marketing society, acknowledging her effective leadership and innovative ideas. A few months later, the Gannett Communications Center was dedicated in what had been the Little Theatre on the Zanja. A $150,000 grant produced additional academic space, as well as housing for the radio station KUOR. Academic enhancements during the Dawson years included a gift from the Proudian family of Chatsworth of $150,000 to begin an honors program for fifteen freshmen.

Faculty distinguished themselves during these years with publications in

political science, literature, fiction, and chemistry. These included Ralph E. Hone, Eugene Kanjo, William Main, Bruce McAllister, and Robert L. Stuart in the English Department. Barney Child and Philip Rehfeldt created highly acclaimed musical compositions. James B. Ifft produced an admirable oeuvre in chemistry.

Johnston was now thriving. In 1977 the institution was reaccredited and showered with high praise. Johnston students made conspicuous contributions to campus life through their participation in publications, drama, athletics, and honor societies. Many regarded the return of Eugene G. Ouellette

in the fall of 1978 as a good omen. Ouellette immediately focused his efforts on recruitment and admissions.

The combination of the University's budget deficit and President Dawson's waning influence created a juggernaut that would end his reign. In most respects, it would be unfair to label Dawson as the architect of his own demise. Events overtook many of his initiatives and prevented their immediate implementation. Moreover, the institution's financial woes were basically outside his control. Nevertheless, stagnation characterized the last years of Dawson's tenure. The continuing erosion of the University's financial picture and flat enrollment took a toll on campus morale and on the president's ability to lead.

In sharp contrast to the Armacost years, Dawson's presidency witnessed little or no change to the campus physical plant. No new capital construction occurred, and most renovations had to be deferred. A 1975 fire—deemed arson—in Wallichs Theatre inflicted serious damage. The perpetrator was never caught. In a move to infuse its coffers with quick cash, the University sold several parcels of real estate, including large undeveloped tracts in south Redlands, properties downtown, and land north of the University just above the athletic fields. The sales generated badly needed cash but limited future expansion options.

Even worse was the hint of malfeasance. Accounting blunders by the Business Office in the sale of University assets pointed to questionable actions on the part of a few employees. A questionable financial deal surfaced involving an academic administrator. The fiduciary behavior of a member of the Development Office added to the institution's woes. Hints of financial shenanigans only exacerbated the sense of malaise, and the administration could do little to stem the chatter. Anyone familiar with the Redlands campus environment at the time understood that confidences were rarely kept and "witch hunts" took place in relation to many situations. Only during the Great Freeze of 1913 and the Great Depression of the 1930s had the University faced such dire challenges.

For many months, it seemed to the inner circle of the Board of Trustees that Dawson had become overwhelmed by serious financial issues. Individuals in the administration and faculty confirmed the fears. Board Chairman Milo Bekins even attended a secret off-campus gathering with ASUR leaders, who cooked dinner and described their difficulties with Dawson. They urged his removal.

To honor the faith of the founders seventy-five years earlier, the trustees needed stability. Putting the gossip mill out of business was paramount. The concerns of students, faculty, and staff reaffirmed that assessment. Only those far removed from the situation could have been surprised in January 1978 when the Executive Committee of the board suddenly announced Dawson's departure. They granted him a one-year sabbatical and the title of President Emeritus. The negotiations, behind closed doors, had proven difficult. Both town and gown took sides. Nevertheless, the Dawson period was over. Strong, mixed feelings lingered for years, echoes of Clarence Howe Thurber's dismissal as president four decades earlier.

In Thurber's day, however, no one questioned the University's ultimate survival. At this juncture, by contrast, doubt existed in some quarters about whether it could continue to exist. Responsible for keeping the doors open, the trustees showed their mettle and proved their dedication. For the remainder of the school year, the board exercised a greater degree of oversight. Chairman Bekins and the Executive Committee oversaw policy issues, while University attorney Tom McPeters was responsible for day-to-day operations. Soon thereafter the board tapped Donald Kleckner, provost of Whitehead College, to serve as acting president. These actions ensured administrative stability while the trustees pondered weightier questions.

The transition afforded an opportunity to pose soul-searching inquiries about the future of the University. Closed doors concealed serious, painful discussions. Could the University of Redlands survive the massive financial fissure it faced? Could it address faculty salaries that lagged behind national averages? Could it meet the needs of a deteriorating physical plant? This sobering dialogue consumed the attention of the men and · women of the board as they contemplated the solution of the most important issue of all: What sort of person could best lead the University out of this morass? The answer to that critical question could not have mattered more.

9

Righting the Ship

"The Seventh President: Not a Time for Faint Hearts."

— GEORGE H. ARMACOST, RALPH E. HONE, AND ESTHER MERTINS

MOORE ENERGY

When the position of University of Redlands president was advertised nationally in the spring of 1978, the qualifications listed emphasized fundraising expertise and managerial competence. The announcement presented a capsule view of the University, noting that its campus lay in a 130-acre, parklike setting with three schools, the College of Arts and Sciences, Johnston College, and Alfred North Whitehead College. It boasted a total of 3,200 registered students; 1,100 undergraduates lived on campus and another 500 resided nearby. Whitehead College accounted for another 1,600. While the advertisement created the image of a typical campus atmosphere and a healthy enrollment, the trustees understood that many qualified candidates would shy away from what was in fact a troubled institution.

Nonetheless, the search committee received over two hundred applications, and it set a new precedent by having members visit the short-list candidates' home bases to check on their credentials. The search narrowed to two, both of whom were invited to campus. For reasons that no doubt made sense at the time, the committee arranged for both individuals to be on campus concurrently, even lodging them in the same motel. Board Chairman Milo Bekins urged one of the candidates, Douglas R. Moore, president of Minnesota's Mankato State University, to retire to his room for a few hours' relaxation following his interview while he rounded up a quorum of the search committee for further deliberations. Welcoming this reprieve from the stresses of the interview process, Moore and his wife, Becky, returned to the Sandman Motel, where they doffed their formal clothing and prepared to settle in for a much-needed nap.

Suddenly, a sharp knock interrupted their quiet. Moore hastily dressed and opened the door. He found Bekins standing outside, manifesting the guilty air of a Duke-era student caught outside after curfew. With a loud, conspiratorial whisper, the chairman of the board pleaded, "Quick! Let me in. I don't want the other candidate to see me." As Bekins entered the room, Becky Moore—attired only in her bathrobe—heard Bekins inform her husband, "We want you." Apparently wishing to exclude her from the negotiations, Bekins directed Moore into the bathroom. And so it was that the amazed Moore, wedged between the shower and sink in a second-rate motel bathroom, learned that beginning in August he was to become the seventh president of the University of Redlands.

Moore had accumulated extensive administrative experience before he took the reins of Redlands. He had a national reputation as a consultant on higher education, and served on the boards of several professional academic organizations. He had received his undergraduate degree at Texas Wesleyan College in Fort Worth in 1950. From Boston University School of Theology, he earned an S.T.B. (Bachelor of Sacred Theology) in 1957, and a Ph.D. in psychology and counseling in 1964 from Boston University. At one point, he had been a full-time Methodist minister; later he became dean of students, then provost, at Callison College of the University of the Pacific in Stockton, California. He had served as president of Mankato State since 1974.

Moore found himself attracted to the genuine sense of community that existed at Redlands. Acknowledging the serious
issues the University faced, he declared that the "last thing this
institution needs is to engage in self-denigration and to feed
impulses toward pessimism—things are *not* bad here." He
also pointed out that, while strong and accountable leadership
was necessary, it should not and could not be executed in an
autocratic manner but rather in an "open and candid" fashion.

RETRENCHMENT

The new president spent the first year in office studying and
listening. His findings led him to conclude that reorganization
was essential. His inaugural address, on November 16, 1978,
outlined two goals: first, a need for unity, to focus on and demonstrate direction and purpose; and second, a re-commitment
to excellence by increasing faculty salaries and services.

Candidly, President Moore addressed the trustees on the
problem of student enrollment numbers and fiscal shortfalls. At
a special trustees' meeting on March 19, 1979, he presented a
new structure for the University. Although Dawson had implemented a re-organizational plan three years earlier, the new
president felt the University's financial situation required even
more profound change.

Moore now proffered several recommendations, so profound
in their implications that they effectively abandoned the vision
of a multicollege university undertaken scarcely more than a
decade earlier. First, he proposed to redefine the two collateral
colleges as academic centers within the University. A director
would head the administrative apparatus of each and would
report to the vice president of academic affairs. Second, that
vice president would now assume authority over all academic
programs in every unit of the University. This made superfluous
the Johnston College Board of Overseers; thus the third recommendation was for the dissolution of that body. Displaced overseers were offered an opportunity to serve on the President's
Advisory Council; they might also receive consideration for the
Board of Trustees as vacancies occurred. With trustee ratifica-
tion of these three recommendations, Johnston and Whitehead
ceased to exist as semi-autonomous entities.

Other recommendations had ramifications beyond the two
collateral colleges. The fourth proposal called upon University
faculty, staff, and students to create new, comprehensive systems of representative governance. The fifth and last proposal
was an omnibus measure to overhaul the administrative apparatus. Revitalization of student recruitment and admissions
would address the root cause of the financial woes: declining
admission. In the wake of Johnston's and Whitehead's new
status, further opportunities for administrative consolidation
became possible. Finally, greater scrutiny would be given to
contract renewals and vacancies.

Inevitably, the decision to close Johnson as a college was not
universally popular. Hoping against hope to postpone implementation, Johnstonians placed their confidence in Chancellor
Eugene G. Ouellette and the faculty. The die, however, had been
cast, with economic issues paramount behind the decision. In
reviewing the need to stem the flow of red ink, centralize disparate operations, and place the University upon secure financial
footing, Professor Emeritus Robert L. Stuart recalled, "I do not
believe he [Moore] has ever been given enough credit for the

Student Hangouts

In many ways, the student experience at Redlands is inextricably linked to the off-campus places where students gathered to relax, get away from their books, or avoid another institutional meal. Over the years, these local establishments have come and gone, but they all remain vivid in the memories of those who made late-night runs to Donut Hut in Mentone or the further-off Tommy's Burger in Los Angeles, enjoyed happy hour at Cask 'n Cleaver or Gay 90s, or took a date for a soda at Pete's Malt Shop.

Annabill's
B & B Drive-In
Bob's Big Boy
Bob's Donut Shop & Sandwich Grill
Burgerbar
Cask 'n Cleaver
Charlie Jewel's
Cuca's
Curry Ice Cream
Curt's Drive In
Donut Hut (Mentone)
El Burrito
El Gate Gordo
The Falconer
Flamingo Cocktail Lounge
Forest Falls
Fox Theater
Frank and Maria's (Mentone Beach)
Gay 90s
Golden Spoon
Gourmet Pizza Shoppe
Hudlow's Drive In

Jazz & Java
Kramer's Drive In
KUOR (campus radio station)
Law's Coffee Shop (Oak Glen)
Minnie & Clyde's
Mitten's Fountain
MJ's on Q
Moore's Café
Muscle Mike's Tavern
Pete's Malt Shop
Pete's Pie Shop (Yucaipa)
Phil's of Redlands; also,
    Phil's Charcoal Broiler
Pinky's
Pizza Chalet
Putter 'n Putt Miniature Golf
Redman Grill
Reubens
Scott's Drive-In
Shakey's Pizza Parlor
Skateland Recreation Center
State Street West
Taco Blanco
Tod's Coffee Shop
Tommy's Burger (Los Angeles)
Triangle Chocolate Shop
Uncle Howie's Pizza
University Ice Cream Co.
The Vault
V-Bill Corner
Walt's Drive Inn
Willie's Brookside Drive In
Winn's Drug Store and
    Soda Fountain

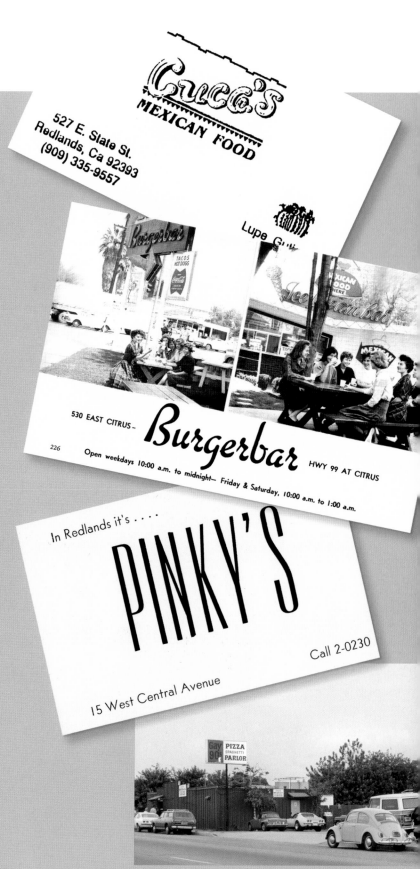

wisdom and courage of his decision to reorganize the University radically."

In *A History of Johnston College*, William McDonald and Kevin O'Neill summarized what happened in one telling sentence: "So the University decided to close the college, but keep the program." They also acknowledged that Johnston was in no position to resist. The subsequent absorption of the college's faculty into the University College of Arts and Sciences involved lengthy and difficult negotiations. Ultimately, however, it enriched the undergraduate University faculty, both in leadership and in scholarship. The core of the Johnston teaching force was retained. Stuart, who later served as Moore's special assistant, acknowledged that, while alarming to many, "the President's [total organizational] decision was wise and saved the University from even greater financial trouble. It did not, however, save us from continuing deficits."

Having made the difficult decision to downsize Johnston, the next challenge was how best to preserve the experimental college's educational experience. Fortunately, Moore was familiar with the challenges faced by a start-up collateral college within an older, established institution, from his days overseeing Callison College at the University of the Pacific. This experience shaped his attitude regarding the inherent educational value of Johnston.

Controversy over the president's appointment of an academic vice president added to the woes. A search committee

recommended three finalists, ranking the acting vice president, Gerald Gates, third. In March 1980, Moore nonetheless rejected their first and second choices and instead selected Gates, who had been a very popular biology professor. Committee members immediately groused about the snub. Still smarting over the closure of Johnston, many of the faculty viewed the selection of Gates as further evidence of presidential imperiousness. Looking back on the episode from the safety of retirement, Robert Stuart opined that Moore had chosen the best candidate after all. Acceptance of the search committee's first preference, he declared, "would have been a disaster." Nevertheless, rumors swirled regarding a no-confidence vote by the faculty, and even the trustees communicated some "stiff" comments regarding Moore's handling of the situation. The president defused the tension with an apology. While admitting errors and acknowledging failure "to work more closely" and to communicate "more effectively," he staunchly defended his choice: "I have no intention of resigning and running from the work before us."

Two months later, Moore touted to the trustees a host of University assets, including strong international programs, Johnston, Whitehead, the beautiful campus, and an atmosphere that nurtured students academically. He also encouraged new initiatives in academic affairs, student life, and athletics. He extended the spirit of renewal to the board itself: "It is time for us to get to work in making this a great place to be and to stop flagellating ourselves and washing our dirty linen in public." To infuse new blood, Moore and the trustees launched a concerted effort to recruit new board members from outside the traditional network of alumni and friends.

Student levels continued to be a major issue, as revenues declined in proportion to shrinkage in matriculation and retention. In four of the five years from 1978 through 1982, all divisions recorded fewer students. Higher enrollments would enhance the residential experience and also bolster costly

tuition subsidies. As President Moore remarked, "Redlands has to get beyond subsistence and get some fat on its bones."

Thus, Moore and his cabinet began a major reorganization of the administrative division. Following the reassignment of long-time Director of Admissions Kenton Corwin '48 as special assistant to the president, Director of Student Activities Charlotte G. Burgess '69, '70 became acting dean of admissions in 1979. Her charge: take a new team of admissions reps and present the Redlands story in areas not yet visited by recruiters. Starting in September, she and her assistant dean, Phillip L. Doolittle '76, increased the applications and matriculation numbers in the face of increased competition among the private liberal arts colleges in Southern California. The effort of larger institutions such as the University of California, Stanford, and even east coast Ivy League schools to attract California's top students further complicated recruitment. Steven C. Hankins replaced Burgess in 1981, when she became dean of students, and by 1984 President Moore was able to delight in the results of their labors. Both undergraduate residential programs and the Whitehead Center for returning adult students boasted higher enrollments.

After years of deferred maintenance, the physical plant cried out for attention and care. No major improvement to the dining

and religious gatherings, the Chapel was showing wear and tear. New paint, lighting, carpeting, and a sound system literally lifted spirits.

To enable these various improvements, the University took out bonds arranged through Moody's Investors Services. However, interest rates on the bonds further stressed the annual budget and endowment income.

A 1976 bequest from the estate of Mary Kimberly Shirk, longtime Redlands resident and philanthropist,

facility had been undertaken in two decades, and the update of the Commons in 1980 proved popular. Cosmetic enhancements were made to Duke Hall and Grace Parker Hall of Letters. Also pointing to a newly invigorated atmosphere and cautious optimism on campus was the decision to give the Memorial Chapel a facelift. After nearly sixty years of hosting speakers, performances,

created an endowment to bring important women to campus to address issues of the day. Over the years, the line-up

of speakers included such diverse luminaries as Pearl Bailey, Jane Fonda, Betty Ford, and Gail Sheehy.

A DIAMOND JUBILEE

The seventy-fifth anniversary of the University, in 1982, served both as a tonic and an energizer. A committee of sixty volunteers was assembled to oversee and implement the planning of the event. The anniversary became the focus of both an internal and external public-

relations outreach. Three years in the making, it was chaired by Trustee Larry E. Burgess '67, archivist at the A. K. Smiley Public Library, and staffed by the indefatigable alumni director, Merilyn Bonney. The anniversary year occasioned major events, academic programs and symposia, a musical and a gala, special publications, and a spectacular fireworks display.

A timely offer by the aerospace giant TRW's San Bernardino branch to underwrite the entire printing and mailing expense for the year enabled an event unprecedented in University history. From the opening convocation, honoring seventy-five of the University's most distinguished alumni and a keynote address given by attorney and diplomat Warren M. Christopher '46, to the closing dinner at the San Bernardino Hilton, the University set a new benchmark. An important outgrowth of the Diamond Jubilee was the formation of a "friend-raising" group for residents of Redlands and surrounding communities. To be called Town and Gown, the organization was to support on-campus social programs and underwrite scholarships for local and regional students. The central fundraising vehicle for the scholarships became the innovative and highly successful annual luncheon, "A Woman's Place Is Every Place," which

honors women of achievement from San Bernardino and Riverside counties. From its very beginning, Town and Gown has drawn a wide audience of residents of these locales. At present its scholarship endowment stands at more than $500,000, and its membership has grown from the initial one hundred to seven hundred.

Although the management of the Redlands Symphony Orchestra was transferred to an independent non-profit organization in 1979, the University has continued to be a major guarantor of the budget and to supply the facility for performances. From 1980 the symphony had been ably conducted by Professors Jack Wilson and James Jorgenson. When the conductor's position opened up, Jon Robertson was hired. He immediately began to make adjustments in the staging of concerts, added new selections to the repertory, and created a professional, unionized orchestra, always including in its ranks two or three outstanding School of Music students. The orchestra has gained a reputation throughout Southern California and has received many state arts grants for its excellence.

It Takes a Village

Looking back on collegiate careers years after the fact, most alumni probably recall one or two professors or administrators who made a difference in their lives. But no university could function without the help of those who work behind the scenes. From the groundskeepers to the dishwashers, from department secretaries to

mechanics, staff members keep the University humming. Often serving the institution longer than the average faculty member, staff handle most of the day-to-day tasks—no less essential to the University's mission than a history lecture or chemistry lab.

Staff members most likely to be remembered by students would be housekeepers or food servers, the people with whom they interacted on a regular basis. For example, many residents of Cortner Hall and Billings House during the 1960s and 1970s probably recall Virgie Margee, the gregarious housekeeper who was responsible for the two buildings. Virgie used to regale the women of Billings House with tales of the Cortner men's outrages—sloth, snakes, and sniping.

Those same students may well remember food server Tess Happe, who was often anything but. Students from a slightly later generation may recall Norm Venables, then director of the campus food service. His father, Dick, made banana bread every day. Wanda Webb joined the Saga team in 1981 and continued to swipe IDs as a cashier for Bon Appetit during the 2005–06 school year. Webb starts everyone's mealtime with a smile and her signature greeting, "How are you today, honey?" Whether the customer is the freshest freshman, a grizzled professor, or a senior vice president, they are all "honey" to her.

Not all staff members have regular contact with students. Harriet Barents ran a coffee lounge in the basement of the Administration Building. The space, closed to students, became a haven for faculty and staff, a welcome respite from a day's hard work. Each morning the smell of freshly baked chocolate-chip cookies wafted through the building. For employees drawn in by the aroma, Barents's shop became a mecca for fine conversation and local gossip. When she retired in 1987 after a twenty-year run, the University made no attempt to continue her unique niche. Vending machines occupied the former coffee lounge, and a longstanding locus of cordiality and conviviality faded from the scene.

The individuals mentioned above represent but a small sampling of the memorable characters employed by the University during its century of existence. Their example must stand to represent the professionalism and dedication of their peers and coworkers, without whom the University could not function.—JDM

RETRENCHING REDUX

President Moore sought to emphasize the importance of the liberal arts. This initiative came at a time when many parents and students viewed college primarily as a ticket to well-compensated employment. Moore decried the "obsession" with career preparation. "Our educational efforts," he declared at the opening convocation in 1983, "must first and last be focused on life, on how to live, and not on 'making a living.'"

Despite all of the positive elements put in place for the Diamond Jubilee, the financial picture remained problematic. After meeting with the administration and Executive Committee, the full board authorized deletion or cutbacks in eighteen academic programs. The president hoped the retrenchment would curb deficits, allow more concentration on existing programs, and encourage their improvement. "We must make a few things excellent [rather] than many things mediocre," he said. In 1983 he called for the termination of a number of faculty positions. The proposed cutbacks were intended to help the University provide more competitive faculty salaries, which remained below national norms.

Much anxiety prevailed on campus that fall. When word leaked out about the possible changes, students demonstrated, asking that cherished majors such as dance, theater, geology, and physical education be retained. They continued to express dismay over the next three years, with the last of the protests caused by dance-program cuts occurring in May 1986. Some alumni harbored what they believed to be justified resentment for the elimination of their majors; many, especially geology graduates, curtailed their support of the University.

Balancing the need to achieve financial solvency with that of being sensitive to student demands and alumni complaints proved to be very difficult. Many faculty, students, and alumni came to see the reluctant decision by the Board of Trustees to eliminate eighteen programs as dogmatic and not fully thought out. Complicating the situation were the duplicitous actions of some faculty whose departments suffered cutbacks or elimination. Privately, they informed the president of their assent to the recommendations, but then publicly decried these actions in the press. Vice President of Academic Affairs Daniel Cohen, who replaced Gates in 1985, was charged with implementing the controversial curricular reforms. Following Cohen's departure for another position, William Jones assumed the academic leadership post.

A HOUSE CAN BE A HOME

In 1984 the University chose to commemorate the centennial of the City of Redlands, looming four years hence, by replanting a grove of Washington navel orange trees at a long-abandoned field on Colton Avenue at Grove Street. This act proved a metaphor for renewed growth and faith in the future. The grove and others that followed on campus became working green space; profits from the annual crops were placed in a fund for ongoing upkeep. The Centennial Grove's first crop was harvested in January 1988.

Changes in neighborhood demographics by 1986 prompted an important decision. For many months, President Moore had deliberated about the utility of the President's Mansion as a personal residence. While its campus location seemed ideal for this function, there were drawbacks. Long gone were the orange groves and sleepy lane that had led to it. Privacy was now hard to come by. Subdivisions sprouted where trees once stood, and traffic sped down Grove Street. Many residents in surrounding homes strolled through the grounds at all hours. Early one morning, Becky Moore entered her kitchen, only to be confronted by strangers. A group of perplexed students wandering the grounds had found a back service door ajar and decided to peer in. She quickly concluded that the duties

of presidential wife did not extend to being gawked at in her bathrobe while trying to enjoy her morning coffee. The time had come for a change. Ultimately, the University purchased a new president's home on the hill in an exclusive area south of town just below Sunset Drive. It served as the president's residence through the tenure of Moore's successor, James R. Appleton. When Appleton retired, in 2005, he purchased it in accordance with a prior contractual agreement.

Moore proposed that the former President's Mansion be renamed Alumni House. In May 1986, Alumni House became the home to Alumni Relations, Town and Gown, and the Faculty Club. The house provides a venue for these organizations' activities, including official meetings and social gatherings, as well as limited housing for visiting alumni and dignitaries. In many ways, therefore, President Jasper Newton Field's once-controversial residence continues to serve as the social hub of the campus.

An issue lingering since the era of President Victor L. Duke became the focus of President Moore in the summer of 1986. He called for the closure of Colton Avenue between Grove and University Streets. Throughout the rest of the summer and fall, the City Council, city officials, neighbors, students, alumni, and staff were embroiled in an often acrimonious debate. The issue of public safety combined with the logic of future planning had produced the Colton Avenue initiative. Moore had correctly predicted that the city's future housing plans east of Grove along Colton Avenue would make Colton a major four-lane artery, with thousands of cars passing through campus daily. By December opponents had geared up for a fight. Redlands had a population of nearly 50,000 while the campus had but 1,400 resident students. The city refused to close a major east/west artery. Colton Avenue would have to wait for another day.

FOOTING REGAINED

Despite the acrimony generated by the Colton Avenue initiative, a series of positive events characterize Douglas Moore's last years in office. Accomplishments covered all facets of the University, from its relationship with the City of Redlands to the physical plant and to campus life in general.

The social turmoil that roiled the entire country during the early 1970s and post-Vietnam War period had inflicted wounds on the town and gown relationship. Moore sought to heal these rifts by including townspeople in appropriate functions and initiating many new ones specifically for them, including access to lectures, athletic events, and campus festivals. To bring more collegiality to campus and to provide a forum for intellectual interchange, he inaugurated the President's High Table lecture series. He often attended the Faculty Club's regular Friday luncheons. Additions to the curriculum and to the physical plant enriched the town's quality of life. Truesdail Speech Center inaugurated a new communicative-disorders service. The facility offered both graduate and undergraduate students a training ground, and additional faculty introduced new areas of expertise to the center's offerings. The clinic extended professional services to the local community. In early 1980, upcoming major renovations to the campus prompted a seismic study to evaluate each building's need for retrofitting; a secondary purpose was to assess the ability of the campus to house nearby residents who might be displaced by an earthquake or other disaster.

New personnel and programs in student life also enlivened campus life. The hiring of Donald Shockley as chaplain reinvigorated traditional offerings and inspired new programs for multifaith groups. An alcohol-awareness program for students was inaugurated in 1984. Ever since the University opened its doors, students had often informally volunteered service to the Redlands community. In 1982 a student-coordinated program to assist senior citizens was established. Its success helped to sow fertile ground for a major initiative for community-service learning in the 1990s.

For the trustees, the main challenge of early 1980s was to eradicate the University's dependence on tuition to meet the budget. Working together, the president, the trustees, and the Development Office devised a plan to broaden the base of planned giving. They sought to increase commitment by alumni and friends to the annual fund. In 1986 a multi-million-dollar fundraising campaign began to take shape. Consultants, trustees, alumni, and selected potential donors conducted a series of meetings on campus to raise awareness. But on the brink of launching the campaign, human tragedy interceded.

One day in December, 1986, President Moore felt unwell. He then suffered a major heart attack. Doctors stabilized him, but he remained hospitalized in critical condition. Further analysis indicated immediate need for open-heart surgery. The campus was stunned. The rancor and ill-will surrounding Moore's controversial initiatives and cutbacks seemed to pale, as many feared his illness would retard the University's newly restored vigor. Even in the darkest times, Moore had manifested a genial personality, subtle humor, and a sense of accommodation for opposing opinions. Many of the president's harshest critics realized that his inherent honesty and genuine willingness to seek mutual compromise made him someone with whom they could work.

During Moore's recovery from surgery, University staff arranged a temporary downstairs office because he was anxious to get back to work. Slowly, but deliberately, he did. While at home on March 21, 1987, he complained to his wife about feeling weak and tired. Shortly afterward, he died. He was fifty-six years old.

At the memorial service for Moore in the Chapel, a capacity crowd of 1,500 shared the joy, sorrow, and regret over a productive life cut short. Grief and sympathy for Becky Moore and her children pervaded the room, along with an uncomfortable feeling that perhaps the mountain of stressful challenges had contributed to the tragedy of the president's premature death.

The acting presidency of William Jones, formerly academic vice president, witnessed the inevitable pushing of disparate agendas and jockeying for internal position that often accompanies the sudden loss of the person in charge.

In retrospect Moore's tenure should be viewed as an important transitional period, during which the University repositioned itself in structure, attitude, and focus. That it was a time of healing is illustrated by the re-energized supporters daunted during the Dawson years. The emerging leadership during this period of two alums who later chaired the Board of Trustees illustrates this point: H. Jess Senecal '52 (chair from 1987 to 1991) and Richard Hunsaker '52 (chair from 1992 to 2003).

Douglas R. Moore managed to reverse the University's long decline and generate considerable forward momentum. His legacy ensured that his successor stood poised to usher the chronically troubled University of Redlands into an era of prosperity unparalleled in its history. All that was needed was the right leadership. Fortunately, the trustees were on top of their game. They wasted no time in opening a search and had a new president in place by summer's end.

Chapter 10: 1987–2006

How Far the Dream?

"It is my opinion that our University, no matter how intellectually stimulating, is incomplete unless we maintain a simultaneous commitment to intellectual and moral excellence. This commitment, however, must always be tempered by individual choice—the freedom to make informed decisions. We must be intentional, while not jeopardizing openness."—JAMES R. APPLETON, APRIL 19, 1989

ENDING ONE CENTURY, BEGINNING ANOTHER

Writing about recent times discomfits the historian. By trade we sift through events, deeds, individuals, emotions, processes, triumphs, and tragedies of the past. A long lens helps us to refract their causes, impacts, and legacies. A short lens reveals a view that is too immediate, which leads often to badly crafted history. Two decades makes for good journalistic reviews but, with such a short lens, bad history. Achievements and capital improvements are readily documentable. Less apprehensible is the impact of curricular change or social mores and laws affecting student life. Any assessment of the long-term significance of such matters would be tenuous. With many of the actors still treading the stage, the historian must carefully consider every word he writes.

As a matter of professional conceit, we historians also prefer a certain detachment from our subject: the better to ensure objectivity. Yet your present author can hardly claim any pretense to objectivity, having served on the University of Redlands Board of Trustees since 1987. During much of that time, I also chaired the Campus Planning Committee. Heading a trustee committee also puts one automatically on the Executive Committee. These perches have guaranteed me

a front-row seat from which to observe the decisions, construction projects, and changes that comprise the tenure of the University's latest president. In addition, I am married to the vice president and dean of student life. While this vantage point certainly affords a tremendous opportunity for an insightful chapter, the historian in me counseled prudence. Years of professionalism emphasizing detachment are not easily discarded.

Thus, in writing this chapter, I faced a dual set of concerns, rather like a double-edged sword. If the need to assess the recent past posed one dilemma, my undeniable insider status posed a second one. How to tackle this uniquely personal challenge nagged me from the moment I agreed to write this book. Finally, the coin fell into the slot: I realized that only solipsistic hubris could lead me down the path of ignoring my personal participation in the events of these years. And so to render the University's recent past, I resolved to employ a different approach, one that breaks from the style and tone of the previous chapters. This chapter is less a story than a personal essay. Absent are many of the assessments that critical distance from events affords. My point of view is related in the first-person at the beginning and end of the chapter, and therefore the tone here is more intimate. I can only hope that the resulting overview

will guide whoever authors the sesquicentennial history fifty years hence. To that individual goes the responsibility of writing a complete account of these years.

SEARCHING FOR THE DESIRED NON-CANDIDATE

Over the summer of 1987, the Board of Trustees considered a number of individuals for the presidency. As is often the case, few candidates in an applicant pool are appropriate. Some are happy in their present situation. Some choose not to jeopardize existing positions by drawing attention to a bid for another one. Still others fear the sting of rejection. Fortunately, "head-hunter" services can frequently divine such candidates, often because they have been nominated for the job rather than applying for it themselves. The successor to Douglas R. Moore was found in this way. And yet not everyone involved recalls the process similarly.

One September evening in 1987, an old acquaintance telephoned me at home out of the blue. Then employed at the University of Southern California, the caller gushed excitedly over the board's selection of James R. Appleton as the eighth president of the University of Redlands. Having served as vice president for development at USC and as a dean of students,

Appleton, my friend assured me, possessed fundraising skills, energy, and vision. He would lead the university to new horizons of development. "Jim is simply the best!" he concluded.

As a "supposedly" knowledgable trustee, I made every effort to react as if I knew what the blazes the informant was telling me. The presidential search committee had been scrupulously close-to-the-vest in its approach. The C.I.A. should maintain such secrecy! This was the first I had heard of the decision. My wife and I had gone to school with the caller, who had learned the news from the nominee himself; Appleton was his boss. The ties of a close-knit community can fray almost imperceptibly.

A NEW PRESIDENT, RENEWED ENERGY

On a sunny Founders' Day in April 1988, James R. Appleton delivered his inaugural address; he had been at his new job since the previous November. The occasion for a formal inauguration provided an opportunity, he noted, to celebrate "this event, the rich past, challenging present, and the bright future for our University." A crowd of 2,500 welcomed him at the Alumni Greek Theatre and joined in a festive reception on the Quad following the music and speeches.

standoffs, as he called them — to create an atmosphere "of harmony and amazing faculty support." He continued, "This is a great student body!," signaling the importance of student engagement in the learning process. He noted the critical role of the physical plant and the need for refurbishment and expansion. He praised the dedicated staff. In assessing the financial situation, he outlined his aim to balance the budget and increase the endowment.

Appleton had been vice-president for development at USC since 1982. For ten years prior to that, he had been the university's vice-president for student affairs and had served as president of the National Association of Student Personnel Administrators. With a B.A. from Wheaton College in Illinois, and an M.A. and Ph.D. from Michigan State University, Appleton had accrued a diverse set of credentials and experience. He had coauthored *Pieces of Eight: The Rites, Roles, and Styles of the Dean* (1978) and contributed numerous articles to professional journals. The president's wife, Carol, a teacher, designer, and artist, brought to Redlands a cultural background that complemented her husband's experience. The couple was poised to launch Redlands into the future with appropriate energy and enthusiasm.

In his address, the president alluded to the issues facing the University. "It begins with the faculty," he stated, pointing to "their commitment, their teaching, their scholarly activity and research contribution to the quality of their teaching." Faculty development, improved salaries, and a sound working relationship with the administration became hallmarks of Appleton's tenure. Over the years, he would seek to address the strong mood of discontent that he had inherited—"we–they"

The majority of Appleton's remarks focused on the liberal arts tradition and the responsibility of Redlands to reaffirm its importance to society and to "restore respect for fundamental values and ethical behavior." Reminding his audience of the mind-and-heart relationship articulated by the University's first president, Jasper Newton Field, Appleton observed, "Though the final measure that a society may apply to us is our ability to inculcate employable skills, not how to get along with neighbor or self, we educate for life at least in the same proportion as we educate for livelihood."

THE BUILT ENVIRONMENT

During the Appleton years, it may be safely said that the University of Redlands experienced a third building boom, echoing the rapid growth of the years of Presidents Victor L. Duke and George Henry Armacost. Earth movers, cranes, and construction fences became familiar sight. New structures sprouted to support academics, student life,

Gown Honors the Town With an Orange Grove

If early Redlands settlers in the 1880s came for the glorious vistas, healthful climate, and oxymoronic California winters, many could afford their sun-drenched second homes thanks to the emergence of citrus as a cash crop. The burgeoning town's name soon spread far and wide on labels adorning orange packing crates (see page 6). Citrus was the town's first real industry.

After World War II, however, suburbanization and population shifts to the Sunbelt meant the conversion of acres of orange trees to tract homes and shopping malls. By 1984 the only on-campus remnant of the orange groves whose bounty had once supplemented university coffers was a gnarled grove blighting campus just below Alumni House. With the city set to celebrate its centennial four years later, William T. Hardy, Jr. '66, Charlotte G. Burgess '69, '70, and Larry E. Burgess '67 conceived and executed a plan to raze the existing grove, send a fundraising appeal to hundreds of alumni and town residents, arrange for the acquisition of Washington navel trees, and replant the 2 1/2-acre grove with 225 new specimens in just five days.

Fury characterized the initial local reaction. According to the *Redlands Daily Facts*, "People were irate—and here the grove was dead except for spots." When neighbors realized a new grove would be planted, joy displaced anger. "You can't imagine what a lift it was when I drove down Colton and spied the newly planted grove. . . . Thanks for preserving a bit of Redlands' citrus history", wrote one woman. "Here's something you don't see anymore in Redlands", stated the paper, "The replanting of an orange grove. . . . Not tract homes, but real orange trees."

The Centennial Grove was a gesture of solidarity between town and gown. A $10 donation covered the cost of one tree and additional funds were used for the grove's upkeep. Robert G. Wiens '56 and Marion Draper Wiens '57 contributed the value of one tree for each member of their immediate family who attended the University—four children and one daughter-in-law in addition to themselves. Some took a proprietary interest in the new plantings. One woman wished to designate which specific trees were hers, and another inquired whether she could pick the oranges from her two trees when they matured. In a sly postscript, she added, "I'll bring the vodka for the O. J. party."

That party occurred in January 1988 when donors were invited to campus to celebrate the mature trees' first harvest. General manager of Foothill Groves and one of the grove's 1984 progenitors, William T. Hardy, Jr. '66, estimated the first-year crop at 1,500 pounds. He projected that the grove might one day produce up to seventy-five bins of fruit worth about $7,000. At this first harvest party, each celebrant went home with a special "navelty" item: a ten-pound bag of oranges.

While the Centennial Grove remains the largest on campus, new rows of orange trees now stand in several other locations. Today, the mature trees generate enough profit to provide for their upkeep, but their chief value is in their capacity to remind town and gown alike of their common roots and in the fragrance of the blossoms each spring. —JDM

and athletics; the University even built its own power plant. Rejuvenation of the physical plant became one of the president's enduring accomplishments. Older buildings received badly needed facelifts and underwent seismic upgrades; some received new tenants as departments shuffled to new quarters. Rewiring brought many buildings into the Internet age, but ordinary wires quickly became outdated: in 2006 the University was in the midst of installing a wireless network in order to create a "plug and play" campus. In all, 199,014 square feet of building space were constructed under President Appleton's watch. Capital expenditures equaled $157,997,620. This resulted in a greatly improved and competitive campus environment.

Because of Appleton's able leadership, the demands of capital improvement were met thanks to generous gifts. First came a significant donation from Chairman of the Board Richard C. Hunsaker '52 and Virginia Moses Hunsaker '52. Their commitment enabled a building to be constructed in two parts anchored by a plaza. Completed in 1994, it houses the Irvine Student Commons, Student Life offices, ASUR, a bookstore, and a post office, as well as various seating areas, meeting rooms, and the Heritage Lounge, where historical University photos and memorabilia are displayed. Appleton called it "a much needed living and dining room for the campus."

The University's science buildings, overdue for renovation at the least and replacement at best, had been aptly described by a consultant as perfect examples of the history of science but not useful for its current practice. This sardonic remark led to a concerted effort to obtain new facilities. A contribution from the Stauffer Foundation kickstarted a fundraising effort that, with the addition of federal money and private support, resulted in the Stauffer Science Complex, a cluster of four buildings with laboratory facilities appropriate for the twenty-first century. A

grant from the Hedco Foundation made possible Hedco Hall for Biology and Chemistry. Just across a wide plaza dotted with trees and benches stands Gregory Hall, the gift of Arthur G. Gregory, Jr. '41 and Louise Gregory in honor of Arthur's father, A. G. Gregory, a founding trustee of the University. These first two buildings opened in 2000. Five years elapsed before completion of the second phase.

Shortly after he announced his departure from the presidency, the trustees determined to name the third building after James and Carol Appleton. Running west along Grove Street and featuring faculty offices and classrooms for students studying physics, mathematics, and computer science, Appleton Hall closely resembles Hedco and Gregory. Just to the west of Appleton lies the most innovative building on campus. Appropriately enough, the Environmental Studies Center is an environmentally sound, "green" building. Half the structure is underground. Berms were built up against the new walls, then landscaped, all to reduce heating and cooling costs. Named Lewis Hall after Redlands Congressman Jerry Lewis, who helped secure federal funds to make the center possible, it is south of Williams Hall (West Hall) and boasts a teaching amphitheater. An audience of more than two hundred invitees gathered under a canopy on Saturday, December 3, 2005, to dedicate Lewis and Appleton Halls. Lewis had just opened that fall; Appleton was to follow in January 2006. With the completion of these two facilities, Redlands, a liberal arts university, had positioned itself at the cutting edge of the rapidly evolving worlds of science and technology.

Another issue, unresolved for many years, concerned the closure of Colton Avenue. While President Moore's bold challenge to the city in 1986 had become a lightening rod for criticism and resistance, he nevertheless succeeded in setting the stage for compromise. The Appleton administration took a new approach in the mid-1990s. Appleton and Senior Vice President for Finance and Administration Phillip L. Doolittle '76 opposed a city proposal to make Colton a four-lane artery. Doolittle ingeniously suggested to the city planners, the same people who had scuttled the previous proposal, that they establish a joint project to control floods caused by storm run-off. This would involve the installation of storm drains under Colton Avenue. Rather than recommend that the street be closed, Doolittle offered up signals to regulate traffic flow. This would

direct large trucks to other major streets such as Citrus and Lugonia Avenues. A landscaped median would keep pedestrians from crossing except at the lights. It would also beautify the streetscape while enhancing the unity of the campus. This idea was warmly embraced by the City Council, as well as other municipal officials and citizens, including a city bureaucrat who later took credit for the concept! The University picked up more than two-thirds of the $2 million project costs.

If the construction of outstanding new facilities is one legacy of the past two decades, restoring those built by earlier generations was also an achievement of Appleton's tenure. The process began under President Moore in the early 1980s, when the University obtained bonds from the California Education and Facilities Authority (CEFA). The program enables small private schools to float bonds by tapping the deeper resources of the state in order to rehabilitate existing facilities. The Appleton administration earmarked the CEFA funds for a variety of projects. Sarah Grace Parker Hall of Letters and Hornby Hall were renovated, as were student-oriented facilities such as Melrose Hall. CEFA money helped repurpose Willis Center for administrative uses, after its traditional occupants decamped to Hunsaker University Center.

Heretofore, the principal and interest on the bonds was paid with undesignated monies and was laddered to account for such gifts against bond costs in future years. This was a perfectly acceptable way to cover expenses, but it limited the amount the quasi-endowment could achieve in the future. After a decade and a half of balanced books, Doolittle felt confident that the bonds could be retired through the University's annual budget. This constituted an important fiscal decision, indicating the enhanced strength of Redlands's financial position.

ATHLETICS — NEW ACHIEVEMENTS

On the last day of practice in 1996, before they would fly to Evanston, Illinois, to participate in the Collegiate III National

In Their Own Words: Field and Appleton

The job of a university president has changed in form and content over the past century, as the two documents that follow affirm, but one task has remained primary: fundraising. The first is a letter written by founding President Jasper Newton Field to the Board of Trustees in 1913; the second, a reaction to that letter written ninety-one years later by President James R. Appleton. His comments illustrate that, while the goals remain the same, the techniques and stakes have both evolved. — JDM

Tucson, Arizona, March 4, 1913

My dear Brothers:

On January 31st I went to San Diego to see Miss Emerson, who had already given us $2,000, knowing that she had some property with no one depending on her. I suggested that she give the University another $1,000, which would enable her to endow two scholarships. It appealed to her, and also to a niece taking care of her. They both felt, however, that a nephew by the name of Bailey should be consulted, as he had the oversight of her affairs. After this I went to Hollywood and saw Mr. Bailey, who is himself a Baptist. He seems to be a fine man. He said he was perfectly willing that Miss Emerson should give me [her money]. She is now eighty-three years of age and quite feeble.

I saw Mrs. Julia A. Libby, of Santa Ana, and suggested that it would be fine if she could arrange to give us $6,500 more and have the President's Home entirely her gift to the University. She said it would be nice, and that she would think about it. I believe the prospect is good, and only regret that I could not follow it up before leaving.

I ventured to make a fourth visit with Mrs. Baldwin, of Los Angeles. She said if we located the university in Los Angeles she would give us $40,000, but not a cent if we located anywhere else. The first time I called on her some years ago she called my attention to what she had said, and remarked that when a woman's mind is made up it is made up. The second time I called she showed signs of getting away from that notion. The third time I called, about a year ago, she said "maybe some time I will help you." A few weeks ago she said [that] she expected $10,000 in cash [in July], and that then she would give us a gift. I let her know very decidedly that $10,000 would come in mighty good play. She laughed heartily during the conversation, knowing of course that I knew how positive she was at first, and that it was interesting to me to see her capitulating. . . . The prospect is splendid for a good contribution from her, if she lives until July, and I told her she must live until then anyway.

A few days before leaving I had a long talk with Brother A. T. Currier. He said that he did not feel like signing an endowment pledge, but that it had been his plan to remember the institution in his will. I replied then, Brother Currier, it is all right if you prefer to do it that way, but please do not put it off until it is too late as others have done. He smiled and replied, I am making my will right now, and have been at it for two months, and the University of Redlands is included. . . .

I am now in Tucson on the way East. Stopped off in Imperial Valley, addressed the churches at Holtville and El Centro last Sunday, and the high school of El Centro on Monday morning. I knew there was not much money down there for us yet, but I got $50.75 in cash. . . . We will get some of their young people.

President Appleton's September 28, 2004, impression of the letter from president Field.

How interesting, some nine decades later, having just announced a $100 million Centennial development campaign, to reflect on the work of our founding president, Jasper Newton Field.

There are some similarities, aren't there? Consideration of larger gifts, such as discussed with Mrs. Baldwin, are often the result of many meetings. The time commitment to fund development on the part of the president, in 1913 as well as today, is illustrated so well in this letter. Also, while gifts to the annual fund are essential, consideration of trusts and will designations are crucial to the long-term health of the University. I also note that fund development was then, and is now, integrated with the representation of the University for purposes of admissions and general good will. And a bit of humor never hurts. I smiled when I read that the prospect of a gift from Mrs. Baldwin was "splendid . . . if she lives until July, and I told her she must live until then anyway."

Yet a number of significant differences can be read between these lines.

President Field was off campus for days and sometimes weeks at a time. This would not be possible today given the complexity of the responsibilities assumed by the president with an operational budget in excess of $103 million. My trips must be considerably more focused. Moreover, Dr. Field's report leads one to believe that he was initiating these various calls without much advanced staff work. Today, our professional staff might have made several of these calls, trust options would be articulated, and I would be advised on where I might be most useful. This doesn't reduce the importance of the president in fund development, but it does change the focus considerably as now the president is a part of a team of researchers, professional staff, attorneys, financial consultants, and volunteers.

Assuming this detailed report to the Executive Committee includes all the gifts resulting from the president's efforts from January 24 to March 4, I'm afraid I would be quite discouraged with only five gifts and two prospects in such a span of weeks. I also note that President Field's work on these trips seems almost exclusively to be with Baptist folks and, of course, this has changed significantly over the years. Many major contributors to the University of Redlands today respect our traditions but are outside this religious fold (and fewer chicken dinners are scheduled . . .). And, stating the obvious, there were no alumni of this fledgling university, while today a major portion of our gift income is given by our graduates.

We have President Field to thank for his paving the way for fund development on behalf of the University. I fear that this intention was not carried out with the same enthusiasm or results by many of our presidents. So we've had some catch up to accomplish in the context of this Centennial Celebration—to increase the number of endowed faculty chairs and student scholarships, enhance our international education program, complete needed facility improvements and additions, and add to the annual program and operational resources of the University.

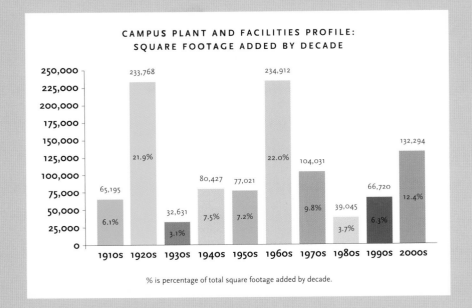

CAMPUS PLANT AND FACILITIES PROFILE: SQUARE FOOTAGE ADDED BY DECADE

% is percentage of total square footage added by decade.

Championship tournament, the members of the women's water-polo team—the defending national champion— were called out of the water after warm-ups by Coach Tom Whittemore, who announced that he had a surprise for them. Guessing what it was likely to be, the squad hustled onto the deck, then out the door into waiting vans. A few moments later, they arrived at the gleaming Thompson Aquatic Center, still unfinished. Whittemore had conspired with the construction manager and dean of students to allow his players to hold their final practice in the facility, which was not set to open officially until the next season. The team, which went on to win the second of the Bulldogs' seven national titles, thus became the first swimmers in the new outdoor pool's history. The tale intrigues because it combines two elements that characterize Bulldog athletics during the final decades of the twentieth century: the creation of new facilities and the explosive growth in women's sports.

BOTTOM: Originally constructed in 1949 on the current site of Hunsaker University Center, the football stadium was disassembled and moved to its current location along Brockton Avenue in 1970 to make way for Armacost Library and the anticipated Johnston College campus. The facility was renamed in 1988 for longtime Bulldog athletic director Ted C. Runner. The Appleton years saw the rejuvenation of Ted Runner Stadium. Seismic upgrades to the grandstands accompanied the construction of a new press box in 1998, and in 2000 new exterior landscaping included a graceful, arched entryway named for the late football coach Frank Serrao. Another coaching legend was honored in 2005, when a refurbished track was dedicated to Ashel Cunningham.

BELOW LEFT: A generous gift from Harold W. Thompson '39 and Dorothy M. Thompson made possible the construction of a new, outdoor aquatic center, located on Brockton Avenue adjacent to Ted Runner Stadium. The NCAA-regulation-length pool not only provides a home for Redlands swimming, diving, and water polo squads, which have enjoyed unprecedented success since it opened, it is a popular recreation spot for students, faculty, and staff.

BELOW RIGHT: Donald D. Farquhar '44 and Kathryn "Kay" Wilson Farquhar '46 provided funding for a soccer complex in 1997. The Farquahr Fields include a practice field, an equipment/restroom building, and a men's and women's performance field with berm seating.

Intercollegiate athletics shared in the building boom enjoyed by the campus as a whole. Older facilities like the football stadium and Currier Gymnasium received upgrades, and benefactors made possible several entirely new venues. For years there had been discussion about naming the stadium. Early on in his presidency, Appleton decided to move quickly. At an October 1988 ceremony, the facility was named for long-time coach and twenty-six-year Athletic Director Ted C. Runner '48, who was retiring. Much admired by many generations of student athletes, Runner had played football and track at Redlands. Looking closely at what he saw, Appleton quietly observed that the stadium itself was badly in need of major renovation. Over several years, the University was able to strengthen the bleachers, construct a press box, and replace the old track. The new

Mondo running surface added spring to the step of Bulldog athletes. Named for legendary Coach Ashel Cunningham, the track was dedicated on September 17, 2005. Noting that an all-weather track had been needed for years, student Evan Baughman '06, a four-year track competitor, wrote that "athletes want to train

in the best conditions possible, and now we have those at the Ashel Cunningham track." He added, "New facilities bring new fans. . . . There is nothing quite like running that final lap with the roar of the crowd pushing you along the home stretch."

One of the more venerable campus structures, Currier Gymnasium also benefited from renovated bleachers during the Appleton years. The project to convert Currier's long-closed pool into an auxiliary gymnasium was completed in 2006. The new multipurpose space now permits men's and women's teams to practice simultaneously and creates more opportunities for intramural sports to take place there when varsity athletes hit the showers.

Three entirely new facilities helped ease the pressure on Currier's cramped locker and storage facilities. Briefly bucking the trend of relocating Bulldog athletics to the northern reaches

football grandstand, the pool, boasting thirteen twenty-five-yard lanes for swimming and a thirty-meter-wide area for water polo, immediately sparked an impressive run of league championships for all aquatic sports. The pool has enabled Redlands to attract major post-season tournaments and has enticed many eastern and midwestern teams to sunny California for a mid-winter respite.

One year later, the Farquhar Soccer and Recreation Fields debuted. Named for donors Donald D. Farquhar '44 and Kathryn Wilson Farquhar '46, the complex, which includes game and practice fields, lies north of Brockton Avenue and east of the football stadium. Like the pool, the new home pitch propelled the soccer teams to league championships. The 2001 men's soccer team advanced through the NCAA Division III tournament to the final, where it took second place.

Much of the demand for expanded athletic facilities reflected increased participation by women in intercollegiate athletics. That development stemmed from changing cultural attitudes in the nation about gender roles embodied by Title IX, which some historians now see as among the most influential pieces of social legislation of the twentieth century. Women's varsity athletics at Redlands currently includes three fall sports (soccer,

of campus, a new softball field opened in 1994, located on the site of the former women's athletic field behind Gannett Center. A dedication plaque indicates the new home turf was "made possible by the generous donation of Bill and Sue Johnson, February 12, 1994."

The Johnsons were parents of Laura J. Johnson '94. A popular and useful addition to campus, the diamond quickly earned the nickname "Field of Dreams" because it was designed by the same firm that constructed out of an Iowa corn pasture, the pristine ball field used in the movie *Field of Dreams*. The field was the site of the first round of the NCAA regionals in 2005 and 2006, reflecting the championship caliber of the softball squads.

Two other additions were sited in close proximity to Ted Runner Stadium across Brockton Avenue from campus. Harold W. Thompson '39 and Dorothy Thompson supported the construction of the aforementioned aquatic center, dedicated in 1996. Fronting Brockton just behind the homeside seating outside the

cross country, and volleyball), two winter sports (basketball and swimming and diving), and a whopping six spring sports (golf, lacrosse, water polo, track and field, softball, and tennis).

The story of women's water polo at Redlands is of particular interest for a number of reasons. Redlands and the league in which it competes—the Southern California Intercollegiate Athletic Conference (SCIAC)—became leaders in championing the sport. The Bulldogs have racked up a number of impressive firsts in the twelve seasons since women's water polo was given varsity status, including nine SCIAC titles, seven national titles, and a coveted berth in the NCAA tournament for Division I schools. In 1994 SCIAC became the very first all-sports conference in the nation to sanction a varsity championship in women's water polo. Prior to that, the few schools sponsoring teams affiliated in "conferences" specific to the sport, without regard to the leagues in which their other teams played. Later, many of these institutions decided to stage their own season-ending tournament to determine a national champion. The women's event, dubbed the Collegiate III National Championships, has been staged three times at the Thompson Aquatic Center. The number of institutions supporting women's water-polo teams has increased every year.

Tom Whittemore has guided the team since its founding. He arrived in Redlands in 1988 to coach men's and women's swimming and diving and men's water polo, but he also took on the challenge of guiding the women's water-polo club. The team included many players who were complete beginners. Bulldog Hall of Fame inductee Michele M. Wright '94 was a dominating figure in sports at Redlands in those early years. Women's water polo had earned varsity status by her senior year, when the team won its first SCIAC Championship. Although Redlands did not garner a national title until 1995, Wright's leadership and tenacity influenced a core group of athletes who would power the team to glory in subsequent years. Between 1995 and 1999, the Bulldogs racked up five consecutive national championships and added three more, in 2002, 2004, and 2006.

The influence of the University of Redlands and SCIAC on women's water polo as a competitive sport can be demonstrated by two other developments. First, upon increasing its tournament field from four to eight in 2005, the NCAA rewarded SCIAC for its leadership in advancing the sport nationally by inviting the conference leader to the national championship tournament. A singular honor for a conference composed entirely of Division III schools, the automatic berth sends the SCIAC champs into competition against the sport's Division I powerhouses, such as the University of California, Los Angeles, and Stanford University. That first automatic berth eventually went to Redlands. The second indicator of Redlands's importance to the sport may be gleaned from the composition of the NCAA rules committee for women's water polo, which was chaired in 2005 by Leslie Evans Whittemore '94, '96, the University's head coach of men's and women's swimming and diving. The committee also included

BELOW: Scream Night is an enduring sorority tradition. Here, members of Beta Lamda gather on the Chapel steps at the 1994 event.

OPPOSITE PAGE: The 1996 women's water-polo team received a singular honor in May 1996, when they marked the last practice of the season by becoming the first swimmers in the new, outdoor pool at the Thompson Aquatic Center. The next day, the squad flew to Evanston, Illinois, to compete in the Collegiate III National Championship tournament, where they won the second of the Bulldogs' five consecutive (seven overall) national titles. Front row (left to right): Danielle M. Altman '97, Jennifer M. Argue '96, Rachel N. Tolber '98, Lisa M. Todd '98, Chelsea D. Cooke '96, '98, and S. Justine Albritton x98. Back row: Jennifer M. Stoskopf '97, Joanna M. Bell '97, Nicole Fonnesbeck '96, Sarah E. Taylor '99, Wendy A. Naftzger '98, Teresa J. Lawson '99, and Amanda Cooper '99, '02.

STUDENT LIFE: NEW INNOVATIONS

Student life thrives as ever, even if contemporary tastes make the trappings appear different than in days gone-by. One significant change involves student housing. Any college admissions officer will tell you that it is a competitive world out there, and twenty-first century undergraduates like modern bells and whistles. Commodious living options are one such preference. From its inception, the University favored a residential campus plan, and nearly eighty percent of current students live on campus. The annual room-draw procedure continues to elicit both jubilation and frustration. However, juniors and seniors who seek to spread their independent wings can opt for off-campus alternatives. While some students receive permission to reside in private apartment complexes or even to rent houses, the University, following a national trend, opened its own alternative to the traditional dormitory in 2003. The Brockton Avenue Apartments on the north end of Grove Street provide their student residents with more privacy than a residence hall, plus their own kitchens. Such is the apartments' popularity that there is always a waiting list.

three-time national champion Danielle M. Altman '97, who now coaches the sport at the University of California, Santa Barbara. While other women's varsity teams at Redlands have enjoyed success, none can match the accomplishments of the water-polo teams or claim the same influence on their sport's growth.

The founding of the Bulldog Bench and of the Hall of Fame honored the importance of athletic achievement to University alumni and local residents. The Bulldog Bench is a booster and fundraising organization. It sponsors an annual golf tournament and continues to help finance athletic-department endeavors. There were precursors of the Bulldog Bench in the early 1970s, but the Bench really got its start in 1983 with the inauguration at Redlands of the Intercollegiate Athletic Hall of Fame. The Hall of Fame was created to acknowledge the achievements of the University's most gifted and dedicated student athletes. Virginia Reed Coffey '26 provided the Bulldog Bench and Athletic Director Ted Runner with the means to establish the endowment to support the Hall of Fame. Located in Currier Gymnasium, as of 2006 it includes one hundred eighty-one individuals and nine varsity teams representing a variety of sports.

The Hunsaker Center occupies a central position in daily life for today's students, just as the Dog House did for earlier generations. The building is home to ASUR, and it offers several meeting rooms for use by student groups and organizations. Feature films play in a first-floor screening space. They may not always be current, but they are free! The Plaza Café has a performance area for students bands, which often draw large crowds. A "Redlands Idol" singing competition, aping the popularity of the television sensation "American Idol," was a popular draw in 2005 and 2006. Professional bands chosen from a variety of musical genres enliven Hunsaker Plaza with an outdoor, Wednesday evening concert series that soothes minds weary from a day's study.

Fraternities and sororities continue to play an important role in student activities, as do service organizations. Clubs catering to various ethnic groups are headquartered in the Multicultural

A High-Water Mark in Bulldog Athletics

While intercollegiate athletics spans the full century of the University's existence, perhaps the team to enjoy the most notable success is one of the newest: the women's water-polo squad. Promoted to varsity status in 1994, the team has since claimed eight SCIAC Championships and seven Collegiate III National Championships (1995–99, '02, '04, '06). In 2005 the Bulldogs became the first Division III school invited to the NCAA championships. Coach Tom Whittemore has guided the team since its inception.

The Bulldogs began a five-year run of national titles in 1995. The potent offensive combination of Danielle M. Altman '97, Joanna M. Bell '97, and Nicole Fonnesbeck '96, backed by defensive stand-out Laurie A. Archer '97, led Redlands to their first championship. Jennifer M. Argue '96, Wendy A. Naftzger '98, Jennifer M. Stoskopf '97, and Lisa M. Todd '98 augmented the core group the following year, as Redlands retained the mantle in 1996.

In 1997 the Collegiate III organizers saluted the move of Bulldog aquatics from the dated facilities of Currier Gymnasium to the large outdoor pool of the sleek new Thompson Aquatic Center by staging the water-polo championship at Redlands. The Bulldogs repaid this honor by winning their third crown, in home waters. The national title was sweet compensation for having narrowly lost that year's SCIAC championship game. Altman and Bell were seniors on that team, while Teresa J. Lawson '99 and Jennifer L. Roth '99 ensured that next year's squad would not lack for experienced leaders. Indeed, that duo, assisted by Sarah E. Burdge '00, Cheryl L. Burkett '00, G. Marie Willison '00, and freshmen Rozalynd A. McCree '01 and Kathryn Reichert '01, breezed through the 1998 championship run, as Redlands crushed all comers. The Bulldogs made it a five-year reign in 1999, with Maureen L. Collin '02 tending the nets.

Following a semifinal defeat in 2000 and a disappointing overtime loss in the 2001 final (once again at Redlands), the Bulldogs reclaimed the national crown in Minnesota in 2002. Lauren N. Ayers '02, Laura J. Bonny '03, Kauanoeokawanaa M. Brooks '02, Linnzi M. Kennedy '02, and National Division III Player of the Year Sarah B. Rosenberger '03 led that team, which also chalked up regular-season triumphs over two nationally ranked Division I schools. Quintuple overtime in 2003 produced another heartbreaking defeat in the final, but the squad rebounded in 2004 to win a seventh national title, vanquishing Pomona-Pitzer in the title tilt and, in so doing, avenging earlier regular season and SCIAC championship losses to their rival. Corinne

J. Flowers '05, Natalie M. Hower '07, Kelly A. Phillips '07, Lora M. Plumlee '04, Jane A. Rempalski '04, Meghan M. Rosenberger '06, and Amanda K. Zimel '05 led the way.

Recognizing SCIAC's role in the growth of the sport, the NCAA invited the conference champion to participate annually in its tourney when it doubled the field from four teams to eight in 2005. The previous year's core team, joined by Caitlin P. O'Dell '07 and Alice E. Penney '05, won the Bulldogs' ninth conference championship. In so doing, the Bulldogs bypassed the opportunity to bid for an eighth Collegiate III title to compete in the more prestigious NCAA tournament. After losing in the opening rounds to traditional Division I powers USC and Michigan, the Bulldogs became the first Division III team to win an NCAA tournament game when they defeated Division I Wagner College for seventh place. — JDM

Center. Modern trends are reflected in the presence of a Diversity Office that has responsibility for the Women's, Multicultural, and PRIDE Centers (the latter, which replaced the Gay, Lesbian, Bisexual Student Union, stands for People Representing Individuality, Diversity, and Equality). Other students engage the campus community by joining residence life teams as mentors and advisors.

The University's founders had always encouraged training of the body as well as the mind. While antiquated physical-

education requirements no longer stand between undergraduates and their bachelor's degrees, opportunities abound for students to engage in recreational sports. Colleges and universities nationwide have begun to commit sizable sums for up-to-date fitness centers, priding themselves on creating environments that rival the finest private health clubs. New facilities at Redlands reflect the importance students place on converting leisure time into fitness time. The University budgeted $3.5 million to expand a small gymnasium on Brockton Avenue.

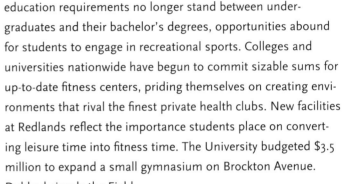

Dubbed simply the Field House (a purely descriptive name, and not an invocation of the University's first president, Jasper Newton Field), it not only supports varsity athletics with a first-rate venue for weight training but is also open to the entire student body. Finished in 2002, the center enjoys constant use and has become a principal draw in recruiting new students.

Other facilities also cater to recreational athletes. Capitalizing on the advantage of the outstanding California weather are an outdoor basketball court and sand volleyball pit on the lawn between the backsides of Hunsaker Center and Cal-Founders Hall. They are equipped with lights, so that students can burn off excess energy well into the evening. The new auxiliary gym at Currier hosts pick-up games of basketball and volleyball; and the Thompson Aquatic Center offers morning, afternoon, and evening hours for the recreational or fitness-minded swimmer. The pool is also sometimes the site of outdoor film screenings for moviegoing students who watch while they bob in the water on inner tubes. On hot days, it is not surprising to see as many students sunning themselves as swimming. Believe it or not, many even appear to be reading their assignments!

BELOW: As part of Yeoman initiation, the incoming class must covertly steal the president's chair and leave him with a new one in its place. To get his chair back, President Appleton had to appear at the commons and sing the alma mater. Left to right: James Appleton, Kristine M. Brown '99, Gregory Van Hyfte '99, Vanessa B. Al-lyn '99, Kelly W. Brown '99, and Katherine L. Curtis '99.

BOTTOM: Stealing the Fairmont Hall rock has become a quirky campus tradition. The custom often includes gallons of paint and can turn the lawn into a soggy mess.

For those more interested in competition, a lively intramurals program offers something for nearly everyone: flag football, coed Ultimate Frisbee, water polo, tennis, coed softball, soccer, beach volleyball, racquetball, and two varieties of basketball: three on three and five on five. For those who have not quite grown up, coed kickball and dodge ball recall the days of elementary-school recess. Coed sports offer a way for young men and women to interact that would have been taboo for their peers in the University's early years. If the Baptists thought dancing could induce a decline in morals, what would they have said about coed contact sports like Ultimate Frisbee?

TOWARD MORE DIVERSITY

Ethnic and cultural diversity was a major focus at the University in the 1990s. A 1989–90 grant from the Ford Foundation resulted in the introduction of race and ethnicity into the existing curriculum and in the creation of several new courses. These actions came after much debate. Intensifying the need for diversity studies was the backlash from the riots in Los Angeles in 1991 in the wake of the Rodney King verdict. The specter of a burning Los Angeles inspired many administration and faculty-led discussions. In the mid-1990s, a Hewlett Corporation grant underwrote campus dialogue on race and diversity, and a minor in minority studies was approved. In 1995 the faculty position of director of race and ethnic studies was established. By 2001 it had became an academic major. Shortly thereafter, support from the James Irvine Foundation furthered diversity initiatives.

Encouraged by President Appleton, the faculty in 1999 embraced an initiative to increase the hiring of more professors of color. It also called for growth in the number of students of color. The University added six faculty positions for this purpose. Because of intense national competition for such candidates, Redlands often found itself outbid by wealthier colleges and universities. So a creative concept of interdisciplinary hirings was initiated. In 2001 six additional teaching posts were authorized to enhance diversity. (Interdisciplinary and off-campus programs received augmented funding.) As a result, several programs were instituted: women's studies, Asian studies, and later American studies, now all majors. A director of diversity affairs was added to the Office of Student Life.

REDLANDS AND THE NEW AMERICAN COLLEGE

A major new initiative was born in 1990 with Appleton's encouragement. Schools such as Redlands, which had outgrown its roots as a small college but was not so large as to be considered a research university, sought a new way to define themselves. In a lecture entitled "The Ugly Duckling of Higher Education," Vice President for Academic Affairs Frank Wong

Preserving History: The University Archives

Established in 2001, the University Archives serves as the institutional memory for the University of Redlands, and plays an integral role in managing its information resources regardless of media or format. The archives collects and preserves documents, photographs, and ephemera, and sound and video recordings, which tell the history of the University and the evolution of its various academic programs, administrative decisions, and student activities. This evidence helps to foster a vigorous and dynamic institution by preserving traditions and vital information that define the unique qualities of the University of Redlands.

It was not until the early 1980s, as planning for the University's seventy-fifth anniversary began, that a professional-level archive program began in earnest.

With its rich collections of historical documents and artifacts, the University Archives serves as both a repository and research center open to the entire University community. Here can be found more than fifty scrapbooks detailing student life and activities since 1909, one hundred years of campus newspapers and other publications, numerous volumes of official proceedings of the faculty and trustees, hundreds of audio recordings, films of the campus dating to 1929, sports memorabilia, and tens of thousands of photographs that are part of the institution's collective memory.

More than a museum or repository for old documents, the archives provides a vital service to a wide variety of campus offices, alumni, and other constituencies.

As the University enters its second century, the archives will continue to solicit and acquire significant materials that document the unique story of the University of Redlands. — JDH

proposed a new paradigm for higher education. Wong's brainchild resulted in the creation of a consortium of institutions known as the Associated New American Colleges (ANAC). The goals of ANAC are best summarized by scholar of higher education George Keller in his 2004 book *Transforming a College*:

> The consortium . . . [is] devoted to creating a more practical and contemporary liberal arts education. Wong advocated a mix of some professional training, some research and some community or regional service with the traditional liberal arts courses, unlike the "pure" liberal arts education of, say, a Reed, Carleton, or Swarthmore. In 1995, the late Ernest Boyers, president of the Carnegie Foundation for the Advancement of Teaching, was captivated by the concept of a new layer of American academic institutions that were not research universities, exclusively liberal arts colleges, or career-oriented state colleges and universities. Boyer invited Wong's little group to Princeton, New Jersey, to help organize the ANAC. The ANAC institutions are medium-sized (3,000 to 7,000 students) and are devoted to a core liberal arts education combined with preprofessional or professional studies and service opportunities. The ethos is student centered, not faculty centered, and faculty are expected to be dedicated to expert teaching, as well as to scholarship and research. The goal is to turn out graduates who have a historically grounded and applied competence, not just theoretical knowledge, young women and men who can use knowledge for constructive action and wise policy making in society.

Redlands was a founding member of ANAC and continues to be an active participant in its annual meetings. Currently, other ANAC member schools include Butler University, Drake University, Ithaca College, Pacific Lutheran College, Susquehanna University, the University of Evansville, Valparaiso University, and fifteen others. Invisible to most students, the

relationship with similarly situated schools enables administrators to discuss trends unique to institutions of their size and to share approaches to common problems. Annual meetings often center on specific themes, such as the relationship between student-life and academic-affairs offices, the control of tuition inflation, and the role of professional schools within the liberal arts. Without doubt, Redlands has benefited from this meeting of minds.

A COMMUNITY SERVICE TRADITION

The opening in 1989 of an office of community service signaled the centralization of volunteer activity, a rich tradition that has been integral to the culture of the University from its opening day. Operating under Student Life, the office began

as a clearinghouse, matching student outreach with community needs. The program evolved into a broad menu of offerings, with students devoting many hours to such diverse activities as youth services, senior healthcare, public safety, and arts and culture.

The importance of this initiative was underscored in 1994 when the faculty endorsed a three-unit community-service activity course that would be required in order to receive a Redlands degree. The new Office of Community Service Learning reports both to Student Life and Academic Affairs, and focuses its efforts on the May Term. Tony D. Mueller '90, the program's director, stated: "The decision to keep the word 'community' was intentional and, together with the new focus on learning, it spoke to the reciprocal relationship between town and gown as well as service and learning."

Requiring eighty hours of service at a non-profit agency or school, as well as reflective and evaluative work, the course mirrors closely the Johnston Center program in which students established their own learning objectives. By 2006 University students were delivering more than seventy-five thousand hours a year of public service, only twenty thousand of which were required! Professor Emeritus Robert L. Stuart, in a lecture to the faculty on October 14, 2004, wryly noted that his colleagues, having been unanimous in their endorsement of compulsory community service for students, seemed to feel no need to include such a commitment as part of their own annual evaluations. Community service had been a condition of tenure review during the George Armacost administration and during some of Eugene E. Dawson's tenure.

WHITEHEAD DIVIDES INTO TWO

For some time, the administration and its academic offices had discussed the future of the Whitehead College program. Intensive competition among colleges and for-profit universities to attract adults seeking a degree or completing one had both positive and negative impact on Whitehead. Enrollment at some of its regional branches had increased but had decreased at others. The University's adherence to the liberal arts component as a requisite part of any professional degree program at times disadvantaged recruiting. Given Southern California's penchant for instant access, instant success, and instant gratification, the "drive-thru" version of other institutions' programs proved alluring, if not academically challenging.

By 2000 Whitehead College no longer generated sufficient income to justify its structure. After much analysis, the trustees accepted a plan whereby Whitehead ceased to exist as a separate college. In its place, two schools emerged: the School of Business was inaugurated, and the School of Education, originally founded in 1924 and folded into Whitehead as a program in the 1980s, was restored to its earlier independent status. In 2002 a renovated Hornby Hall opened to serve as headquarters for the business school. The education school opened on Brockton Avenue in the north portion of the former Commons, renamed University Hall. The deans of education and business have revamped their curricular and recruiting procedures. Evolving are two programs that will bear a distinctive Redlands stamp, firmly rooted in the liberal arts.

Addressing the ubiquitous issues of ethics in business, alumnus David Banta '63, '65, along with his wife, Stephanie, endowed a center to discuss, study, and propose action among students and faculty. The Banta Center for Business, Ethics and Society, University of Redlands School of Business became active as a new force in the curriculum in 2006.

THE WINDS OF CHANGE

President Appleton concentrated much of his time, but not all of it, on fundraising. With liberal arts colleges such as Pomona

and Grinnell enjoying billion-dollar-plus endowments, the Redlands trustees determined to increase the University's. First came the announcement in 1989 of a $45 million campaign. This comprehensive initiative also served as a template to test the waters for a larger effort for the upcoming centennial. When the goal was reached in 1993, planning began for a $100 million effort to be called the "Centennial Campaign." It was formally announced in 2004 at a black-tie dinner on the Quad with special guest former Secretary of State Warren Christopher '46. Demonstrating Appleton's seasoned fundraising abilities, the University succeeded in amassing the entire $100 million by 2006.

The December 3, 2004, Executive Committee meeting was the occasion for a bombshell. Appleton and Board Chairman Richard Fisher '65 jointly announced the president's intent to leave his office by July 31, 2005, concluding an eighteen-year tenure. At first there was silence, then a discernable tearing of eyes all around, and then an earnest discussion filled with words of praise and expressions of affection, followed by discussion of presidential selection, transition, and the future of the Centennial Campaign.

The next day, with Carol Appleton in attendance, the president made the announcement to the full board. He cited the importance of timing: the balanced $104 million budget (the latest in sixteen straight years of balanced budgets), the growth in endowment, the enhanced infrastructure. It is better, as Appleton noted, "to . . . change in a time of strength than in a time of weakness." Next he reminded the board that, with the University's centennial approaching, the institution must be platformed for its future. A new president should be on board by then; he or she would need a year to become grounded. Finally, he explained that the trustee executive evaluation and compensation committee "provided him the opportunity to assume the title of chancellor," which would permit him to undertake "selected initiatives," most importantly to continue the success of his fundraising efforts.

James Appleton's tenure saw the endowment grow from $24 million to over $120 million. Enrollment in 1988 stood at 1,280; by 2005 it had reached 2,450 undergraduates and 1,965 in the professional schools of business and education. The faculty expanded from 145 in 1988 to 222 in 2005. With over $140 million spent to upgrade the physical plant and technology infrastructure, and with endowed faculty chairs having increased from two in 1988 to twelve in 2005, Chairman Fisher could report to the University constituency "great strides academically through internal restructuring and strategic development."

The search for Redlands's ninth president began. With it came ongoing and new responsibilities. Some major projects initiated under Appleton's direction would fall to the new president to finish, notably the completion of Phase II of the Stauffer Science Complex and a co-generation plant that would allow Redlands to produce its own electricity. The latter project was quite complex. Prompted by anxiety over escalating energy

costs, the University committed itself to a multi-million-dollar investment in a natural gas-driven mechanical center which generates seventy percent of the campus's electrical power and provides heat and cooling to buildings on the University's east side. The center became operational in 2006. Funded from a tax-exempt bond issue, it represents an initiative by the University to shield itself from the State of California's mercurial electricity market.

The presidential home had challenged President Field and then came to haunt him. The issue resurfaced during the search for the ninth president: the campus needed a new presidential residence. President Moore had decided to leave the mansion on campus for an off-site home, which the University purchased for his use. Following Moore's death, the Appletons occupied it with an option to buy. Electing to remain in Redlands in retirement, the couple acquired the house. Because the need for new presidential accommodations coincided with a formidable surge in the Southern California real-estate market, a trustee committee's search for a new presidential home turned out well but seemed nearly as complex as their search for the president. Finally, after many months, the trustees agreed to purchase a house on Smiley Heights Drive for the University's new leader.

Meanwhile, the presidential search committee, comprised of seventeen dedicated individuals representing trustees, faculty, administrators, staff, and students, worked assiduously through the spring of 2005. From more than one hundred applicants, they winnowed the final selection down to three. For each finalist, there was a dinner in Alumni House at which trustees could become acquainted with the candidate and his wife.

I think my own preferences in the search crystallized during the visit of Stuart and Michelle Dorsey. As the Dorseys talked of their interests and answered myriad questions, I felt a strong sense of continuity. Deep into the preparation of this book at the time, I remembered the photographic image of President Field entertaining the faculty in this same room, around the same table (see page 39). I felt moved by how eerily similar was this event to its forebear ninety-five years earlier. If the choice of a president represented a fork in the road, I could not help but wonder whether the ghosts of presidents of yore were with us even now, helping us to determine which possibility would best serve the University's future needs.

A chance remark by Dorsey forged a stronger link to the past. In his 1908 letter to Chairman of the Board Mattison B. Jones accepting the post, Field humbly questioned his own

worthiness for the honor. Professing to "shrink from the consequence of refusal," Field ultimately accepted the presidency, which he obviously viewed as no less a calling than the ministry he already served. Almost a century later, in a December 21, 2004, letter to the board formalizing his departure, James Appleton echoed the founding president's view of the job, acknowledging that he and his wife had considered the presidency of the University as more "a calling than a job." Now, at this dinner, Stuart Dorsey responded to a question about how he felt regarding the fit between Redlands and himself in the following words: "In terms of the search and of this University, I look at it as more of a calling than a job."

"Well, there you have it," I thought to myself. From Field to Appleton to Dorsey, the best people impelled to seek leadership

roles are those who truly value commitment. The same sense of commitment also distinguishes the ranks of administrators, faculty, and staff. By meal's end, I sensed we had found our man. I felt confident Stuart and Michelle Dorsey exemplified the principles we sought.

The board reached a similar conclusion weeks later, on May 27, 2005. At an executive session in University Hall (the old Commons), whose sole purpose was to select the new president, trustees heard the search committee's unanimous recommendation. A lively discussion ensued, during which members of the committee were peppered with questions and observations from the rest of us. Trustees who could not be present physically chimed in on the telephone. After two hours of analysis, the board unanimously endorsed Stuart Dorsey as the ninth president of the University of Redlands. He reported to work on August 1, 2005. The Dorsey era had begun.

THE NEW MAN IN TOWN

Stuart Dorsey earned a B.S. in economics from the University of South Dakota, and M.A. and Ph.D. degrees, also in economics, from Washington University, St. Louis. His fields of specialization are labor economics and monetary theory. After graduate school, he served three years as assistant professor at Western Illinois University. He moved to Washington, D.C., spending one year as a research economist at the U.S. Department of Labor, and then as staff economist for the U.S. Senate Committee on Finance, from 1982 to 1984. He returned to academia as associate professor of economics at West Virginia University, Morgantown, and in 1989 was named the George F. Collins, Jr. Professor of Business and Finance at

Baker University in Baldwin City, Kansas. He was appointed vice president and academic dean of Baker in 1996, serving in this position until being named vice president for academic affairs at the University of Evansville (Indiana) in 2002. At Baker Dorsey was honored by faculty and students for teaching, research, and administration. He was active in the Midwest region of the Association to Advance Collegiate Schools of Business (AACSB). He is a coauthor of *Pensions and Productivity* (1998) and has published over one dozen articles in economics journals. His research has centered on the economic foundations of private pensions. A former vice president of the Midwest Economics Association, he completed the Institute for Educational Management program at Harvard University in 2003.

Michelle Dorsey immediately became involved in local organizations, affirming once again the century-old tie between town and gown. She demonstrated her energy and personality when she served as master of ceremonies at the Town & Gown scholarship fundraiser "A Woman's Place Is Every Place" in March 2006. She also joined the board of Family Service Association, the city's oldest social service organization.

Chilly, rainy weather on Saturday, March 18, 2006, belied the glow and warmth inside Memorial Chapel. The inauguration of Redlands's ninth president essentially was an extended University family affair, with hugs, smiles, a few tears of joy, memories, and speeches laced with humor and affection. In his remarks, Dorsey

paid homage to the University, which he termed a "good place that has struggled and prospered, but always endured for ninety-nine years. We believe that we are called here, and we pledge the rest of our working lives in service to the University, its students, faculty, and staff."

In acknowledging the debt owed to President Appleton's leadership and expressing appreciation, Dorsey said, "Jim has supported me at every turn, and continues to provide wise counsel and energetic service to this University. . . . I am grateful for his friendship and his example. . . . Perhaps the greatest accomplishment of the Appleton years has been to raise the sights and spirit of the University." Dorsey credited President Field by observing that "it was largely his vision and energy that drove this improbable venture . . . his speeches and writings revealed his ambitious vision for a first-rate comprehensive University." And citing a quality of the University that has been present from the beginning, Dorsey paid tribute to nearly a century of faculty service: "I think what makes me most proud of our University is that this faculty has never measured itself by the tools our students bring with them, but what they take away when they leave." The second century of the University of Redlands opened on a positive, determined course. The new leader's certainty and self-assurance guarantees that its second century will begin just as did the first: with unbounded confidence.

Afterword

Living in the City of Redlands for more than fifty years has had its advantages. It has permitted me to know some of the early figures instrumental in the University's history. It has also brought me too close sometimes to the community's inner workings and frankly in the gossip. When I agreed to author this history, some wags wondered if I might not write an unattributed, underground version, sort of a collection of historical outtakes. Institutions are human affairs, and even those possessed of mighty intellectual ability, leadership power, youthful inquiry, staff loyalty, and alumni affection are still capable of sometimes regrettable or downright nasty actions. My narrative has ignored most of this in favor of the more important and transcendent issues that comprise the University's story.

The University of Redlands's first history, *Redlands: Biography of a College*, came from the pen of a poet and writer, a man so smitten with the beauty of the written word and of those who held the pen's gift that his views are revealed in sentences that are as much literary as historical. Lawrence E. Nelson wryly observed in his concluding charge to the "veiled historian of the hundredth anniversary" (see Preface) that he had witnessed most of the University's alumni graduate, and had "seen the campus problem-children grow and wax strong in spirit, with the grace of God seemingly upon them until they frequently become honored leaders of men, and occasionally trustees of the college."

Nelson included some poetic fragments that I suspect he wrote:

> Let knowledge grow from more to more
> But more of reverence in us dwell
> That mind and soul according well
> May make one music as before
> But vaster.

These lines capture the essence of an institution as committed then to the pursuit of liberal studies as it is today. Nelson suggested the vision required to create a college, sustain it, grow it, and make it great:

> In the Faith of Our Fathers we go
> Not in Their Tracks
> Their Stars We follow
> Not Their Dead Campfires.

At the memorial service for George T. Stevens '34 early in 2006, family members mentioned interesting notes found among his papers. One of Stevens's observations is particularly telling: "The University was not only to teach knowledge and skills to its students, but to help them acquire wisdom and insight, love of truth and beauty, moral discernment, understanding of self, and respect and appreciation for others." The imperatives of those words continue to challenge some seventy-two years later.

Not long ago, in final essays required in the class I teach in the spring on historical interactions between Southern California, Redlands, and the University, I found two observations about the institution's history that seem highly appropriate for the conclusion of this centennial story. "Today, those of us who are lucky enough to attend the University," stated one student, "have the choice between forty-two areas of study, hundreds of classes, and the opportunity not just to learn what is happening in the world as it is reflected in our classes, but to go out and experience it first hand, thanks to the study-abroad program. The University has come a long way from its ten courses of study, 59 students and nine faculty members." Said the other,

As I stood on the quad three years ago and looked at the beautiful campus that surrounded me and the countless number of freshman un-packing cars, I could truly not have known what my heritage was in attending Redlands. But it is an amazing history and one that has installed great pride in the founding of this place with the support of a local town, to presidents — some dying in office — to students working together to plow the first athletic fields. They all worked together to build the heart and mind of this University.

When President Stuart Dorsey expressed his appreciation that faculty emphasize not what students bring with them, but rather what they take away upon graduating from Redlands, I was reminded of the observation of a 2005 alumnus. As a participant in one of the University's study-abroad programs, he was buffeted by the travails of foreign travel and living, unfamiliar cultural landmarks, and social customs laden with the possibility of faux pas. In the face of these, he declared: "Redlands gave me the confidence to do things I only dreamed of doing."

Chapter Notes

PRIMARY SOURCES

Archives
Unless otherwise noted, the
sources for minutes, manuscripts,
speeches, correspondence, and
other records is the University
of Redlands Archives.

Nelson
Nelson, Lawrence E. *Redlands:
Biography of a College*. Redlands,
Calif.: University of Redlands, 1959.

Emblem
Armacost, George H., Ralph E.
Hone, and Esther N. Mertins.
Whose Emblem Shines Afar.
Redlands, Calif.: University of
Redlands, 1982.

Johnston
McDonald, William, and Kevin
O'Neill. *A History of Johnston
College: 1967–1979*. San Francisco,
Calif.: Forum Books, 1988.

Stuart
Stuart, Robert L. "Hail and
Farewell: Thirty-Four Years at the
University of Redlands." Presented
to the University of Redlands
Faculty Forum, October 14, 2004,
unpublished manuscript.

Minutes
Minutes of the Board of Trustees

Faculty
Minutes of the faculty

Facts
Redlands Daily Facts

Sidebar Authors
Unless otherwise noted, sidebars
were written by the author.

BJG – Brennan J. Gosney '04

JDH – James D. Hofer '78

JDM – John D. Master

VJW – Vanessa J. Wilkie '00

CHAPTER 1

p. 3 For descriptions of the proposed
University landscape plans,
see *University of Redlands, 1908.
Pioneer Notes for the Diaries of
Judge Benjamin Haye* (privately
printed, 1929), pp. 276–77.

For a discussion of Theodore
Steele, see William H. Gerdts and
Will South, *California Impressionism*
(New York: Abbeville Press, 1998).

4 Charles Nordhoff, *California for
Health, Pleasure, and Residence*
(New York: Harper Brothers, 1873).
Chapter 12 of this volume focuses
on the San Bernardino Valley.

5 Nelson. Authorized in 1956 by
the trustees, Nelson's book was
released in 1959 as part of the
Golden Jubilee, marking fifty years
since classroom instruction began
at Redlands. In later years, Nelson
confided to me that so many
of the original founders of the
University and their contemporaries were still alive that it was
difficult to present candidly some
of the more controversial aspects
of the history of the institution.

6 Charles Lummis, *Biblio–Cal Notes*
(Winter 1974).

7–9 For the earliest accounts of the
June 1907 efforts by the citizens
of Redlands to secure a college,
see *Facts, Redlands Review*,
and *The Citrograph*.

CHAPTER 2

12 The full text of Jasper Newton
Field's address to the 1911
Southern Baptist Convention
is housed in the Archives.

14 Minutes and the Executive
Committee Minutes for December
1907 and January 1908 are instruc-
tive as to how the Board organized
and began to pursue the 1909
opening date.

16 The Apr. 19, 1909, Minutes discuss
the offer of funds rejected by the
trustees because of the donor's
racist demands.

19 A delightful source on the early
years from a student perspective
are the scrapbook and privately
printed reflections of Nellie Hill
Lolmaugh, *Way Back When*
(about 1985).

CHAPTER 3

22 The University's first catalogue
(1908–09) presents the philosophy
of its educational instruction and
lists the unit requirements.

For the orange and white colors,
see Nelson, p. 90.

25 The transcript of an oral-history
interview with Lois E. Field on
January 21, 1982, in the A. K. Smiley
Public Library Archives, affords
insights into the first graduating
class.

27 The history of the *Alma Mater*
comes in part from an oral interview the author conducted in 1967
with Elizabeth J. Hidden, later a
professor at Redlands, who was
involved in the creation of
the school song.

30 For details on dancing, see
Minutes 1913.

31 Arguably the best eye-witness
account of the disastrous
January 1913 freeze is contained
in the letters of Daniel Smiley in
the A. K. Smiley Public Library
Archives.

33 The urgency of the University's
financial situation is captured
in the Jan. 21, 1913, Minutes,
p. 146.

34 Concerns about Baptist views
on the Redlands budget
priorities are contained in the
September 1913 Minutes, p. 154.

36 Minutes and Faculty 1914
address the events surrounding
President Field's resignation.

CHAPTER 4

42 Additional material regarding
Duke's thoughts on whether
Redlands should continue as
a university or become a college
may be gleaned from his Dean's
Report, January 18, 1915. See
Facts, Feb. 15, 1967, for a more
recent discussion of this topic.

44 It should be noted that the
rail line used to transport the
Baptist delegates to campus
in 1915 still exists. Metrolink
is currently planning to extend
the line to the University.

46 All across the United States,
the population rejoiced at the
end of World War I. The same
fervor swept the Redlands
campus. Of particular useful-
ness for the period covered in
this chapter is an unpublished
history of the University by
Professor A. Harvey Collins
for the forthcoming twenty-fifth
anniversary of class instruction in
1924. It is a meticulous account
penned by one who lived in
Redlands before the founding
of the University and who
served as an original faculty
member.

CHAPTER 4
(continued)

50 I first began discussing the anonymous friend with Nelson in the 1970s. It became obvious that Nelson was so moved by this individual's generosity, and by the fact that he literally had made the difference between the University's success and possible failure, that he believed someone should be given a clue as to his identity. A professor of English, Nelson began his long career at the University in 1925 (he died in 1978). He possessed a quick mind, a retentive memory, and a trustworthy character that led people to confide in him. He had come to know well the friend's daughter and her husband, both of whom had graduated from Redlands. He believed that long after the principal players had left the scene, it would be fitting and appropriate to acknowledge such fidelity and generosity. Nelson told me to find a photograph of the dedication of the library in 1926, because the anonymous donor could be found in the group portrait. During a luncheon in June 8, 1993, Rita Palmer, Milo C. Treat's great daughter-in-law, confirmed his role as the donor. She indicated that the family always referred to Treat as "the man from Pittsburgh," who had made his fortune by bringing the gas works to the city. Treat's first anonymous gift to the University was modest: $600 for loans to students "to enable them to pursue their courses."

51 For insight into Herbert J. Powell's architectural contributions to the campus, see his privately printed biography, *From City Boy to Cowboy and Back* (n.d.); Frank E. Moore, "The Architecture of Herbert J. Powell" (1988), an unpublished manuscript in the A. K. Smiley Public Library Archives; and letters from Powell also in the Smiley Library.

53–54 For information on architect and landscape expert Norman Foot Marsh, see Jane Apostol, *South Pasadena: A Centennial History* (South Pasadena Public Library, 1987).

57 For the observation about Field's last public duty at the dedication ceremony of the Chapel, see Nelson, p. 189.

60 Professor William Southworth, debate coach, generously shared his unpublished manuscript on the history of debate at the University.

CHAPTER 5

71 Cecil Eaker's poem is published in the Apr. 12, 1933 *Spectrum*.

75 Nelson (p. 212) discussed the Depression's specter at Redlands as only one who lived through it could.

For a discussion of the hiring of Thurber, see Nelson, pp. 22–33.

78 Margaret Lynn, Professor Lynn's widow, maintained that the tremendous strain on her husband caused by the controversy over his teaching greatly impaired his health. For many years, she rented out rooms in her home on The Terrace to students.

79 Benjamin E. Smith, *Two Paths, Emmett Oliver's Revolution in Indian Education* (Seattle: Salish Press, 1995), is an excellent source on Redlands during the Thurber years. Chapter 4 is a delightful account of Oliver's campus recollections.

The origins of the Yeomen are described in *The Bulldog*, 24, 2.

80–85 Issues of *La Letra* during this period portray a level of enthusiasm and optimism on the part of students that is indicative of youthful resilience and ingenuity.

85–89 The author had many discussions with historian Earl Cranston about the Thurber presidency. Debate coach and professor Joseph Baccus provided much insight. President Thurber's daughter, Helen, showed me the beautiful signed and bound testimonial presented to the Thurbers by the citizens of Redlands. The full text of Reverend Dr. Herbert C. Ide's conciliatory address to the faculty is in Faculty, Mar. 11, 1936.

CHAPTER 6

93 Anderson to Jones, Mar. 27, 1938.

The details of Anderson's hiring are contained in Minutes, Apr. 1, 1938.

94 For "Do you think I am the man for the job?," see *The Bulldog*, Aug. 18, 1944.

Anderson's full discussion about enrollment is contained in the Executive Committee Minutes, October 1938.

94–96 Anderson's view of religion and the individual is contained in *Report of Southern California Baptist Convention*, 1938.

See *The Bulldog*, Dec. 13, 1939, for details on the Anderson-student exchange.

98 The John Raitt story is related in *Facts*, Feb. 21, 2005.

100 See *The Bulldog*, Jan. 8, 1943, for details of student reaction to the president's war messages at chapel.

For more information on Executive Order 9066 and the Japanese in California, see Anderson's letters and *Redlands Report* (Spring 1985), pp. 18–19.

101–06 The president's reports to the board from 1942–44 document Anderson's efforts to bring the V–12 to Redlands. For details about dancing and the V–12 on campus, see James G. Schneider, *The Navy V–12 Program: Leadership for a Lifetime,* (Boston: Houghton Mifflin, Co., 1987), pp. 277–78. Robert Campbell, a former ASUR president, supplied additional information about the dancing controversy in a 1985 interview.

106 Anderson detailed the way he entertained in his report to the trustees, 1943-44.

107 For more on Anderson's death and funeral, see *Facts*, Aug. 22, 1944. See also Colena Anderson to Douglas Moore, Oct. 15, 1982, in which the former president's wife remembered her time at Redlands.

CHAPTER 7

109 As one of the three authors of *Emblem*, Armacost used the occasion to chronicle his achievements and to provide his approach to such issues as Johnston College and the Vietnam War years. His confrontation of the relationship between the University and the Baptists are chronicled on pp. 3–4. Armacost's remarks about retirement occurred in a discussion with the author in May 1982. Efforts to meet post-World War II building and space needs are discussed in *Emblem*, p. 17.

Nelson's views of Cortner are found in Nelson, p. 282.

110 The conversation between Allen B. "Curley" Griffin and the author took place during Homecoming, 1982.

CHAPTER 7
(continued)

110 Fundraising challenges are addressed in the Executive Committee Minutes, November 1946.

112 A discussion of enrollment issues is found in the Executive Committee Minutes of August 1947.

113 Further thoughts on the Christian nature of the University and Armacost's concepts can be found n *Emblem*, pp. 16, 36.

121 The infamous 1960 water fight is described in *Facts*, Apr. 27 and May 12, 1960.

123 For the Alumni Association history, see *Emblem*, p. 19.

127 The background of Interim Term is presented in *Facts*, Feb. 29 and Mar. 3, 1968. The antiwar protest quotes are from the October pages of *Facts*.

Armacost's proposals regarding minority studies are outlined in *Facts*, June 4, 1969.

132 Protests over the president's censorship of *The Bulldog* are noted in *Facts*, May 1, 1962.

132 The details of the firebombing of the Administration Building can be found in the *Facts*, April 22 and 23, 1970.

133 Armacost lamented his final years as president during a conversation with the author in April 1970.

134 A summary of the Armacost years is contained in *Emblem*, p. 109.

CHAPTER 8

139–40 Dawson's initial goals are detailed in *Emblem*, p. 137.

140 The fast pace of administrative changes is discussed both in *Emblem* and Stuart.

141–49 For Johnston's origins and the subsequent sequence of events, see *Emblem*, pp. 80–82, 85–89; *Facts*, Oct. 25 and 27, 1965, and Jan. 14, 1970; and *Time*, Oct. 3, 1969. For O'Neill's remarks, see *The Bulldog*, Jan. 28 and Feb. 11, 2005. For Armacost's memorandum, see *The Bulldog*, Oct. 11, 1969, and Johnston, pp. 124–27.

154 For background on Whitehead College, see Al Robertson's unpublished history of the institution.

155–57 For further information on the fiscal issues of the Dawson years, see *Emblem*, p. 145.

158–59 For discussion of protests, see *Facts*, March and April 1974.

162 The fire in Wallichs Theatre is covered in *Facts*, October 1975

CHAPTER 9

165 Becky Moore described the circumstances of her husband's selection as president in a conversation with the author in 2004.

166 For Moore's goals, see *Emblem*, p. 190, and Stuart. For the University's reorganization, see *Emblem*, p. 197.

169 See Stuart for the way Moore made personnel decisions and for his criteria for appropriate administrative behavior. Stuart noted, "The president told me that there were three things he would not tolerate: incompetence, insubordination, and unkindness." For Moore,

according to Stuart, the latter was "the last straw" and, in some cases could lead to dismissal.

173–74 For the controversy generated by the proposal to close Colton Avenue, see *Facts*, Nov. 16 and Dec. 6, 1984.

CHAPTER 10

178–79 For the inaugural address of James Appleton, see his transcript, dated Apr. 29, 1988.

183 For more details on CEFA bond issues, see a memorandum from Phillip L. Doolittle to the Executive Committee, Apr. 19, 2006.

187 Letter from Evan Baughman dated Jan. 31, 2006. The tenor of change may be seen in the pages of the 2005 Annual Trustee Retreat Program, "Transitions," Feb. 24-26, 2005. See also Executive Committee Minutes, Apr. 19, 2006.

188 For more details of the Casavant organ, see "Memorial Chapel Organ Rededication," a brochure printed by the University, May 17, 2003.

193–95 Frank E. Wong, "The Ugly Duckling of Higher Education," presented at the University of the Pacific, Mar. 30, 1990. For more about the new American college, see George Keller, *Transforming a College* (Baltimore: Johns Hopkins Press, 2004).

197 The overview of the University in 2002 is from an internal summary for an Irvine Foundation grant, Part B, pp. 1–27. Also useful is the "Planning Document," 2004–05, Board of Trustees, President's Cabinet and University Council, October 2004.

197 For Appleton's decision to retire, see his memorandum of July 5, 2005, to the University community. For details about Appleton's last few months in office, see *Och Tamale*, 81, 2 (Spring 2005) and 81, 3 (Summer 2005); Board of Trustees executive session, Dec. 4, 2004; University of Redlands press release, "President Announces End to Eighteen-Year Term," Dec. 6, 2004; and Appleton's memoranda to the Board of Trustees, Dec. 21, 2004, and May 16, 2005.

198 The endowment figures are from the 2005–06 report to the Board of Trustees, May 2005.

199–200 For details of the ninth presidential search, see job description, Feb. 17, 2005; and University press release, "University of Redlands Announces New President," June 2, 2005. For Dorsey as the new president, see *Och Tamale*, 82, 1 (Fall/Winter) 2005–06. Details concerning Dorsey's inauguration may be found in his inaugural speech, Mar. 18, 2006. For information about the inauguration and its context, see the introduction of Dorsey by Daniel Lambert, president of Baker College, Mar. 18, 2006.

Appendices

BOARD OF TRUSTEES
(continued)

Shellenberger, George
1967–1975

Shikles, Janet L., '64
1995–2004

Silke, V. Stanley, '18
1946–1957

Simms, Linda Nelson, '62
1991–1994, 1997–present

Smiley, Daniel
1917–1930

Smith, A. Arnholt
1964–1967

Smith, Albert Hatcher
1907–1909

Smith, Carey R.
1907–1913

Smith, Charles H.
1991–1996

Smith, Joel H.
1927–1941

Smith, John Bunyan
1933–1941

Smith, J. Lewis
1909–1912

Snape, John
1925–1926, 1929–1935

Snyder, Conway W., '39
1964–1966

Starring, Francis W.
1930–1934

Steinbach, Robert C., '54
2002–2005

Stevens, Kenneth, T., '73
1995–1996

Strait, J. H.
1907–1929

Sweeney, Martin
1929–1937

Taylor, N. Anthony, '63
1998–2001, 2002–present

Taylor, Richard
1949–1951

Thompson, H. R.
1941–1945

Thompson, Harold W., '39
1986–1995, 1996–1999

Tomlinson, Jr., John G., '66
1995–1998

Townsend, John H., '54
1971–1981, 1982–1991

Troupe, Ronald C., '64
1997–present

Truesdail, Roger W., '21
1935–1974

Turrill, G. S.
1914–1920

Untereiner, Raymond E., '20
1964–1965

Upham, Steadman, '71
1998–present

Vanderknyff, Jr., Jacobus, '65
2000–2003

Van Osdel, Boyce, '33
1954–1981

Walk, William E.
1971–1978

Walker, Ralph
1939–1942

Wallace, Sam S.
1954–1959

Wallichs, Glenn E.
1958–1960, 1963–1968

Wallichs, Dorothy
1973–1978

Warren, George E.
1962–1966

Weisser, Stanley C.
1999–present

Wells, Karl C.
1913–1914

Wennerberg, C. Herbert, '37
1949–1968

West, Jr., W. Richard, '65
1993–2002

Wheeler, Richard H., '35
1974–1975

White, Barbara M., '38
1970–1972

White, Larry
1984–1987

Wiens, Robert G., '56
1979–1982, 1982–1991,
1992–2001, 2002–present

Wiens, Marion D., '57
1984–1987

Wieschendorff, James R., '63
1996–1999

Wightman, F. W.
1935–1938

Wilcox, W. W.
1907–1908

Wilkerson, Margaret B., '59
1999–2004

Wilkinson, H. E.
1919–1925

Williams, A. R.
1963–1968

Williams, Donald E., '51
1981–1986

Williamson, Mrs. J. N.
1934–1943

Willis, Arthur B.
1964–1976

Winslow, James C.
1970–1974

Wood, Dorothy D.
1977–1986

Wood, W. F.
1912–1922

Woollacott, Robert M., '65
1993–2002

Wright, George C.
1913–1914

Wyshak, Lillian Worthing, x '49
1972–1981

Ziilch, Charles N., x '42
1986–1998

BOARD OF TRUSTEES CHAIRS

Richard N. Fisher
5/2000–present

Richard C. Hunsaker
5/1984–5/2000

H. Jess Senecal
5/1981–5/1984

Milo W. Bekins, Jr.
5/1972–5/1981

Frederick Llewellyn
5/1969–5/1972

Wallace L. Chadwick
2/1956–5/1969

Joy G. Jameson
6/1941–11/1955

Mattison B. Jones
12/1907–6/1941

EMPLOYEES OF THE UNIVERSITY WHO HAVE SERVED FOR TWENTY YEARS OR MORE

List compiled by Ann O'Donnell from a number of archival sources. The titles listed here reflect the last job held.

*People who will have served 20 years in 2007, the end of the centennial year.

**Master's degree only

Abbott, Charles H.
George Robertson
Professor of Zoology
1922–1950

Adams, Bess Porter
Professor, English
1938–1965

Adams, J. D.
Machine Shop Supervisor,
Facilities Management
1973–1993

Albert, Orrin W.
Professor, Mathematics
1923–1954

Allison, George E., III
Adjunct Faculty,
School of Business
1985–2005

Allum, Dora H.
Secretary, Political Science
1954–1975

Almond, Paul N.
Adjunct Faculty,
School of Businesss
1987–present*

Anderson, John D.
Adjunct Faculty,
School of Education
1977–2004

Anderson, Kathleen J.
Loan Coordinator,
Financial Aid
1987–present*

20 YEARS OF SERVICE
(continued)

Angel, Ralph M.
Edith R. White Distinguished
Professor, English
1981–present

Aparicio–Laurencio, Angel
Professor, Spanish
1966–1991

Appleton, James R.
University Chancellor
1987–present*

Applewhite, Joseph Davis
Professor, History
1949–1979

Aquino, Priscilla
Office Manager, Assessment
& Student Support Center,
School of Business
1982–2006

Armacost, George H.
University President
1945–1970

Arnold, Robert B.
Adjunct Faculty,
School of Businesss
1987–present*

Austin, Margret J.
Secretary to Director,
Johnston Center for Integrative
Studies and Philosophy
1974–2000

Auton, Graeme P.
Professor, Government
1987–present*

Baccus, Joseph H.
Professor, Speech Education
1930–1963

Bach, Peter J.
Adjunct Faculty,
School of Businesss
1985–present

Balch, David E.
Adjunct Faculty,
School of Businesss
1976–present

Barents, Harriet
Manager, Faculty & Staff
Coffee Lounge
1967–1987

Battjes, Margaret
Bookkeeper, Business &
Finance Office
1947–1968

Baty, Roger M.
Professor, Anthropology;
Farquhar Professor of the
American Southwest
1969–2002

Becker, Gilbert B.
Professor, History
1946–1974

Billings, Frederick H.
Professor, Botony and
Bacteriology
1921–1946

Blanck, W. Robert, '72, '81
Adjunct Faculty,
School of Business
1980–present

Bloxham, Michael J.
Professor, Mathematics
1982–present

Blume, Frank R.
Professor, Psychology
1960–1961, 1971–1996

Boese, Raymond C.
Professor, Music
1959–1982

Bohrnstedt, Wayne R.
Professor, Music
1953–1993

Bonney, Merilyn H.
Director, Alumni Relations
1976–1996

Bowman, Douglas C.
Professor, Religion
1969–1997

Bragg, David B.
Professor, Mathematics;
Director, Fletcher Jones
Academic Computer Center
1967–1999

Brandt, Judith A., '90
Assistant Campus Director
and Admissions Officer,
School of Business
1986–present

Brawley, Judy C.
Administrative Assistant to
the University Registrar
1984–2006

Brett, Julia A.
Adjunct Faculty, English
1985–present

Brigola, Alfredo L.
Professor, Romance Languages
1957–1981

Bristoll, Roseline E.
Administrative Assistant to
the Housing Director,
Student Life
1985–2005

Bromberger, Frederick S.
Professor, English
1948–1984

Brown, Gilbert L., Jr., '39, '39
Vice President, Development
1939–1972

Brownfield, John P.
Professor, Art
1965–2004

Brubacher, Elaine S.
Professor, Biology
1980–present

Bruington, Paul L.
University Treasurer
1929–1950

Brun, Anne B.
Administrative Assistant,
Alfred North Whitehead Center
Admissions
1979–2000

Buclatin, Bayani B.
Adjunct Faculty,
School of Businesss
1987–present*

Burgess, Charlotte
Gaylord, '69, '70
Vice President and Dean,
Student Life
1969–present

Caminiti, David L., '65, '73
Adjunct Faculty,
School of Education
1980–present

Campbell, Josephine
Acquisitions Assistant, Library
1956–1983

Carlson, Richard F., '57
Professor, Physics
1967–2001, 2002–2004

Carrick, Nancy E.
Professor, English; Vice
President, Academic Affairs
1980–present

Cartlidge, Francis Annette
Professor, Music
1916–1946

Caudle, Patricia M., '86**
Director, Financial Operations;
University Controller
1983–present

Chakrapani, N.
Professor, Computer Science
1985–present

Childs, Barney
Professor, Music
1971–2000

Clark, Donna L.
Administrative Assistant,
Physical Education & Athletics
1969–1972, 1974–2006

Clark, Margaret Davis
Associate Professor, Art
1940–1971

Clopine–Ikerman, Margaret U., '80**
Admissions Officer, Alfred North
Whitehead Center
1978–2001

Cohen, Robert
Adjunct Faculty,
School of Businesss
1976–2006

Cohen, Sheldon D.
Adjunct Faculty,
School of Businesss
1981–2002

Collins, A. Harvey
Professor, History
1909–1934

Combs, Stanley L.
Professor, Education
1948–1973

Coppernoll, Elmer E.
Electrician, Facilities Management
1920–1944

Cornell, Portia A., '65
Senior Lecturer, Mathematics
1973–present

Cortner, George P.
University Business Manager
1915–1946

Corwin, Kenton W., '48
Director, Administrative Services
1954–1988

Cox, Aaron J.
Professor, Physics
1970–present

Cragg, Nadine A.
Professor, Physical Education
1930–1964

20 YEARS OF SERVICE
(continued)

Crampton, Marlyn J.
Office Assistant, College of Arts & Sciences Admissions
1977–1998

Cranfill, Linda V.
Cashier, Business & Finance Office
1968–present

Crawford, Lorene
Secretary, Communicative Disorders Clinic
1972–1992

Cummings, Jack B., '50, '65
Vice President, University Relations
1955–1981

Cunningham, Ashel
Professor, Physical Education; Director, Athletics; Coach, Football and Basketball
1912–1921, 1926–1953

Cushman, Cecil A.
Professor, Physical Education; Coach, Football
1923–1959

Dana, Stephen W.
Professor, Geology
1945–1986

Davies, Ellis Ryhs
Professor, Physical Education; Coach, Track and Swimming
1928–1964

Dermer, Cary E.
Adjunct Faculty, School of Businesss
1983–present

Deyo, Christine A., '99
Assistant to the Vice President, Academic Affairs
1980–1987, 1989–present

DiGiacomo, Stephen
Plumber, Facilities Management
1974–present

Dillow, H. Ben
Professor, Speech; Dean, Special College Programs
1969–2004

Dittmar, Henry G.
Professor, History
1948–1978, 1991–1998

Dole, Kenneth L.
University Physician
1921–1946

Doolittle, Phillip L., '76
Senior Vice President for Finance and Administration and Chief Financial Officer
1976–1977, 1979–1981, 1990–present*

Dornbach, Vernon E., Jr.
Professor, Art
1957–1986

Downing, Clarence E.
Professor, Religion; University Pastor
1950–1974

Driscoll, Paul M., '89**
Dean, College of Arts & Sciences Admissions
1981–present

Duke, Victor Leroy
Professor, Mathematics; University President
1909–1933

Durall, Maurice J.
Professor, Communicative Disorders
1967–1999

Dusenberry, Lorna
Data Recorder, Alumni Relations
1966–1990

Eadie, Douglas G.
Will C. and Effie M. Crawford Professor of Religion
1947–1981

Ebel, Bartel E.
Professor, German
1924–1952

Edwards, Gregor
Adjunct Faculty, School of Businesss
1987–present*

Eng, Robert Y.
Professor, History
1980–present

Engel, Robert D.
Professor, Engineering and Applied Mathematics
1967–1993

Erlanger, David
Adjunct Faculty, School of Businesss
1986–present

Fink, Harry A.
Adjunct Faculty, School of Businesss
1980–present

Finsen, Lawrence E.
Professor, Philosophy
1979–present

Fisher, Robert E.
Professor, Art
1971–1993

Franklin, Carol A.
Professor, Education
1976–present

Fulmer, Lee
Professor, Physical Education; Coach, Golf
1955–1982

Gates, Gerald O.
George Robertson Professor of Biology
1966–1999

Gauger, Doris, '75
Supervisor, Student Health Services
1962–1987

Geary, Patricia C.
Professor, English
1987–present*

Golz, John L.
Professor, Music
1953–1981

Gonzalez, Olga C.
Professor, Spanish
1968–present

Goodman, Ruth
Visiting Lecturer, Education
1946–1972

Green, Fredarieka
Assistant Professor, Music
1925–1946

Greenway, Frank L., Jr.
Professor, Business Administration
1946–1980

Gregory, Wilbur S.
Professor, Psychology
1947–1974

Griffin, L. Susan
Administrative Assistant, School of Business
1987–present*

Griswold, David R.
Instructor, Community School of Music
1985–present

Gross, Thomas F.
Professor, Psychology
1980–present

Hall, Verda
Secretary to the Dean, Special and International Programs
1951–1974

Halvorsen, Marcia L.
Professor, Economics
1975–1996

Hanson, Howard
Superintendent, Grounds and Safety
1950–1973

Harrison, Benjamin S.
Professor, English
1931–1958

Harvill, Lawrence R.
Professor, Engineering and Applied Mathematics
1964–1998

Haverty, Ruth
Supervisor of Accounting, Business & Finance Office
1953–1978

Heath, Bradley A.
Adjunct Faculty, School of Businesss
1986–present

Hendon, Larry H., '47
University Treasurer
1948–1975

Hennen, Nettie
University Employee
1930–1952

Hester, James D.
Will C. and Effie M. Crawford Professor of Religion
1967–2000

Hidden, Elizabeth
Professor, Education
1926–1954

Higginson, Margaret J.
Library Assistant
1973–1982, 1988–2000

Hile, Esther
Librarian; Director, University Library
1931–1963

Hill, Edith A.
Professor, Romance Languages
1910–1947

Hollenberg, George J.
Professor, Biology
1939–1964

Hollenberg, J. Leland
Professor, Chemistry
1959–2001

Hone, Ralph E.
Professor, English
1956–1978

20 YEARS OF SERVICE
(continued)

Howell, Charles D.
George Robertson
Professor of Biology
1952–1976, 1976–1977

Hunt, Linda L.
CTC Credential Analyst,
School of Education
1973–present

Huntley, William B., Jr.
Will C. and Effie M. Crawford
Professor of Religion
1974–present

Hurlbut, Howard S., Jr., '59
Professor, English and
Russian Studies
1958–1959, 1959–2003

Husky, Bonnie L.
Coordinator, College of Arts &
Sciences Student Accounts
1973–present

Hynes, J. Gordon
Will C. & Ellie M. Crawford
Professor of Religion
1948–1973

Isom, H. Novella, '84
Supervisor, Telephone Services
1969–1993

Jacobsen, Arthur D.
Professor, Economics
1923–1946

Jennings, Irmengard K., '79
Director, Community
School of Music
1984–present

Jennings, Louise
Professor, Business
Administration, Secretarial
Science, Economics,
American History
1939–1965

Jones, J. William
Professor, Music
1945–1970

Jones, S. Guy
Professor, Chemistry
1909–1949

Jordan, Cheryl T.
Adjunct Faculty,
School of Education
1987–present*

Jorgenson, James R.
Professor, Music
1957–1988

Kanjo, Eugene R.
Professor, English
1953–1991

Karpman, E. Gail
Textbook Coordinator,
School of Business
1981–2004

Keays, James H., '62
Professor, Music
1972–present

Keays, Mary Lee
Adjunct Faculty,
School of Music
1980–2001

Keith, Mary Newton
Assistant Professor,
Mathematics
1922–1943

Kennedy, William H., '76
Associate Librarian;
Associate Director,
Armacost Library
1980–present

Killpatrick, Allen R.
Professor, Mathematics
1969–present

Kirchner, Harold D.
Professor, Business
Administration
1954–1983

Klausner, William J., '41
Professor, Sociology
1948–1979

Kopka, Georgia J.
Administrative Assistant,
Communicative Disorders
1985–2006

Krantz, Reinhold J.
Professor, Chemistry
1947–1980

Kyle, James W.
Professor, Ancient Languages
1909–1945

Lacy–Stapert, Paula
Data Records Specialist,
Registrar's Office
1980–present

Larose, Susan S.
Library Assistant
1986–present

Larson, Larry E., '83, '85
Adjunct Faculty,
School of Businesss
1987–present*

Lawrence, Marilyn J.
Administrative Assistant,
Student Leadership &
Involvement Center
1973–1974, 1983–present

Lee, Jesse S.
Engineer, Facilities
Management
1928–1948

Lindberg, Stephan M.
Campus Mail Clerk,
Office Services
1986–present

Little, JoAnn
Administrative Assistant,
College of Arts & Sciences
Admissions
1971–1978, 1978–1981,
1981–1991

Lloyd, Gordon
Professor, Government
1970–1999

Lockwood, Marjorie, '75
Secretary to the University
Treasurer
1956–1984

Long, Louanne Fuchs
Professor, Music
1962–present

Maatman, Katherine
Head Operator,
Telephone Services
1958–1978

Madler, H. Peter
Professor, European Studies;
Resident Director,
Salzburg Program
1963–1965, 1969–1999

Main, William W.
Professor, English
1956–1979

Malcolm, James R.
Professor, Biology
1981–present

Marquez, Hector P.
Professor, Spanish
1979–1999

Marsh, Herbert Eugene
Professor, Physics and
Engineering
1912–1946

Marshburn, A. Lawrence
Librarian; Director,
Armacost Library
1957–1982

Martin, Walter C.
Professor, Music
1965–1988

Martinez, Frank R.
Lead Groundsworker,
Facilities Management
1973–1993

Martinez, Jeff
Associate Professor,
Physical Education;
Director, Athletics
1983–present

Mattingly, Caroline S.
Professor, English
1928–1957

Mayer, Frederick
Professor, Philosophy
and Humanities
1944–1966

McAllister, Bruce H.
Edith R. White Distinguished
Professor of English
1971–1972, 1974–1997

McAndrew, Theta
Secretary to the University
Business Manager
1947–1968

McBride, Michelle, '75**
Adjunct Lead Faculty and
Program Support Specialist,
School of Business
1980–1986, 1993–present

McCoy, Gerald W.
Adjunct Faculty,
School of Businesss
1985–present

20 YEARS OF SERVICE
(continued)

McDonald, William E.
Professor, English; Virgina
C. Hunsaker Distringuished
Teaching Chair
1969–2005

McElroy, Penny A.
Professor, Art
1986–present

McNeill, James E.
Paint Shop Supervisor,
Facilities Management
1976–1999

Melzer, Josette
Professor, French
1969–1993

Mertins, Esther N.
University Registrar
1929–1969, 1973–1974

Michalski, Walter J., '78
Adjunct Faculty,
School of Businesss
1981–2001

Miller, Kenneth E.
Associate Professor,
Physical Education;
Coach, Baseball
1981–1983, 1984–2003

Miller, Ward S.
Professor, English
1949–1973

Miranda, Donna M.
Operator, Telephone Services;
Staff, Food Services
1973–1980, 1994–present*

Moburg, Leon F.
Professor, Art
1958–1992

Moreno, Charles
Staff, University Commons
1925–1958

Moreno, Ralph
Groundskeeper, Facilities
Management
1921–1971

Morlan, Robert L.
Professor, Political Science
1949–1985

Morrison, Judith A.
Professor, Communicative
Disorders
1981–present

Mueller, Kurt W.
Adjunct Faculty,
School of Businesss
1982–present

Mueller, Tony D., '90**
Director, Community Service
Learning
1985–present

Napoli, Anna M.
Associate Professor,
Psychology
1969–present

Nelson, Lawrence E.
Professor, English
1925–1961

Ng-Quinn, Michael
Professor, Government
1985–present

Nichols, Egbert R.
Professor, Speech Education
1913–1952

Niggle, Christopher J.
Professor, Economics
1983–present

Niss, Beverly A., '90**
Associate Registrar
1985–2006

Norton, Nancy A., '62, '68
Adjunct Faculty,
School of Education
1985–present

O'Donnell, Anastasia T.
Administrative Assistant,
Academic Affairs
1972–1974, 1975–present

Ogren, Kathy J.
Professor, History;
Director, Johnston Center
for Integrative Studies
1985–present

O'Neill, Kevin D.
Professor, Philosophy
1969–present

Ouellette, Eugene, '57, '58
Professor, Communicative
Disorders
1964–1997

Owada, Yasuyuki
Professor, Anthropology;
Director, Johnston Center
for Integrative Studies
1969–1999

Parker, William R., '64
Professor, Speech;
Director, Speech Clinic
1946–1969

Pflanz, Barbara C.
Professor, German
1964–present

Phelps, Barbara R., '45, '68
Adjunct Faculty,
School of Education
1986–present

Phillips, Lester H.
Professor, Political Science
1947–1976

Pierce, Alexandra
Professor, Music
1968–2001

Pierce, Mary Clark
Librarian
1953–1978

Pierpoint, Charles O.
University Business Manager
1946–1969

Poole, Robert R.
Professor, Mathematics
1964–1990

Porch, Grace J., '81
Operator, Telephone Services
1969–2000

Poston, David G.
Professor, History and
General Studies
1947–1973

Pound, Leanne B.
Student Loan Coordinator,
Business & Finance Office
1972–1996

Prendergast, Caroline Mattingly
Professor, English
1928–1958

Price, Eva Rebecca
Associate Professor,
Romance Languages
1926–1951

Prihoda, Marilyn A.
Secretary, Communicative
Disorders
1967–1991

Rabinowitz, Fredric E.
Professor, Psychology;
Assistant Dean, College
of Arts & Sciences
1984–present

Rehfeldt, Philip R.
Professor, Music
1969–2004

Richey, Sandra L.
Library Assistant
1974–present

Rickabaugh, Cheryl A.
Professor, Psychology
1987–present

Rickard, Jeffrey H., '69, '70
Professor, Music; Director,
University Choir
1970–present

Riddick, M. Patricia
Program Assistant, Alfred North
Whitehead College
1977–1998

Rider, Larry P.
Professor, Communicative
Disorders
1973–2004

Rio-Jelliffe, Rebecca
Professor, English
1958–1996

Roberts, Julian L., Jr.
Professor, Chemistry
1961–2001

Robertson, Jon
Conductor, Redlands
Symphony Orchestra
1982–present

Rott, Harry T.
Coordinator, Athletic
Equipment
1980–present

Ruff, Erwin E.
Professor, Music
1942–1981

Runner, Dwanna M.
Executive Secretary to the
University Chancellor
1964–1967, 1986–2004,
2005–present

Runner, Theodore C., '48
Professor, Physical Education;
Director, Athletics, Coach,
Track and Field and Football
1953–1988

Sager, Jon
Adjunct Faculty,
School of Businesss
1977–present

Sales, Fred John
Professor, Education
1930–1952

Sanderson, Judson, Jr.
Professor, Mathematics
1956–1988

Sandos, James A.
Professor, History;
Farquhar Professor of the
American Southwest
1981–present

20 YEARS OF SERVICE
(continued)

Sargent, Ruth Eddy
Associate Professor,
English
1925–1947

Scherer, Mary E.
Professor, Mathematics
1980–2001

Serbein, John G.
Director for Planned
Giving, Development
1987–present*

Serbein, Jeannie
Director, Student Employment
1985–present

Serrao, Frank R.
Professor, Physical Education;
Coach, Football
1964–1984

Serrao, Joan D. D.
Coordinator of Data
Processing, Alumni
Relations
1966–1995

Sherman, Betti
Professor, Physical
Education
1958–1982

Siddell, Marvin J.
Adjunct Faculty,
Business Administration
1983–2004

Smith, Gary H., '64, '67
Professor, Physical Education;
Coach, Basketball
1965–1967, 1971–present

Smith, Lois
Assistant Director,
Custodial Services for
Residence Halls
1954–1974

Smith, Lowell Kent
Professor, Biology
1967–present

Smith, Marc Jack
Professor, History;
Dean of the Faculty
1946–1975

Sommer, Diana J., '82**
International Student Advisor,
Student Services
1978–2003

Sordon, Susan E.
Professor, Communicative
Disorders
1970–present

Southworth, E. William
Professor, Speech
1972–present

Spelman, Leslie P.
Professor, Music
1937–1968

Sponheim, Valerie J., '79, '82
Assistant Dean, Student Life
1979–present

Stewart, Barbara K., '73
Adjunct Faculty,
School of Music
1985–present

Stewart, Donald Judson, '27, '31
Adjunct Instructor, Accounting;
Graduate Manager, Student
Activities; Manager,
University Bookstore
1931–1971

Stone, Bernice
Cataloging Supervisor, Library
1947–1974

Stone, Clarence E.
Adjunct Faculty, School
of Business
1974–1987, 1987–present

Stuart, Robert Lee
Professor, English
1969–2004

Sunn, Larry A., '81**
Adjunct Faculty, School
of Businesss
1981–2003

Svenson, Arthur G.
Professor, Government
1981–present

Swanson, Jean
Librarian; Director,
Armacost Library
1987–present*

Sweeney, Ruth Carol
Adjunct Faculty,
School of Businesss
1984–2004

Swisher, Iona A.
Executive Secretary
to the Vice President,
Academic Affairs
1969–1989

Switzer, Barbara
Adjunct Faculty,
School of Businesss
1987–present*

Symmes, Eleanor Ann, '17
Librarian
1912–1944

Taylor, Paul L., '63**
Professor, Physical Education;
Coach, Baseball
1955–1983

Taylor, Sandra L.
Manager, Office Services
and Purchasing
1983–present

Tebbetts, James R.
Lead Electrician,
Facilities Management
1972–1998

Tharp, David
Associate Professor, History
1982–present

Thompson, Alastair W.
Director, Alfred North
Whitehead College
Admissions
1978–2002

Thompson, Judith C., '83**
Assistant Campus Director,
School of Business
1981–present

Tilton, Howard Cyrus
Professor, Economics,
Political and Social Science
1914–1944

Tinnin, Alvis Lee
Professor, French
1969–1990

Toalson, J. Elizabeth
Executive Secretary to the
President
1965–1987

Torp, Jon R.
Adjunct Faculty,
School of Businesss
1980–1988, 1995–present*

Tritt, Edward Clinton
Professor, Music
1945–1975

Tschann, Judith A.
Professor, English
1978–present

Umbach, William E.
Professor, German;
Dean of Graduate Studies
1952–1979

Valenty, John
Adjunct Faculty,
School of Businesss
1985–present

Van Buren, George A., '79
Adjunct Faculty,
School of Business
1982–present

Vance, W. Scott, Jr., '75, '81
Technical Director for Audio
and Adjunct Faculty, Music
1981–present

Van Osdel, Edgar Bates
Professor, Geology and
Astronomy
1921–1946

VanVranken, Dora
Professor, German
1965–1999

Verdieck, James E.
Professor, Physical Education;
Coach, Tennis
1946–1983

Vincent, Rex
Superintendent, Facilities
Management
1923–1969

Waggoner, J. Phillip, '62
Director, Student Counseling
and Career Development Center
1964–1967, 1968–1986

Walker, Christopher N.
Professor, Communicative
Disorders
1978–present

Walker, Harley P.
University Employee
1930–1957

Walsh, Lawrence F.
Adjunct Faculty,
School of Businesss
1986–present

Wasielewski, Patricia L.
Professor, Sociology
1982–present

Watson, Drage H.
Professor, Education
1973–1997

Webb, Wanda
Cashier, Food Services
1981–2005

Weiss, Michael G.
Adjunct Faculty,
School of Businesss
1984–present

Welborn, Stephen I.
Professor, Accounting
1982–present

20 YEARS OF SERVICE

(continued)

Weltner, B. Irene
Supervisor, Currier Gym
1980–2000

Whitehead, Evelyn
Supervisor, Mailroom &
Duplicating Services
1962–1984

Wilbur, Shirley A., '82**
Assistant Campus Director,
School of Business
1979–present

Wiley, Grace A.
Assistant to the
University Treasurer
1924–1957

Wilke, Clarence D.
Supervisor of Grounds,
Facilities Management
1967–1987

Wilkerson, Kristi
Office Manager,
Hospitality Services
1985–present

Willey, Emily B.
Assistant Professor,
Home Economics
1945–1968

Williams, Edward K.
Professor, Liberal Studies
and Director of Graduate
Advising, Alfred North
Whitehead College
1969–1989

Williams, Nadine
Director, Student Career
Planning & Placement
1962–1977, 1980–1985

Williford, Elaine R.
Office Manager, Food Services
1975–present

Wilson, John D.
Associate Professor, Music;
Director, Opera and
Musical Theatre
1968–1990

Woodrow, Harold Wright
Professor, Chemistry
1930–1962

Woolway, Ralph
Electrician and Engineer,
Facilities Management
1950–1973

Wright, Ray
Ranch Foreman and Engineer;
Facilities Management
1938–1970

Zatkin, Judith
Adjunct Faculty, School of
Businesss
1987–present*

ENDOWED ACADEMIC POSITIONS

The Edith R. White
Distinguished Professor of
English and Creative Writing

The Robert A. and Mildred
Peronia Naslund Dean's Chair
in the School of Education

The Hedco Chair in
Environmental Studies

The Will C. and Effie M.
Crawford Professor of Religion

The Fletcher Jones
Professor of American Politics

The Hunsaker Distinguished
Teaching Chair

The John Stauffer Director
for the Center for Sciences &
Mathematics

The Hunsaker Endowed Chair
of Management

The Farquhar Professor of the
American Southwest

The David Boies
Professor of Government

The Omer E. Robbins
Chaplain to the University

The H. Jess and Donna Colton
Senecal Endowed Dean's Chair
in Business

The Ken and Lynn Hall Chair
in Public Policy

The William R. and Sue
Johnson Endowed Chair
in Finance

The John and Linda Seiter
Endowed Chair in Business

The Ronald D. and Cheryl
N. Lossett Endowed Visiting
Professorship

The Forest and Dolores
Grunigen Endowed Visiting
Professorship in Business

Endowed Lectures

The Oliver de Wolf and Edith
M. Cummings Lecture on
World Peace

The Decker–Dana Lectureship

The Eaton Lectureship

The Kathryn A. Green
Lecture Series

DISTINGUISHED SERVICE AWARDS

Ruth Violett Abbey '23
1958

Edith Ericksen Abramson '50
1975

Roger Ackley '37
1980

Barbara Powers Allen '59
1989

Leroy Allen '36
1984

Albert Anderson '44
1966

Leo Anderson '24
1959

J. Russell Andrus '25
1957

Verda Armacost
1964

Mary Ann Adet Baker '61
1974

Maydelle Baker '25
1959

David Banta '63
1997

Wendell Barner '84, '86
2004

Christina Davies
Beeson-Bailey '33
1976

John Peter Beiden '32
1984

Hilton Bell '31
1957

Ivan Bell '28
1963

Doug Bender '76
1995

George Benson '55
1990

Robert Bingham '32
1959

Daniel Boone '51
1978

Judith Moore Bowman '65
2002

J. Delmar Branch '23
1968

Sam Brown, Jr. '65
1977

Mary-Carol Walberg
Burdett '46
1986

Nelson Burdett '47
1992

Charlotte Gaylord
Burgess '69, '70
1982

Larry Burgess '67
1982

Gary Byrne '64
1987

Robert Campbell '43
1985

Steven Carmichael '67
1991

Marilyn Magness Carroll '75
1979

Wallace Chadwick '20
1958

Alvin Chang '42
1969

Warren Christopher '46
1966

Helen Stroebe Clark '32
1961

Richard Cline '25
1965

May Coggins '20
1964

Allan Cole '34
1972

John Cole '49
1968

George Cortner
1965

Jane Towar Corwin '49
1993

Kenton Corwin '48
1993

Mary Anderson Covington '42
2003

Robert Covington '41
1972

Earl Cranston
1970

Joyce Blayney Crawford '45
1981

Jack Cummings '50
1962

Oliver Cummings '21
1981

Sally Rider Cummings '56
1989

Ashel Cunningham
1960

Herbert Cunningham '50
1979

Jesse Curtis, Jr. '28
1960

Cecil Cushman '38
1959

David Danielson '75
2000

Lillian Rigby Dean '36
1988

John Demmon '63
2005

William Dickenson '64
1994

Phillip Doolittle '76
1988

Carl Doss '44
1994

Muriel Bernice Duncan '31
1965

Nancy Wheeler Durein '65
1998

James Edson '53
1982

Janet McLean Edwards '55
2001

R. H. Edwin Espy '30
1968

Willard Espy '30
1982

Wm. Glenn Evans '39
1968

Donald Farquhar '44
1998

John Fawcett '41
1991

Maryetta Huntoon Ferre '70
1999

Richard Fisher '65
1996

Hugh Folkins '42
1961

Harold Ford '42
1981

James Fox '29
1962

Martha Logan Fox '31
1962

Morris Fox '34
1965

Walter Gage, Jr. '35
1958

Milton Gair '22
1957

Robert Gardener '73
1996

Marland Garth '38
1993

Harold Geistweit '17
1959

Blossom Mills George '32
1977

Gordon Gibbs '32
1981

Russell Goodwin '29
1967

John Grant '82
1999

Judith MacConaghy Graunke '71
1990

W. Harry Green '26
1965

Allen Griffin '34
1979

Sanford Gunter '30
1961

James Guthrie '35
1960

Joel Habener '60
1975

Edwin Hales '33
1970

Margaret Wickliffe Hall '29
1961

Ann Halligan '76
1996

William Hardy '41
1992

William Hardy, Jr. '66
1987

Nora Vitz Harrison '77
2002

Donald Haskell '60
1987

Marie Stevens Haskell '62
1991

Mary Vasse Hawk '56
1990

William Hawk '54
1985

Dick Hays '56
1976

A. R. Schultz '28
1963

Louise Hoffman Schultz '27
1985

Laurence Scott '39
1999

H. Jess Senecal '52
1997

Elsie Elliott Severance '18
1977

Rogers Severson '62
1988

Charles Shackelton '63
1993

Donald Sham '27
1947

Edward Shattuck
1966

Ann White Shaw '43
1964

Janet Lamb Shikles '64
1979

Leo Sievert '19
1952

James Silke '53
1965

V. Stanley Silke '18
1960

Linda Nelson Simms '62
1995

Dudley Sipprelle '57
1982

A. LaMont Smith '35
1963

Benjamin Smith '37
2003

Gary Smith '64
2000

Conway Snyder '39
1962

Bernice Brown Sorrells '34
1966

Maurice Sorrells '32
1966

Bernice Ward Stevens '38
1987

· George Stevens '35
1956

Donald Stewart '27
1957

Ronald Styn '63
1992

Susan Shikles Styn '65
1992

Edward Taylor '50
1974

N. Anthony Taylor '63
1997

Byron Thompson '33
1972

Iola Tillitt Threatt '55
1995

William Threatt '53
1991

Harley Tillitt '37
1986

Sylvia Payne Tillitt '37
1994

Jerry Tinker '61
1989

Howard Tipton '58
1976

John Tomlinson '66
2006

Ronald C. Troupe '64
1999

Roger Truesdail '21
1947

Kenneth Turknette '57
1988

Steven Turner '79
1995

William Turnquist '53
1976

C. Paul Ulmer '28
1973

Ray Untereiner '20
1961

Alice Van Boven '33
1978

Boyce Van Osdel '33
1958

Harriet Van Osdel '35
1969

C. Merle Waterman '20
1957

Gary Weatherford '58
1981

Alma Phillips Wedberg '19
1952

Katherine Talbert Weller '71
1984

C. Herbert Wennerberg '37
1959

W. Richard West '65
1992

Richard Wheeler '35
1970

Barbara McNaboe White '38
1980

Margita Eklund White '59
1974

Thomas Whitecloud '39
1973

Marion Draper Wiens '57
1984

Robert Wiens '56
1989

James Wieschendorff '63
1988

Margaret Buford Wilkerson '59
1979

John Will '38
1967

Lois Fair Wilson '45
1982

Dorothy Wagner Wise '48
1967

David Wong '31
1947

Harold Woodrow
1962

Lloyd Yount '23
1968

Charles Ziilch '42
1996

Dorothy Marti Ziilch '42
1996

Index

Page numbers in italics refer to illustrations.

Photography Credits

Unless otherwise noted, all photographs are in the collection of the University of Redlands Archives. Wherever possible, photographs have been credited to the original photographer and are used with permission.

Page VIII by Bob Torrez.

Pages X–XI by David E. Kuhlmann '05.

CHAPTER 1

Page 2 courtesy of A. K. Smiley Public Library.

Page 4 courtesy of Indiana State Museum and Historic Site.

Pages 6, 7, 8, 9 (top right and bottom right) courtesy of A. K. Smiley Public Library.

CHAPTER 2

Pages 12, 17, 18 (bottom right), 19 (both images), courtesy of A. K. Smiley Public Library.

CHAPTER 3

Pages 22 (top right), 23 (bottom left and top right), 25 (top left), 28 (bottom) courtesy of A. K. Smiley Public Library.

Page 36 (bottom left), courtesy of the family of C. Merle Waterman '20.

CHAPTER 4

Pages 44 (left and bottom right), 45 courtesy of the family of C. Merle Waterman '20.

Pages 46 (bottom right), 57 (center right) courtesy of A. K. Smiley Public Library.

Page 61 (bottom right), 69 courtesy of the family of C. Merle Waterman '20.

CHAPTER 5

Page 76 courtesy of A. K. Smiley Public Library.

Page 84 courtesy of Larry E. Burgess '67.

Page 86 (bottom) courtesy of the family of George T. Stevens, Jr. '35.

Page 90 (center) courtesy of the National Museum of the American Indian.

CHAPTER 6

Pages 92, 95 (bottom) courtesy of A. K. Smiley Public Library.

Page 105 (all images) courtesy of Lois Fair Wilson '45.

Page 106 courtesy of Jean Hentschke Baker '47.

CHAPTER 7

Page 112 (bottom right) by Hap Byers.

Page 114 (bottom right) by Sigmund Snelson '53.

Page 117 (bottom) by Sigmund Snelson '53.

Page 137 (top) courtesy of A. K. Smiley Public Library.

CHAPTER 8

Pages 138, 149, 152, 153 (top), 158 (top), 159, by Kenneth R. Creasman '77, Scott E. Kuethen '80, Mark S. Meyers '77, and Jodi Shiarella '77.

Page 156 by Hap Byers.

Page 157 by H. Robert Case.

Page 159 courtesy of Kenneth R. Creasman '77, Scott E. Kuethen '80, Mark S. Meyers '77, and Jodi Shiarella '77.

CHAPTER 9

Page 164 courtesy Viva S. Rose '81.

Page 167 (bottom) courtesy of Kenneth R. Creasman '77, Scott E. Kuethen '80, Mark S. Meyers '77, and Jodi Shiarella '77.

Pages 168 (left), 170 (top left and bottom right) courtesy of Kimbeth L. Coventry '82.

Page 174 by David Current.

Page 175 courtesy of Viva S. Rose '81.

CHAPTER 10

Page 176 by David E. Kuhlmann '05.

Pages 181 (bottom), 182 (bottom right) by Bob Torrez.

Page 182 (top right) by David E. Kuhlmann '05; (bottom left) by Bob Torrez.

Pages 183, 186 (top and bottom) by David E. Kuhlmann '05.

Pages 187 (center right) courtesy of the Lawlor Group; 187 (bottom left) by David E. Kuhlmann '05.

Page 189 (top right) courtesy of the Lawlor Group.

Page 191 by Bob Torrez.

Pages 192 (center right), 193 (top right) courtesy of Gregory J. Van Hyfte '99.

Page 198 (bottom) by David E. Kuhlmann '05.

Page 199 (bottom left) by Steve Woit for the Lawlor Group.

Pages 201 (top left and bottom), 202 (top) by Carlos Puma.

Page 202 (bottom) by Marge Beasley.

AFTERWORD

Page 205 by David E. Kuhlmann '05.